The Essay

An Introduction

Robert DiYanni

Mc Graw Hill

Boston   Burr Ridge, IL   Dubuque, IA   Madison, WI   New York
San Francisco   St. Louis   Bangkok   Bogotá   Caracas   Kuala Lumpur
Lisbon   London   Madrid   Mexico City   Milan   Montreal   New Delhi
Santiago   Seoul   Singapore   Sydney   Taipei   Toronto

McGraw-Hill Higher Education ℞

A Division of The **McGraw-Hill** Companies

THE ESSAY: AN INTRODUCTION
Published by McGraw-Hill, an imprint of The McGraw-Hill Companies, Inc. 1221 Avenue of the Americas, New York, NY, 10020. Copyright © 2002 by The McGraw-Hill Companies, Inc. All rights reserved. No part of this publication may be reproduced or distributed in any form or by any means, or stored in a data base or retrieval system, without the prior written consent of The McGraw-Hill Companies, Inc., including, but not limited to, in any network or other electronic storage or transmission, or broadcast for distance learning.
Some ancillaries, including electronic and print components, may not be available to customers outside the United States.

This book is printed on acid-free paper.

1 2 3 4 5 6 7 8 9 0 DOC/DOC 0 9 8 7 6 5 4 3 2 1

ISBN 0-07-249861-7

Editorial director: *Phillip A. Butcher*
Executive editor: *Sarah Touborg*
Developmental editor II: *Alexis Walker*
Senior marketing manager: *David Patterson*
Project manager: *Karen J. Nelson*
Manager, new book production: *Melonie Salvati*
Media producer: *Todd Vaccaro*
Freelance design coordinator: *Pam Verros*
Cover design: *JoAnne Schopler*
Cover Art: *Pablo Picasso (1881-1973) Two Girls Reading © copyright ARS, NY. Private Collection*
Typeface: *10.5/12 Bembo*
Compositor: *GAC Indianapolis*
Printer: *R. R. Donnelley & Sons Company*

Library of Congress Cataloging-in-Publication Data
DiYanni, Robert.
    The essay: an introduction / Robert DiYanni.
        p.   cm.
    A revision of "The essay" portion of the larger four-genre book: Literature : reading fiction, poetry, drama, and the essay. 4th ed. c1998.
        Complements: Literature : reading fiction, poetry, and drama. 5th ed. c2002.
        Includes index.
        ISBN 0-07-249861-7 (alk. paper)
        1. Essay. 2. Essays.   I. DiYanni, Robert. Literature. II. Title.
PN4500 .D59 2002
808.4—dc21   2001037072

www.mhhe.com

Brief Contents

*Stories, poems, plays, and text discussions new for the Fifth Edition.

Contents

Preface

The Essay: An Introduction presents an approach to literary works that emphasizes reading as an active enterprise involving both thought and feeling. Students are introduced to the art of interpretation through illustrated discussions of the formal elements of the essay. At the same time, they are invited to consider why they respond as they do to an essay and how their responses change during subsequent readings. They are asked, in short, to relate their experience of reading an essay to their experience of life. They are encouraged to value their emotional reactions in line with their previous experiences of life and language and to see essays as a significant reflection of life and an imaginative extension of its possibilities.

The Pedagogy: Experience, Interpretation, Evaluation

From first page to last, *The Essay: An Introduction* is designed to involve students in the dual act of **reading** and **analysis**. The genre of the essay is introduced in a three-part explanatory overview of the reading process organized around the approach to texts of Robert Scholes's *Textual Power* (Yale University Press, 1985), modified and adapted to my own approach to teaching literature. Scholes identifies three aspects of literary response: reading, interpretation, and criticism. The three-part structure of my introduction to *The Essay* breaks down as follows:

1. The EXPERIENCE of the essay
2. The INTERPRETATION of the essay
3. The EVALUATION of the essay

Our *experience* of the essay involves first of all our immediate and valuable subjective impressions and emotional responses. *Interpretation* involves intellectual commitment and analytical thinking. In our *evaluation* of the essay we assess its aesthetic distinction and consider its social, moral, and cultural values.

Comprehensive Introduction to the Genre: Reading and Writing about Essays

The Essay discusses the **types** of essays (speculative, argumentative, narrative, and expository) and introduces their traditional **elements**—voice, style, structure, and thought—through discussions tied to specific essays. Throughout these discussions, students are asked to return to other works and reconsider them from different perspectives.

To demonstate specific strategies for critical **reading,** I have provided an illustration of the "act of reading": an interpolated reading of Gretel Ehrlich's "About Men."

Paralleling the schema for reading and analysis is a similarly organized introduction to **writing** about the essay—including three sample student essays, examples of writing topics, documentation procedures, and a general review of the writing process.

Two Essayists in Context

Key essays of E. B. White and Maxine Hong Kingston are highlighted and contextualized with extensive biocritical introductions, excerpts from the authors' comments on their writing, and criticism by literary scholars. In addition, connections between the two writers are suggested by a general introduction and by Questions for In-Depth Reading.

The Collection of Essays

A word about the choice of the essays. The classic and contemporary selections reflect a wide range of styles, voices, subjects, and points of view. Complex and challenging works appear alongside more readily accessible ones. *The Essay* contains both in sufficient variety for instructors to assign the more accessible selections for students to read and write about on their own, while reserving the more ambitious selections for class discussion.

Timeline

The inside covers of this edition feature a **timeline** that situates major essays in the larger historical and cultural context, thus providing a jumping-off point for students wishing to investigate this context for research projects or to achieve a deeper understanding of the texts.

Acknowledgments

The Essay: An Introduction represents the cooperative efforts of many people. This single-genre spinoff owes its existence ultimately to Steve Pensinger, who originally encouraged me to develop the first edition of the four-genre full-size book, *Literature: Reading Fiction, Poetry, Drama, and the Essay*. For both *The Essay* and for the Fifth Edition of *Literature,* its parent, I have had the pleasure of working with McGraw-Hill colleagues Sarah Touborg, executive editor; Alexis Walker, development editor; Anne Stameshkin, editorial assistant; and Karen Nelson, project manager. Each provided me with the kind of high-quality professional assistance I have come to expect from McGraw-Hill. It continues to be a pleasure to work with them and with their publishing colleagues.

I have also benefited from the suggestions of many colleagues around the country who teach the introductory writing and literature courses, many with earlier editions of this book. The following reviewers provided thoughtful criticism and valuable suggestions for the Fifth Edition of *Literature*:

Michael Aaij, University of Alabama
Beverly Bailey, Seminole Community College
Rosemary Baker, SUNY Morrisville
Mary K. Bayer, Grand Rapids Community College
Mark Bernier, Blinn College
Aniko Constantine, SUNY Alfred
Jim Creel, Alvin Community College
Theresa M. Dickman, Cumberland College
Tina D. Eliopulos, Community College of Southern Nevada
Audley Hall, NorthWest Arkansas Community College
Diane Hyer, Truett-McConnell College
Mary D. Jamieson, Broward Community College
Carol Jamison, Armstrong Atlantic State University
Thomas M. Kitts, St. John's University
Andrea Krause, Hesston College
Carol Swain Lewis, Three Rivers Community College
Steven Lynn, University of South Carolina
Patricia Menhart, Broward Community College
Paul Resnick, Illinois Central College
Katherine M. Restaino, Fairleigh Dickinson University
Denise Rogers, University of Louisiana
Jeff Schonberg, Angelo State University

The following instructors graciously responded to a survey for this revision:

Jacqueline Agesilas, Antillean Adventist U.; **Anthony J. Bialas**, Springfield Technical C. C.; **Robert Blake**, Elon College; **Jo Ann Bornze**, Bearer College; **Bradley Bowers**, Barry U.; **Anthony Boyle**, SUNY Potsdam; **Barbara M. Britsch**, Lourdes College; **J. F. Buckley**, Ohio State U., Mansfield Campus; **Leslie L. Burbick, Jr.**, Kentucky Mountain Bible College; **Cheryl Burghdurf**, Champlain College; **Carl J. Carlsen**, North Shore C. C.; **John Carlson**, Waldorf College; **Ellen Casey**, U. Scranton; **Margaret Corgan**, Kings College; **Wayne Cox**, Anderson College; **Sandra S. Coyle**, College of St. Joseph; **Mary Cross**, Fairleigh Dickinson U.; **Alys Culhane**, Coastal Carolina U.; **David Daniel**, Emerson College; **Andrea Defusco**, Boston College; **Elizabeth J. Deis**, Hampden Sydney College; **John A. Desando**, Franklin U.; **Dale Dittmer**, U. S. Carolina, Salkehatchie; **Claire Doyle**, North Country C. C.; **Annick Durand**, Rivier College; **Jill Evans**, Kettering College of Medical Arts; **Barbara L. Farley**, Ocean County College; **Earl Fitz**, Vanderbilt U.; **Christine Flanagan**, Camden C. C.; **Charles E. Gannon**, Eckerd College; **Michael S. Glaser**, St. Mary's College of MD; **Wilfrid G. Harnlin**, Goddard College; **Lee Hartman**, Howard C. C.; **Carol F. Heffernan**, Rutgers U,. Newark; **Karen C. Henck**, Eastern Nazarene College; **Paul K. Hesselink**, Covenant College; **Joseph F. Higgins**, Chattahoochee Valley C. C.; **Susan G. Hillabold**, Purdue U., North Central; **David E. Hoegberg**, Indiana U., Purdue; **Cindy E. Huggins**, U. Maine at Machias; **Anthony Hunt**, U. Puerto Rico, Mayaguez; **Barbara Hunt**, Washtenaw C. C.; **Jamie W. Hutchinson**, Simon's Rock of Bard; **Margaret Jennings**, St Joseph's College; **Anne Kaler**, Gwynedd Mercy College; **Barbara Kane**, Becker College Leicester; **Beth Ann Kemper**, Campbellsville U.; **Elizabeth Kerlikonskie**, Kellogg C. C.; **Bonnie K. Landis**, Anderson U.; **Karen Lee**, Northeast Iowa C. C.; **Barry H. Leeds**, Central Conn State U.; **Anthony Maulucci**, Three Rivers C.T. C.; **Nancy McCabe**, Presbyterian College; **Alexander Menocal**, U. North Florida; **Janet Minc**, U. Akron, Wayne College; **Deronda Mobelini**, Hazard C. C.; **Scott E. Moncrieff**, Andrews U.; **James Mooney**, Immaculata College; **Joe Murray**, St. Leo College; **David Myslewski**, U. Pittsburgh, Bradford; **Betty P. Nelson**, Volunteer State C. C.; **Miriam Nevins**, Dominican College; **Robert Newman**, SUNY Buffalo; **Charles L. O'Neill**, St Thomas Aquinas College; **Ann M. Parrish**, Atlantic Union College; **Deborah C. Payne**, American U.; **Linda Pelzer**, Wesley College; **Lela Phillips**, Andrew College; **Roger M. Phillips**, Alpena C. C.; **Carol Pippen**, Towson U.; **Alan Rauch**, Georgia I. of Tech.; **Dennis Read**, Denison U.; **Cecilia Ready**, Villanova U.; **F. D. Reeve**, Wesleyan U.; **Angela Salas**, Adrian College; **Craig Saper**, U. of the Arts, Philadelphia; **Katherine Scheil**, Saint Joseph College; **David Seelow**, SUNY Old Westbury; **Cathy W. Sewell**, Chesapeake College; **Alan B. Shaw**, Monroe C. C.; **Cynthia Miecznikowski Sheard**, U. Kentucky; **John E. Skillen**, Gordon College; **Thomas R. Sluberski**, Concordia College; **James Snowden**, Cedarville College; **Barbara E. Sowders**, Eastern Kentucky U.; **Alonzo Stevens**, Voorhees College; **Barbara P. Thompson**, Columbus State C. C.; **Fiona Tolhurst**, Alfred U.; **Jean Trounstine**, Middlesex C. C.; **Earl J. Wilcox**, Winthrop U.; **Dana B. Wilde**, U. Southern Maine; **Rosemary Winslow**, Catholic U.; **Sharon K. Witty**, Des Moines Area C. C.;

Arthur I. Wohlgemuth, Miami Dade C. C., Kendall; and **Christa Zorn-Belde**, Indiana U., Southeast.

I have had the additional pleasure of working with Professor Tom Kitts of St. John's University. Professor Kitts has written a practical and graceful instructor's manual for the Fifth Edition of *Literature;* this manual serves as a rich and rewarding source of practical and provocative classroom applications.

Finally, I want to thank my wife, Mary, whose loving and steadfast assistance enabled me to complete this book on schedule. She is a treasure beyond compare.

ROBERT DiYANNI

CHAPTER ONE

Reading Essays

THE EXPERIENCE OF THE ESSAY

Our experience reading essays may differ somewhat from our experience reading fiction, poetry, and drama. In contrast to the imaginative representations of reality that are depicted in the other genres, the essay is typically factual. Thus in essays we expect to find information, data, facts rather than fictional plots, poetic speakers, or dramatic characters. The primary purpose of essays is not to delight or move us (though essays may accomplish both of these things), but to instruct and persuade us. Their usual purpose is to explain a set of circumstances and persuade us to view them in a particular way. Many of the essays we have read, in fact, and very likely those we have written, either explain ideas or present arguments.

Because of the primacy and explicitness of ideas in the essay, the genre has long had an uncertain status as literature. Instead of the suggestiveness of language and concern with symbolic form associated with other genres, the essay is typically more direct and explicit. It usually subordinates narrative incident and figurative language to the exposition of ideas. To emphasize the primacy of ideas in the essay, however, is not to deny that essays can be imaginative, dramatic, or poetic. In fact, reading essays only for ideas and information while ignoring style and language is to miss much of the pleasure they afford. We will therefore read the essay as literature, in the same way we read the other genres. And in doing so, we will attempt to discover its distinctive literary pleasures. We can begin by considering the opening paragraphs of the following essays:

MARK TWAIN

[1835–1910]

"Cub" Wants to Be a Pilot

When I was a boy there was but one permanent ambition among my comrades in our village on the west bank of the Mississippi River. That was to be a steamboatman. We had transient ambitions of other sorts but they were only transient. When a circus came and went, it left us all burning to become clowns; the first Negro minstrel show that ever came to our section left us all suffering to try that kind of life; now and then we had a hope that, if we lived and were good, God would permit us to be pirates. These ambitions faded out, each in its turn; but the ambition to be a steamboatman always remained.

LOREN EISELEY

[1907–1977]

The Judgment of the Birds

It is a commonplace of all religious thought, even the most primitive, that the man seeking visions and insight must go apart from his fellows and live for a time in the wilderness. If he is of the proper sort, he will return with a message. It may not be a message from the god he set out to seek, but even if he has failed in that particular, he will have had a vision or seen a marvel, and these are always worth listening to and thinking about.

Each of these writers invites us to respond in a different way. Each invites us to enter a world of thought and experience—the world as the writer knows and experiences it. Twain evokes the world of nineteenth-century America when the Mississippi was alive with cargo and passengers. The focus in his opening paragraph, however, is less on the life of the river than on the ambitions of boys. As we read such a passage, we bring to it our own experience, our own goals and ambitions and dreams. We may remember when we were young, how we thought we might "grow up to be" whatever we dreamed about becoming. And we also realize that, like the young boy narrator, many of our ambitions simply faded. Some perhaps have remained, and we are now pursuing them.

Our sense of Twain's essay is influenced by our ability to remember a similar experience from our younger years. We may see the humor in the young boy's enthusiastic response to circuses and minstrel shows, a response that seems natural, suitably unrealistic, and overly romantic, given the realities of growing out of impossible dreams. (Though perhaps we don't see it that way at all since we once wished—and still do—to become something fabulous or important: a circus performer, a wandering minstrel, or a world leader.) We may also see and respond favorably to the way one such dream takes hold. This dream affects a person so strongly that he or she won't give up on it—ever. We ourselves may have such dreams. And whether or not we have pursued them with the tenacity Twain implies in his opening paragraph, such dreams are relevant to our experience of reading his essay.

Loren Eiseley's introductory paragraph invites us to consider a different possibility: that anyone seeking mystical visions and deep understanding must isolate himself from the social world, presumably to tune in either to his spiritual self or to nature. Eiseley at this point doesn't say which. He does insist that when such people do not find the answers or explanations they are looking for, they do nonetheless experience something extraordinary, something that less mystical and less adventurous types should find instructive and thought-provoking.

We experience Eiseley's writing differently from the way we experience Twain's. Eiseley sounds more serious, more academic, more philosophical. His style is less conversational; his voice is less personal, less immediately engaging. However, he too invites us to bring our experience to bear on what he is saying. To follow his thoughts, we need to consider what we know about mystics and visionaries, whether they indeed somehow receive "messages" that are otherworldly, yet relevant, to our lives, or whether they have wild imaginations that enable them to believe in such happenings. We may wonder what Eiseley can possibly mean by these suggestions. We may or may not have any real knowledge of what he is talking about. And that may influence us to become skeptical of his assertions or perhaps to become curious about where his essay will lead us.

The point is that in both instances, that of Twain's boy with his ambitions and Eiseley's mystical adult, we respond largely at first by considering our own experience, by seeing what the writers say in relation to what we have previously encountered or imagined. Something similar happens, but with a slightly altered perspective, when we read the opening of the following essay by Alice Walker.

ALICE WALKER

[b. 1944]

In Search of Our Mothers' Gardens

When the poet Jean Toomer walked through the South in the early twenties, he discovered a curious thing: black women whose spirituality was so intense, so deep, so *unconscious,* they were themselves unaware of the richness they held. They stumbled blindly through their lives: creatures so abused and mutilated in body, so dimmed and confused by pain, that they considered themselves unworthy even of hope. In the selfless abstractions their bodies became to the men who used them, they became more than "sexual objects," more even than mere women: they became "Saints." Instead of being perceived as whole persons, their bodies became shrines: what was thought to be their minds became temples suitable for worship. These crazy Saints stared out at the world, wildly, like lunatics—or quietly, like suicides; and the "God" that was in their gaze was as mute as a great stone.

Walker invites us into yet another world. We may or may not understand from this single paragraph what she is suggesting, but our response to what she describes will certainly be affected by what we know either directly or indirectly of being used as a sexual object; of what we know about suffering, prejudice, and sanity; of what we know about our mothers and grandmothers. Our experience as males or females will affect our reading of this essay, as will the color of our skin or the direction of our lives. We may respond with confusion, shock, amazement, outrage, pity—but we do respond somehow emotionally. Walker clearly invites more than an intellectual response. Before she is through with us, she will ask some frightening questions, questions that are certainly disheartening for women, particularly black women. "What did it mean," Walker asks, "for a black woman to be an artist in our grandmothers' time?" And again: "Did you have a genius of a great-great-grandmother who died under some ignorant and depraved white overseer's lash?" And once again: "Or was her body broken and forced to bear children (who were more often than not sold away from her)—eight, ten, fifteen, twenty children—when her one joy was the thought of modeling heroic figures of rebellion, in stone or clay?"

What kind of questions are these? Questions certainly to which we are invited to respond with feeling. We may agree or disagree with the picture Walker conjures up. We may see it as a wildly lunatic fantasy or as gripping human history. But see it we do, and react to it we must. Nor do we have to have seen or experienced directly what Walker describes to respond to her depiction of nineteenth-century black women. All we have to do is imagine it. Our capacity to imagine introduces one additional way in which we bring experience to bear on our reading of literature. For experience does not mean only what we ourselves have actually lived through; it also includes what we have seen, heard, read about, learned, and are capable of imagining.

With these thoughts in mind, we turn now to a short essay, "The Ring of Time," by E. B. White. As you read, keep track of your responses. Consider, for example, whether White provokes your thinking, stirs your feelings, triggers your memories, engages your imagination.

E. B. WHITE

[1889–1985]

The Ring of Time

After the lions had returned to their cages, creeping angrily through the chutes, a little bunch of us drifted away and into an open doorway nearby, where we stood for a while in semidarkness, watching a big brown circus horse go harumphing around the practice ring. His trainer was a woman of about forty, and the two of them, horse and woman, seemed caught up in one of those desultory treadmills of afternoon from which there is no apparent escape. The day was hot, and we kibitzers were grateful to be briefly out of the sun's glare. The long rein, or tape, by which the woman guided her charge counterclockwise in his dull career formed the radius of their private circle, of which she was the revolving center; and she, too, stepped a tiny circumference of her own, in order to accommodate the horse and allow him his maximum scope. She had on a short-skirted costume and a conical straw hat. Her legs were bare and she wore high heels, which probed deep into the loose tanbark and kept her ankles in a state of constant turmoil. The great size and meekness of the horse, the repetitious exercise, the heat of the afternoon, all exerted a hypnotic charm that invited boredom; we spectators were experiencing a languor—we neither expected relief nor felt entitled to any. We had paid a dollar to get into the grounds, to be sure, but we had got our dollar's worth a few minutes before, when the lion trainer's whiplash had got caught around a toe of one of the lions. What more did we want for a dollar?

Behind me I heard someone say, "Excuse me, please," in a low voice. She was halfway into the building when I turned and saw her—a girl of sixteen or seventeen, politely threading her way through us onlookers who blocked the entrance. As she emerged in front of us, I saw that she was barefoot, her dirty little feet fighting the uneven ground. In most respects she was like any of two or three dozen showgirls you encounter if you wander about the winter quarters of Mr. John Ringling North's circus, in Sarasota—cleverly proportioned, deeply browned by the sun, dusty, eager, and almost naked. But her grave face and the naturalness of her manner gave her a sort of quick distinction and brought a new note into the gloomy octagonal building where we had all cast our lot for a few moments. As soon as she had squeezed through the crowd, she spoke a word or two to the older woman, whom I took to be her mother, stepped to the ring, and waited while the horse coasted to a stop in front of her. She gave the animal a couple of affectionate swipes on his enormous neck and then swung herself aboard. The horse immediately resumed his rocking canter, the woman goading him on, chanting something that sounded like "Hop! Hop!"

In attempting to recapture this mild spectacle, I am merely acting as recording secretary for one of the oldest of societies—the society of those who, at one time or another, have surrendered, without even a show of resistance, to the bedazzlement of a circus rider. As a writing man, or secretary, I have always felt charged with the safekeeping of all unexpected items of worldly or unworldly enchantment, as though I might be held personally responsible if even a small one were to be lost. But it is not easy to communicate anything of this nature. The circus comes as close to being the world in microcosm as anything I know; in a way, it puts all the rest of show business in the shade. Its magic is universal and complex. Out of its wild disorder comes order; from its rank smell rises the good aroma of courage and daring; out of its preliminary shabbiness comes the final splendor. And buried in the familiar boasts of its advance agents lies the modesty of most of its people. For me the circus is at its best before it has been put together. It is at its best at certain moments when it comes to a point, as through a burning glass, in the activity and destiny of a single performer out of so many. One ring is always bigger than three. One rider, one aerialist, is always greater than six. In short, a man has to catch the circus unawares to experience its full impact and share its gaudy dream.

The ten-minute ride the girl took achieved—as far as I was concerned, who wasn't looking for it, and quite unbeknownst to her, who wasn't even striving for it—the thing that is sought by performers everywhere, on whatever stage, whether struggling in the tidal currents of Shakespeare or bucking the difficult motion of a horse. I somehow got the idea she was just cadging a ride, improving a shining ten minutes in the diligent way all serious artists seize free moments to hone the blade of their talent and keep themselves in trim. Her brief tour included only elementary postures and tricks, perhaps because they were all she was capable of, perhaps because her warmup at this hour was unscheduled and the ring was not rigged for a real practice session. She swung herself off and on the horse several times, gripping his mane. She did a few knee-stands—or whatever they are called—dropping to her knees and quickly bouncing back up on her feet again. Most of the time she simply rode in a standing position, well aft on the beast, her hands hanging easily at her sides, her head erect, her straw-colored ponytail lightly brushing her shoulders, the blood of exertion showing faintly through the tan of her skin. Twice she managed a one-foot stance—a sort of ballet pose, with arms outstretched. At one point the neck strap of her bathing suit broke and she went twice around the ring in the classic attitude of a woman making minor repairs to a garment. The fact that she was standing on the back of a moving horse while doing this invested the matter with a clownish significance that perfectly fitted the spirit of the circus—jocund, yet charming. She just rolled the strap into a neat ball and stowed it inside her bodice while the horse rocked and rolled beneath her in dutiful innocence. The bathing suit proved as self-reliant as its owner and stood up well enough without benefit of strap.

The richness of the scene was in its plainness, its natural condition—of horse, of ring, of girl, even to the girl's bare feet that gripped the bare back of her proud and ridiculous mount. The enchantment grew not out of anything that happened or was performed but out of something that seemed to go round and around and around with the girl, attending her, a steady gleam in the shape of a circle—a ring of ambition, of happiness, of youth. (And the positive pleasures of equilibrium under difficulties.) In a week or two, all would be changed, all (or almost all) lost: the girl would wear makeup, the horse would wear gold, the ring would be painted, the bark would be clean for the feet of the horse, the girl's feet would be clean for the slippers that she'd wear. All, all would be lost.

As I watched with the others, our jaws adroop, our eyes alight, I became painfully conscious of the element of time. Everything in the hideous old building seemed to take the shape of a circle, conforming to the course of the horse. The rider's gaze, as she peered straight ahead, seemed to be circular, as though bent by force of circumstance; then time itself began running in circles, and so the beginning was where the end was, and the two were the same, and one thing ran into the next and time went round and around and got nowhere. The girl wasn't so young that she did not know the delicious satisfaction of having a perfectly behaved body and the fun of using it to do a trick most people can't do, but she was too young to know that time does not really move in a circle at all. I thought: "She will never be as beautiful as this again"— a thought that made me acutely unhappy—and in a flash my mind (which is too much of a busybody to suit me) had projected her twenty-five years ahead, and she was now in the center of the ring, on foot, wearing a conical hat and high-heeled shoes, the image of the older woman, holding the long rein, caught in the treadmill of an afternoon long in the future. "She is at that enviable moment in life [I thought] when she believes she can go once around the ring, make one complete circuit, and at the end be exactly the same age as at the start." Everything in her movements, her expression, told you that for her the ring of time was perfectly formed, changeless, predictable, without beginning or end, like the ring in which she was traveling at this moment with the horse that wallowed under her. And then I slipped back into my trance, and time was circular again—time, pausing quietly with the rest of us, so as not to disturb the balance of a performer.

Her ride ended as casually as it had begun. The older woman stopped the horse, and the girl slid to the ground. As she walked toward us to leave, there was a quick, small burst of applause. She smiled broadly, in surprise and pleasure; then her face suddenly regained its gravity and she disappeared through the door.

It has been ambitious and plucky of me to attempt to describe what is indescribable, and I have failed, as I knew I would. But I have discharged my duty to my society; and besides, a writer, like an acrobat, must occasionally try a stunt that is too much for him. At any rate, it is worth reporting that long before the circus comes to town, its most notable performances have already been given. Under the bright lights of the finished show, a performer need only reflect the electric candle power that is directed upon him; but in the dark and dirty old training rings and in the makeshift cages, whatever light is generated, whatever excitement, whatever beauty, must come from original sources—from internal fires of professional hunger and delight, from the exuberance and gravity of youth. It is the difference between planetary light and the combustion of stars.

(1956)

When we read such an essay as "The Ring of Time," we do more than look for the writer's point, though we do that as well. Before we consider what the writer is saying we can consider our responses to what he describes. Did some parts of the essay engage you more than others? Did you relate E. B. White's experience and feelings to your own? Did you find yourself agreeing or disagreeing with something he said?

As with any work of literature, we often derive more from reading an essay after sharing our responses with others. If possible, talk about "The Ring of Time" with your classmates and teacher. See how their responses amplify your own. Most literary works trigger different associations and reactions in their readers. Gaining a sense of the variety of readers' responses and seeing also what is common among them can provide both assurance that others see the work as we do and alternative perspectives from which to understand it.

Such discussions prepare us to reread the essay. This second reading differs from the first because our knowledge of the work is greater and our sense of how it might be approached is augmented. Now we can turn from the subjectivity of our first responses to a more objective consideration of the writer's point. We may, in fact, often begin doing this during our first reading, but we do it more consciously and thoroughly during the second, in which our goal is interpretation.

THE INTERPRETATION OF THE ESSAY

Our experience of reading an essay is enhanced by thinking about its ideas as we interpret it. Interpretation involves four interrelated acts: observing details, connecting or relating them, developing inferences on the basis of these connections, and forming a conclusion in light of the inferences we draw. In reading White's "The Ring of Time" we focus on its subject and theme. We begin with a few questions.

What is the subject of "The Ring of Time"? What does White seem most concerned with—the circus, performance, practice, writing, time? Something else? What ideas about these subjects surface in the essay? What is the author's attitude toward them?

Let's consider just one of the subjects of White's essay—his reflections on time. One thing White suggests is that time is circular—a ring—that it goes around and around, seeming endlessly to repeat itself. The image of the ring of time, called to our attention by the title, suggests that things don't change, that they remain essentially the same. Details supporting this cyclical view of time include the description of the mother holding the rein as her feet make small circles on the ground while she leads the horse around the ring. (Notice the many words that describe *circle* in the first paragraph.)

The circularity of time is further accented and clarified in this sentence from the sixth paragraph: "The rider's gaze, as she peered straight ahead, seemed to be circular, as though bent by force of circumstance; then time itself began running in circles, and so the beginning was where the end was, and the two were the same, and one thing ran into the next and time went round and around and got nowhere." But almost as soon as White says this, he contradicts himself by saying that although the girl "believes she can go once around the ring . . . and at the end be exactly the same age as at the start," she was really "too young to know that time does not really move in a circle at all." With this counterview, White provokes us to think about time, to decide whether it is circular or linear, to consider, in part, whether things change or remain the same. Of course, we may conclude that time can be experienced both ways, that the two views White presents are complementary rather than contradictory. We can make such a compromise if we think of the seventeen-year-old girl growing up and losing her beauty and agility—if we recognize time's linearity, its inevitable sequence of changes. We can recognize that on the other hand, even though the girl moves through time in a linear fashion, she is also part of a larger family unit, which itself is part of a still larger social context— the circus and its performers. And these larger units don't change. One day she will replace her mother at the center of the practice ring. One day she will hold the reins for another young performer, her daughter perhaps, who will practice and perform as she does now. Time, White seems to say, forms both a line and a circle.

Next we provide in more detail an interpretation of George Orwell's "Marrakech." The essay has been printed in sections with intervening comments to illustrate the four aspects of the interpretive process.

GEORGE ORWELL
[1903–1950]

Marrakech

As the corpse went past the flies left the restaurant table in a cloud and rushed after it, but they came back a few minutes later.

The little crowd of mourners—all men and boys, no women—threaded their way across the market-place between the piles of pomegranates and the taxis and the camels, wailing a short chant over and over again. What really appeals to the flies is that the corpses here are never put into coffins, they are merely wrapped in a piece of rag and carried on a rough wooden bier on the shoulders of four friends. When the friends get to the burying-ground they hack an oblong hole a foot or two deep, dump the body in it and fling over it a little of the dried-up, lumpy earth, which is like broken brick. No gravestone, no name, no identifying mark of any kind. The burying-ground is merely a huge waste of hummocky earth, like a derelict building-lot. After a month or two no one can even be certain where his own relatives are buried.

When you walk through a town like this—two hundred thousand inhabitants, of whom at least twenty thousand own literally nothing except the rags they stand up in—when you see how the people live, and still more how easily they die, it is always difficult to believe that you are walking among human beings. All colonial empires are in reality founded upon that fact. The people have brown faces—besides, there are so many of them! Are they really the same flesh as yourself? Do they even have names? Or are they merely a kind of undifferentiated brown stuff, about as individual as bees or coral insects? They rise out of the earth, they sweat and starve for a few years, and then they sink back into the nameless mounds of the graveyard and nobody notices that they are gone. And even the graves themselves soon fade back into the soil. Sometimes, out for a walk, as you break your way through the prickly pear, you notice that it is rather bumpy underfoot, and only a certain regularity in the bumps tells you that you are walking over skeletons.

Comment   Orwell's description accentuates the extreme poverty of Marrakech and the little regard in which human life is held. The gravediggers, for example, "hack" and "fling" the dirt, then "dump" the body in the ground. Moreover the dead individual is seen not as a person (is it man, woman, or child?) but as a "corpse," an inert object. Additional details reinforce the lack of dignity in death and the lack of value accorded human life. Orwell compares the burial ground to an abandoned building lot, run down and neglected. The grave plots are unmarked, which suggests that the people of Marrakech are as anonymous in death as they were in life.

The third paragraph reinforces the poverty of Marrakech's people. Many have only the rags that they will buried in. Besides accentuating their poverty and anonymity, Orwell goes further by questioning whether they are really human beings at all. They live in squalor; they die easily, readily, more like insects than people. Orwell compares them to insects by highlighting their vast number and lack of individuality. Our question here may be: Does Orwell not value them as human beings? Or is he pointing out how they live in hopelessness, poverty, and futility to awaken his readers to these facts?

Notice too that Orwell slips in a sentence of generalization, suggesting that colonial empires are built on the kinds of attitudes and conditions he describes. This comment can be taken as an indictment of colonialism or as a simple assertion of fact, of how things are, with such suffering a necessary evil that colonialism nust accommodate. This political question is crucial: our sense of Orwell's point and purpose in "Marrakech" hinge on our response to it.

The first part of the essay ends with a description of the makeshift cemetery. Here is the second section:

I was feeding one of the gazelles in the public gardens.

Gazelles are almost the only animals that look good to eat when they are still alive, in fact, one can hardly look at their hindquarters without thinking of mint sauce. The gazelle I was feeding seemed to know that this thought was in my mind, for though it took the piece of bread I was holding out it obviously did not like me. It nibbled rapidly at the bread, then lowered its head and tried to butt me, then took another nibble and then butted again. Probably its idea was that if it could drive me away the bread would somehow remain hanging in mid-air.

An Arab navvy working on the path nearby lowered his heavy hoe and sidled slowly towards us. He looked from the gazelle to the bread and from the bread to the gazelle, with a sort of quiet amazement, as though he had never seen anything quite like this before. Finally he said shyly in French:

"*I* could eat some of that bread."

I tore off a piece and he stowed it gratefully in some secret place under his rags. This man is an employee of the Municipality.

Comment   As we read this vignette about the gazelle, we look for some connection to what went before. Not until the Arab navvy (a manual laborer who excavates roads, canals) makes his appearance does the connection become apparent: he's hungry and poor. His shy, indirect request for food suggests that he wants to preserve his self-respect and dignity. There seems to be some tension between this desire and the urgency of his need. What makes the situation more poignant is that the man does not devour the bread but instead hides it under his rags. Presumably he is saving it, which implies that for him bread is a precious commodity. The final detail of the section is important: this man has a job. With this detail Orwell implies how extreme the poverty of Marrakech is.

Having read the two sections, what connections do you see? How does your sense of the first two parts prepare you to read the third?

When you go through the Jewish quarters you gather some idea of what the medieval ghettoes were probably like. Under their Moorish rulers the Jews were only allowed to own land in certain restricted areas, and after centuries of this kind of treatment they have ceased to bother about overcrowding. Many of the streets are a good deal less than six feet wide, the houses are completely windowless, and sore-eyed children cluster everywhere in unbelievable numbers, like clouds of flies. Down the centre of the street there is generally running a little river of urine.

In the bazaar huge families of Jews, all dressed in the long black robe and little black skull-cap, are working in dark fly-infested booths that look like caves. A carpenter sits crosslegged at a prehistoric lathe, turning chair-legs at lightning speed. He works the lathe with a bow in his right hand and guides the chisel with his left foot, and thanks to a lifetime of sitting in this position his left leg is warped out of shape. At his side his grandson, aged six, is already starting on the simpler parts of the job.

I was just passing the coppersmiths' booths when somebody noticed that I was lighting a cigarette. Instantly, from the dark holes all around, there was a frenzied rush of Jews, many of them old grandfathers with flowing grey beards, all clamouring for a cigarette. Even a blind man somewhere at the back of one of the booths heard a rumour of cigarettes and came crawling out, groping in the air with his hand. In about a minute I had used up the whole packet. None of these people, I suppose, works less than twelve hours a day, and every one of them looks on a cigarette as a more or less impossible luxury.

As the Jews live in self-contained communities they follow the same trades as the

Arabs, except for agriculture. Fruitsellers, potters, silversmiths, blacksmiths, butchers, leatherworkers, tailors, water-carriers, beggars, porters—whichever way you look you see nothing but Jews. As a matter of fact there are thirteen thousand of them, all living in the space of a few acres. A good job Hitler wasn't here. Perhaps he was on his way, however. You hear the usual dark rumours about the Jews, not only from the Arabs but from the poorer Europeans.

"Yes, mon vieux, they took my job away from me and gave it to a Jew. The Jews! They're the real rulers of this country, you know. They've got all the money. They control the banks, finance—everything."

"But," I said, "isn't it a fact that the average Jew is a labourer working for about a penny an hour?"

"Ah, that's only for show! They're all moneylenders really. They're cunning, the Jews."

In just the same way, a couple of hundred years ago, poor old women used to be burned for witchcraft when they could not even work enough magic to get themselves a square meal.

Comment   In the third section Orwell takes us into the Jewish ghetto. By now we realize that the essay is largely descriptive and that its descriptive details are tied together by two issues: poverty and anonymity.

We can divide this vignette into two parts. First, Orwell indicates the crowded and filthy conditions in which the Jews live. He compares the children to clouds of flies, primarily to indicate their vast numbers and insignificance. Details about the working conditions reveal their destructive consequences. Orwell doesn't spell out what the future of the six-year-old grandson who works beside his physically deformed grandfather will be. Instead, he accentuates the injustice by describing the fracas over a few cigarettes, which are beyond the purchasing power of people who work "only" twelve hours a day.

The second section of the this vignette depicts the severe prejudice Jews suffer from. The dialogue reveals Orwell's attempt to undermine the unfair caricature of the Jews as rich moneylenders. Prejudice, fear, and hatred run so deep, however, that the Jewish poverty and powerlessness described by Orwell are explained away by a poor European as a "trick." Against this kind of closed-mindedness what can be said? The analogy Orwell draws with witch hunters of an earlier time testifies to the power of prejudice, and it evokes our sympathy for those who suffer unjustly. Orwell's implied criticism of such attitudes transcends the Jewish quarter of Marrakech to all places where human dignity is violated by hatred and prejudice.

This next section is the longest of the essay.

All people who work with their hands are partly invisible, and the more important the work they do, the less visible they are. Still, a white skin is always fairly conspicuous. In northern Europe, when you see a labourer ploughing a field, you probably give him a second glance. In a hot country, anywhere south of Gibraltar or east of Suez, the chances are that you don't even see him. I have noticed this again and again. In a tropical landscape one's eye takes in everything except the human beings. It takes in the dried-up soil, the prickly pear, the palm tree and the distant mountain, but it always misses the peasant hoeing at his patch. He is the same colour as the earth, and a great deal less interesting to look at.

It is only because of this that the starved countries of Asia and Africa are accepted as tourist resorts. No one would think of running cheap trips to the Distressed Areas. But where the human beings have brown skins their poverty is simply not noticed. What does Morocco mean to a Frenchman? An orange-grove or a job in Government service. Or to an Englishman? Camels, castles, palm trees, Foreign Legionnaires, brass trays, and bandits. One could probably live there for years without noticing that for nine-tenths of the people the reality of life is an endless, back-breaking struggle to wring a little food out of an eroded soil.

Most of Morocco is so desolate that no wild animal bigger than a hare can live on it. Huge areas which were once covered with forest have turned into a treeless waste where the soil is exactly like broken-up brick. Nevertheless a good deal of it is cultivated, with frightful labour. Everything is done by hand. Long lines of women, bent double like inverted capital L's, work their way slowly across the fields, tearing up the prickly weeds with their hands, and the peasant gathering lucerne for fodder pulls it up stalk by stalk instead of reaping it, thus saving an inch or two on each stalk. The plough is a wretched wooden thing, so frail that one can easily carry it on one's shoulder, and fitted underneath with a rough iron spike which stirs the soil to a depth of about four inches. This is as much as the strength of the animals is equal to. It is usual to plough with a cow and a donkey yoked together. Two donkeys would not be quite strong enough, but on the other hand two cows would cost a little more to feed. The peasants possess no harrows, they merely plough the soil several times over in different directions, finally leaving it in rough furrows, after which the whole field has to be shaped with hoes into small oblong patches to conserve water. Except for a day or two after the rare rainstorms there is never enough water. Along the edges of the fields channels are hacked out to a depth of thirty or forty feet to get at the tiny trickles which run through the subsoil.

Every afternoon a file of very old women passes down the road outside my house, each carrying a load of firewood. All of them are mummified with age and the sun, and all of them are tiny. It seems to be generally the case in primitive communities that the women, when they get beyond a certain age, shrink to the size of children. One day a poor old creature who could not have been more than four feet tall crept past me under a vast load of wood. I stopped her and put a five-sou piece (a little more than a farthing) into her hand. She answered with a shrill wail, almost a scream, which was partly gratitude but mainly surprise. I suppose that from her point of view, by taking any notice of her, I seemed almost to be violating a law of nature. She accepted her status as an old woman, that is to say as a beast of burden. When a family is travelling it is quite usual to see a father and a grown-up son riding ahead on donkeys, and an old woman following on foot, carrying the baggage.

But what is strange about these people is their invisibility. For several weeks, always at about the same time of day, the file of old women had hobbled past the house with their firewood, and though they had registered themselves on my eyeballs I cannot truly say that I had seen them. Firewood was passing—that was how I saw it. It was only that one day I happened to be walking behind them, and the curious up-and-down motion of a load of wood drew my attention to the human being beneath it. Then for the first time I noticed the poor old earth-coloured bodies, bodies reduced to bones and leathery skin, bent double under the crushing weight. Yet I suppose I had not been five minutes on Moroccan soil before I noticed the overloading of the donkeys and was infuriated by it. There is no question that the donkeys are damnably treated. The Moroccan donkey is hardly bigger than a St. Bernard dog, it carries a load which in the British Army would be considered too much for a fifteen-hands mule, and very often its pack-saddle is not taken off its back for weeks together. But what is peculiarly pitiful is that it is the most willing creature on earth, it follows its master like a dog and does not need either bridle or halter. After a dozen years of devoted work it suddenly drops dead, whereupon its master tips it into the ditch and the village dogs have torn its guts out before it is cold.

This kind of thing makes one's blood boil, whereas—on the whole—the plight of the human beings does not. I am not commenting, merely pointing to a fact. People with brown skins are next door to invisible. Anyone can be sorry for the donkey with its galled back, but it is generally owing to some kind of accident if one even notices the old woman under her load of sticks.

Comment   This section centers on the invisibility of the natives. They are not noticed, presumably because they are not important. They become part of the landscape, a fact which further suggests their lack of distinction, and which also recalls the burial scene of section one. Their dark skins render them invisible.

The information Orwell provides about the land's aridity and the primitive farming tools and methods shows the futility and harshness of their lives. People, especially old women, are reduced to the status of beasts of burden. Orwell acknowledges his acquiescence in the *status quo:* he admits to seeing "firewood" passing rather than the human beings carrying that firewood. It is the abusive treatment of the donkeys, however, not the wretchedness of the women, that initially angers him. Perhaps Orwell suggests here how easy it is to become accustomed to such conditions—as long as one is not subject to them oneself. Perhaps he confesses his guilt, recognizing his deficiencies of perception and sensitivity.

We might note also that the language Orwell uses to describe the dead donkey echoes his description of the human burial in the first vignette. In both instances, the burial reveals a complete disregard for life. Both man and beast serve their purposes, and when they are no longer useful, are unceremoniously disposed of.

The essay concludes with a shift of focus:

As the storks flew northward the Negroes were marching southward—a long, dusty column, infantry, screw-gun batteries, and then more infantry, four or five thousand men in all, winding up the road with a clumping of boots and a clatter of iron wheels.

They were Senegalese, the blackest Negroes in Africa, so black that sometimes it is difficult to see whereabouts on their necks the hair begins. Their splendid bodies were hidden in reach-me-down khaki uniforms, their feet squashed into boots that looked like blocks of wood, and every tin hat seemed to be a couple of sizes too small. It was very hot and the men had marched a long way. They slumped under the weight of their packs and the curiously sensitive black faces were glistening with sweat.

As they went past a tall, very young Negro turned and caught my eye. But the look he gave me was not in the least the kind of look you might expect. Not hostile, not contemptuous, not sullen, not even inquisitive. It was the shy, wide-eyed Negro look, which actually is a look of profound respect. I saw how it was. This wretched boy, who is a French citizen and has therefore been dragged from the forest to scrub floors and catch syphilis in garrison towns, actually has feelings of reverence before a white skin. He has been taught that the white race are his masters, and he still believes it.

But there is one thought which every white man (and in this connection it doesn't matter twopence if he calls himself a socialist) thinks when he sees a black army marching past. "How much longer can we go on kidding these people? How long before they turn their guns in the other direction?"

It was curious, really. Every white man there had this thought stowed somewhere or other in his mind. I had it, so had the other onlookers, so had the officers on their sweating chargers and the white N.C.O.'s marching in the ranks. It was a kind of secret which we all knew and were too clever to tell; only the Negroes didn't know it. And really it was like watching a flock of cattle to see the long column, a mile or two miles of armed men, flowing peacefully up the road, while the great white birds drifted over them in the opposite direction, glittering like scraps of paper.

(1936)

Comment   The description of the Senegalese troops is charged with tension. With his description of the blackness of the troops and their servility, Orwell calls attention to a racial inequality he had implied earlier. Orwell's imagery in the final paragraphs suggests that colonial oppression cannot last forever, that when the oppressed realize their strength and numbers, they will overthrow their imperialist subjugators. It's only a matter of time.

THE EVALUATION OF THE ESSAY

To evaluate an essay means to consider its value for us as readers. Evaluation consists essentially of two different kinds of assessment: (1) a judgment about the work's aesthetic merit; (2) a judgment about the power and validity of its ideas. We will speak briefly about the aesthetic valuation of essays in a moment. First, however, we need to explain what we mean by evaluating an essay's ideas.

When we evaluate an idea, we consider its accuracy as a description, its persuasiveness as an argument, or its suggestiveness as an act of imaginative thinking. In order to evaluate any idea, we first have to abstract it from the discourse of which it is a part. We have to identify it, isolate it, and restate it as a generalization. Evaluation, in short, depends on interpretation. How we understand the point or thesis of an essay (whether this point is explicitly stated or implicitly suggested) will strongly influence how we evaluate that essay.

Once we have a clear understanding of what an essay says, we can assess the values it expresses. Usually these values are those of the writer, since the voice we hear in an essay is typically an author's own rather than that of an imagined character or persona. Our goal in evaluating any essay is to consider how an author's social attitudes, moral convictions, or cultural dispositions affect his or her argument. In making such analyses we bring to bear our own attitudes, beliefs, convictions, and dispositions.

But this kind of thinking about essays represents only one facet of our evaluation of them. Another is our consideration of their aesthetic merit, their success as works of literature. In the same way that we assess the beauty of a poem or the greatness of a play, we can evaluate the aesthetic achievement of an essay. We consider the essay's language or style and its form or structure. We also consider its power to persuade us, move us, or entertain us. To do this we analyze the work, studying how well the writer employs words to create meaning and how well he or she structures and dramatizes ideas. In the first two sections of this introduction, you read E. B. White's "The Ring of Time" and George Orwell's "Marrakech." Although you will be in a better position to evaluate their aesthetic merit after reading Chapter 3, "Elements of the Essay," it should still be useful for you to consider these works from an aesthetic standpoint. You might consider, for example, what aspects of Orwell's or White's language, selection of detail, and organization make them more than mere statements of fact, more than simple descriptions of events. (The commentary provides some implicit direction on this kind of analysis.)

The literary value of an essay also includes its ability to move us, to provide us with a unique experience of intellectual and emotional stimulation. By identifying an essay's effect on us, we acknowledge one of its sources of value.

The other kinds of values we are concerned with as we read essays are the social attitudes, moral beliefs, and cultural dispositions we see as animating the work. How we respond to any essay is determined in part by our understanding of such values and our sense of how they mesh with or collide against our own. Many of the essays in Chapter 7, "A Collection of Essays," reflect strongly held convictions based on particular social, moral, and cultural values. Jonathan Swift's "A Modest Proposal," for example, considers the problem of the Irish poor and what to do about it. E. M. Forster's "Our Graves in Gallipoli" focuses on the problem of war. James Baldwin's "Notes of a Native Son" deals with race relations and family dynamics. In these essays arguments are developed, positions taken, and experience and evidence presented, all based on explicitly delineated social, moral, and cultural values.

Consider the aesthetic value of the following essay from the standpoint of its power to affect you, and from the standpoint of its language and structure. Identify its cultural values and comment on their significance for an understanding of the essay and for an assessment of its meaning to you as a thinking reader. Consider especially the values of the central figures: the wrestler, the doctor, the boy, and the uncle. And consider, finally, how other readers with different racial, cultural, and gender characteristics might respond to the points raised here and to the essay itself.

RICHARD SELZER

[*b. 1928*]

The Masked Marvel's Last Toehold

MORNING ROUNDS.

On the fifth floor of the hospital, in the west wing, I know that a man is sitting up in his bed, waiting for me. Elihu Koontz is seventy-five, and he is diabetic. It is two weeks since I amputated his left leg just below the knee. I walk down the corridor, but I do not go straight into his room. Instead, I pause in the doorway. He is not yet aware of my presence, but gazes down at the place in the bed where his leg used to be, and where now there is the collapsed leg of his pajamas. He is totally absorbed, like an athlete appraising the details of his body. What is he thinking, I wonder. Is he dreaming the outline of his toes. Does he see there his foot's incandescent ghost? Could he be angry? Feel that I have taken from him something for which he yearns now with all his heart? Has he forgotten so soon the pain? It was a pain so great as to set him apart from all other men, in a red-hot place where he had no kith or kin. What of those black gorilla toes and the soupy mess that was his heel? I watch him from the doorway. It is a kind of spying, I know.

Save for a white fringe open at the front, Elihu Koontz is bald. The hair has grown too long and is wilted. He wears it as one would wear a day-old laurel wreath. He is naked to the waist, so that I can see his breasts. They are the breasts of Buddha, inverted triangles from which the nipples swing, dark as garnets.

I have seen enough. I step into the room, and he sees that I am there.

"How did the night go, Elihu?"

He looks at me for a long moment. "Shut the door," he says.

I do, and move to the side of the bed. He takes my left hand in both of his, gazes at it, turns it over, then back, fondling, at last holding it up to his cheek. I do not withdraw from this loving. After a while he relinquishes my hand, and looks up at me.

"How is the pain?" I ask.

He does not answer, but continues to look at me in silence. I know at once that he has made a decision.

"Ever hear of The Masked Marvel?" He says this in a low voice, almost a whisper.

"What?"

"The Masked Marvel," he says. "You never heard of him?"

"No."

He clucks his tongue. He is exasperated.

All at once there is a recollection. It is dim, distant, but coming near.

"Do you mean the wrestler?"

Eagerly, he nods, and the breasts bob. How gnomish he looks, oval as the huge helpless egg of some outlandish lizard. He has very long arms, which, now and then, he unfurls to reach for things—a carafe of water, a get-well card. He gazes up at me, urging. He *wants* me to remember.

"Well . . . yes," I say. I am straining backward in time. "I saw him wrestle in Toronto long ago."

"Ha!" He smiles. "You saw *me*." And his index finger, held rigid and upright, bounces in the air.

The man has said something shocking, unacceptable. It must be challenged.

"You?" I am trying to smile.

Again that jab of the finger. "You saw *me*."

"No," I say. But even then, something about Elihu Koontz, those prolonged arms, the shape of his head, the sudden agility with which he leans from his bed to get a large brown envelope from his nightstand, something is forcing me toward a memory. He rummages through his papers, old newspaper clippings, photographs, and I remember . . .

It is almost forty years ago. I am ten years old. I have been sent to Toronto to spend the summer with relatives. Uncle Max has bought two tickets to the wrestling match. He is taking me that night.

"He isn't allowed," says Aunt Sarah to me. Uncle Max has angina.

"He gets too excited," she says.

"I wish you wouldn't go, Max," she says.

"You mind your own business," he says.

And we go. Out into the warm Canadian evening. I am not only abroad, I am abroad in the *evening!* I have never been taken out in the evening. I am terribly excited. The trolleys, the lights, the horns. It is a bazaar. At the Maple Leaf Gardens, we sit high and near the center. The vast arena is dark except for the brilliance of the ring at the bottom.

It begins.

The wrestlers circle. They grapple. They are all haunch and paunch. I am shocked by their ugliness, but I do not show it. Uncle Max is exhilarated. He leans forward, his eyes unblinking, on his face a look of enormous happiness. One after the other, a pair of wrestlers enter the ring. The two men join, twist, jerk, tug, bend, yank, and throw. Then they leave and are replaced by another pair. At last it is the main event. "The Angel vs. The Masked Marvel."

On the cover of the program notes, there is a picture of The Angel hanging from the limb of a tree, a noose of thick rope around his neck. The Angel hangs just so for an hour every day, it is explained, to strengthen his neck. The Masked Marvel's trademark is a black stocking cap with holes for the eyes and mouth. He is never seen without it, states the program. No one knows who The Masked Marvel really is!

"Good," says Uncle Max. "Now you'll see something." He is fidgeting, waiting for them to appear. They come down separate aisles, climb into the ring from opposite sides. I have never seen anything like them. It is The Angel's neck that first captures the eye. The shaved nape rises in twin columns to puff into the white hood of a sloped and bosselated skull that is too small. As though, strangled by the sinews of that neck, the skull had long since withered and shrunk. The thing about The Angel is the absence of any mystery in his body. It is simply *there*. A monosyllabic announcement. A grunt. One looks and knows everything at once, the fat thighs, the gigantic buttocks, the great spine from which hang knotted ropes and pale aprons of beef. And that prehistoric head. He is all of a single hideous piece, The Angel is. No detachables.

The Masked Marvel seems dwarfish. His fingers dangle kneeward. His short legs are slightly bowed as if under the weight of the cask they are forced to heft about. He has breasts that swing when he moves! I have never seen such breasts on a man before.

There is a sudden ungraceful movement, and they close upon one another. The Angel stoops and hugs The Marvel about the waist, locking his hands behind The Marvel's back. Now he straightens and lifts The Marvel as though he were uprooting a tree. Thus he holds him, then stoops again, thrusts one hand through The Marvel's crotch, and with the other grabs him by the neck. He rears and . . . The Marvel is aloft! For a long moment, The Angel stands as though deciding where to make the toss. Then throws. Was that board or bone that splintered there? Again and again, The Angel hurls himself upon the body of The Masked Marvel.

Now The Angel rises over the fallen Marvel, picks up one foot in both of his hands, and twists the toes downward. It is far beyond the tensile strength of mere ligament, mere cartilage. The Masked Marvel does not hide his agony, but pounds and slaps the floor with his hand, now and then reaching up toward The Angel in an attitude of supplication. I have never seen such suffering. And all the while his black mask rolls from side to side, the mouth pulled to a tight slit through which issues an endless hiss that I can hear from where I sit. All at once, I hear a shouting close by.

"Break it off! Tear off a leg and throw it up here!"

It is Uncle Max. Even in the darkness I can see that he is gray. A band of sweat stands upon his upper lip. He is on his feet now, panting, one fist pressed at his chest, the other raised warlike toward the ring. For the first time I begin to think that something terrible might happen here. Aunt Sarah was right.

"Sit down, Uncle Max," I say. "Take a pill, please."

He reaches for the pillbox, gropes, and swallows without taking his gaze from the wrestlers. I wait for him to sit down.

"That's not fair," I say, "twisting his toes like that."

"It's the toehold," he explains.

"But it's not *fair,*" I say again. The whole of the evil is laid open for me to perceive. I am trembling.

And now The Angel does something unspeakable. Holding the foot of The Marvel at full twist with one hand, he bends and grasps the mask where it clings to the back of The Marvel's head. And he pulls. He is going to strip it off! Lay bare an ultimate carnal mystery! Suddenly it is beyond mere physical violence. Now I am on my feet, shouting into the Maple Leaf Gardens.

"Watch out," I scream. "Stop him. Please, somebody, stop him."

Next to me, Uncle Max is chuckling.

Yet The Masked Marvel hears me, I know it. And rallies from his bed of pain. Thrusting with his free heel, he strikes The Angel at the back of the knee. The Angel falls. The Masked Marvel is on top of him, pinning his shoulders to the mat. One! Two! Three! And it is over. Uncle Max is strangely still. I am gasping for breath. All this I remember as I stand at the bedside of Elihu Koontz.

Once again, I am in the operating room. It is two years since I amputated the left leg of Elihu Koontz. Now it is his right leg which is gangrenous. I have already scrubbed.

I stand to one side wearing my gown and gloves. And . . . *I am masked*. Upon the table lies Elihu Koontz, pinned in a fierce white light. Spinal anesthesia has been administered. One of his arms is taped to a board placed at a right angle to his body. Into this arm, a needle has been placed. Fluid drips here from a bottle overhead. With his other hand, Elihu Koontz beats feebly at the side of the operating table. His head rolls from side to side. His mouth is pulled into weeping. It seems to me that I have never seen such misery.

An orderly stands at the foot of the table, holding Elihu Koontz's leg aloft by the toes so that the intern can scrub the limb with antiseptic solutions. The intern paints the foot, ankle, leg, and thigh, both front and back, three times. From a corner of the room where I wait, I look down as from an amphitheater. Then I think of Uncle Max yelling, "Tear off a leg. Throw it up here." And I think that forty years later I am making the catch.

"It's not fair," I say aloud. But no one hears me. I step forward to break The Masked Marvel's last toehold.

(1979)

QUESTIONS

1. Compare the reactions of the boy and his uncle to the wrestling match they jointly watch. How do you respond to their reactions?
2. Consider the effectiveness of the comparisons employed in paragraphs 1 and 32. What do they contribute to your understanding of the essay? To your evaluation of it?
3. Comment on Selzer's handling of time in the essay. What does he gain by breaking chronology in telling the story of the wrestler?
4. Identify parallel details between the first and second parts of the essay and between its second and third parts as well. What does this use of parallelism contribute to the effectiveness of the essay?
5. Much of the essay is given over to dialogue. To what extent does dialogue generate the emotional power of the essay?
6. In what ways does the surgeon break The Masked Marvel's last toehold? Consider the various meanings of "break."
7. In considering the aesthetic value of an essay, we measure it against others of its type. How would you characterize this essay? How does it measure up against others you have read?
8. What cultural and social values do you find in the essay? What assumptions about men and boys, about doctors and patients underlie its action and meaning?
9. If you value the essay, why do you value it? If you don't, why don't you?
10. If you could ask the author one question, what would it be?

THE ACT OF READING THE ESSAY

There are many ways we can actively engage a literary work. Most require some form of writing as we read; questioning, annotating, making notes or journal entries. Here we will try something different: an imaginary dialogue with the author. This approach to a text is perhaps best suited to the essay, since the genre typically invites agreement with an explicitly stated idea. In choosing the essay form, in fact, writers signal their intention to persuade us of their views. One way of accepting the invitation is to enter into a kind of imaginary conversation with an essay's author.

We illustrate by reading an essay, Gretel Ehrlich's "About Men," then conducting an imaginary interview with Ehrlich.

GRETEL EHRLICH

[*b. 1946*]

About Men

When I'm in New York but feeling lonely for Wyoming I look for the Marlboro ads in the subway. What I'm aching to see is horseflesh, the glint of a spur, a line of distant mountains, brimming creeks, and a reminder of the ranchers and cowboys I've ridden with for the last eight years. But the men I see in those posters with their stern, humorless looks remind me of no one I know here. In our hellbent earnestness to romanticize the cowboy we've ironically disesteemed his true character. If he's "strong and silent" it's because there's probably no one to talk to. If he "rides away into the sunset" it's because he's been on horseback since four in the morning moving cattle and he's trying, fifteen hours later, to get home to his family. If he's "a rugged individualist" he's also part of a team: ranch work is teamwork and even the glorified open-range cowboys of the 1880s rode up and down the Chisholm Trail in the company of twenty or thirty other riders. Instead of the macho, trigger-happy man our culture has perversely wanted him to be, the cowboy is more apt to be convivial, quirky, and softhearted. To be "tough" on a ranch has nothing to do with conquests and displays of power. More often than not, circumstances—like the colt he's riding or an unexpected blizzard—are overpowering him. It's not toughness but "toughing it out" that counts. In other words, this macho, cultural artifact the cowboy has become is simply a man who possesses resilience, patience, and an instinct for survival. "Cowboys are just like a pile of rocks—everything happens to them. They get climbed on, kicked, rained and snowed on, scuffed up by wind. Their job is 'just to take it,'" one old-timer told me.

A cowboy is someone who loves his work. Since the hours are long—ten to fifteen hours a day—and the pay is $30 he has to. What's required of him is an odd mixture of physical vigor and maternalism. His part of the beef-raising industry is to birth and nurture calves and take care of their mothers. For the most part his work is done on horseback and in a lifetime he sees and comes to know more animals than people. The iconic myth surrounding him is built on American notions of heroism: the index of a man's value as measured in physical courage. Such ideas have perverted manliness into a self-absorbed race for cheap thrills. In a rancher's world, courage has less to do with facing danger than with acting spontaneously—usually on behalf of an animal or another rider. If a cow is stuck in a boghole he throws a loop around her neck, takes his dally (a half hitch around the saddle horn), and pulls her out with horsepower. If a calf is born sick, he may take her home, warm her in front of the kitchen fire, and massage her legs until dawn. One friend, whose favorite horse was trying to swim a lake with hobbles on, dove under water and cut her legs loose with a knife, then swam her to shore, his arm around her neck lifeguard-style, and saved her from drowning. Because these incidents are usually linked to someone or something outside himself, the westerner's courage is selfless, a form of compassion.

The physical punishment that goes with cowboying is greatly underplayed. Once fear is dispensed with, the threshold of pain rises to meet the demands of the job. When Jane Fonda asked Robert Redford (in the film *Electric Horseman*) if he was sick as he struggled to his feet one morning, he replied, "No, just bent." For once the movies had it right. The cowboys I was sitting with laughed in agreement. Cowboys are rarely complainers; they show their stoicism by laughing at themselves.

If a rancher or cowboy has been thought of as a "man's man"—laconic, hard-drinking, inscrutable—there's almost no place in which the balancing act between male and female, manliness and femininity, can be more natural. If he's gruff, handsome, and physically fit on the outside, he's androgynous at the core. Ranchers are midwives, hunters, nurturers, providers, and conservationists all at once. What we've interpreted as toughness—weathered skin, calloused hands, a squint in the eye and a growl in the voice—only masks the tenderness inside. "Now don't go telling me these lambs are cute," one rancher warned me the first day I walked into the football-field-sized lambing sheds. The next thing I knew he was holding a black lamb. "Ain't this little rat good-lookin'?"

So many of the men who came to the West were southerners—men looking for work and a new life after the Civil War—that chivalrousness and strict codes of honor were soon thought of as western traits. There were very few women in Wyoming during territorial days, so when they did arrive (some as mail-order brides from places like Philadelphia) there was a stand-offishness between the sexes and a formality that persists now. Ranchers still tip their hats and say, "Howdy, ma'am" instead of shaking hands with me.

Even young cowboys are often evasive with women. It's not that they're Jekyll and Hyde creatures—gentle with animals and rough on women—but rather, that they don't know how to bring their tenderness into the house and lack the vocabulary to express the complexity of what they feel. Dancing wildly all night becomes a metaphor for the explosive emotions pent up inside, and when these are, on occasion, released, they're so battery-charged and potent that one caress of the face or one "I love you" will peal for a long while.

The geographical vastness and the social isolation here make emotional evolution seem impossible. Those contradictions of the heart between respectability, logic, and convention on the one hand, and impulse, passion, and intuition on the other, played out wordlessly against the paradisical beauty of the West, give cowboys a wide-eyed but drawn look. Their lips pucker up, not with kisses but with immutability. They may want to break out, staying up all night with a lover just to talk, but they don't know how and can't imagine what the consequences will be. Those rare occasions when they do bare themselves result in confusion. "I feel as if I'd sprained my heart," one friend told me a month after such a meeting.

My friend Ted Hoagland wrote, "No one is as fragile as a woman but no one is as fragile as a man." For all the women here who use "fragileness" to avoid work or as a sexual ploy, there are men who try to hide theirs, all the while clinging to an adolescent dependency on women to cook their meals, wash their clothes, and keep the ranch house warm in winter. But there is true vulnerability in evidence here. Because these men work with animals, not machines or numbers, because they live outside in landscapes of torrential beauty, because they are confined to a place and a routine embellished with awesome variables, because calves die in the arms that pulled others into life, because they go to the mountains as if on a pilgrimage to find out what makes a herd of elk tick, their strength is also a softness, their toughness, a rare delicacy.

(1985)

Interview

QUESTION: I understand that you published this essay in 1985. I wonder whether you think the cowboy continues to be as romanticized now as he was five or ten years ago. I'm also curious about your sense of where the romanticized stereotype of the cowboy derives from.

RESPONSE: [Here as readers we might imaginatively create the author's responses. And of course we can follow up our train of thought with some of our own speculations. If we are lucky we might, at least occasionally, get the author's actual responses.]

QUESTION: I hadn't really thought before of the maternal side of cowboy life. You are serious, I presume. But now that you bring up the idea, it makes me wonder about the cowboy as a parent generally. Given the long hours and the time away from home, how do these men handle their parental responsibilities?

RESPONSE:

QUESTION: In fact, I wonder if you haven't romanticized the cowboy's image yourself in this essay by suggesting that cowboys are typically "strong silent types." You know, they don't talk much about their feelings; perhaps they don't talk much about anything. And I also wonder how far you mean to suggest that this image of the man who says little is characteristic of American males generally.

RESPONSE:

QUESTION: I'm curious too about why you retitled the essay "About Men" rather than staying with its former title, "Revisionist Cowboy," which *Time* magazine used when it was first published. Which title do you actually prefer? Have you considered any others?

RESPONSE:

QUESTION: How do you respond when ranchers tip their hats and treat you according to the code of western chivalry? Do you think you should be treated like "one of the the guys"?

RESPONSE:

QUESTION: You attribute much of the character of the cowboy to his close relationship with nature. His life, as you intimate, is governed and his character formed by his direct and lasting contact with landscape, animals, weather. Is there a place for a life of the mind, for culture as well as nature in the cowboy's existence?
RESPONSE:

QUESTION: One last question: You seem concerned with debunking certain myths about the cowboy largely by complicating the stereotype. Why do you think such an image came into existence in the first place? And do you think there is a parallel stereotype of the western woman?
RESPONSE:

Imagining a conversation with the writer, imagining the writer's responses to our thoughts and questions promotes our understanding of the implications of the essay. It also stimulates a consideration of dimensions of the subject the writer has not included. And, of course, it encourages us to reread the essay and reconsider its ideas.

We can classify essays in a rough way as speculative, argumentative, narrative, and expository. Speculative essays explore ideas and feelings; argumentative essays make claims and present evidence to support them; narrative essays tell stories and chronicle events; expository essays explain ideas and attitudes. Nearly all essays are persuasive to one degree or another. Whatever their dominant mode and form, most essays attempt to convince readers of something.

SPECULATIVE ESSAYS

Let us glance first at what we have called the *speculative essay*. *To speculate* means to contemplate, conjecture, or surmise. A *speculative essay* is concerned less with making a point overtly and decisively than with exploring an idea, perception, or feeling. The tone of a speculative essay is typically less authoritative and less insistent than the tone of expository or argumentative essays. Speculative essays frequently take their form from the way thought flows in the mind of the writer. Rather than employing a conventional pattern of organization such as comparison and contrast, a speculative essayist will find a looser, less immediately recognizable organization. John Donne's "Meditation XVII: For Whom the Bell Tolls" (page 110), for example, is primarily associative in structure. As Donne's title indicates, his essay is more a meditation than an argument.

Writers of speculative (or meditative) essays seem less interested in advancing arguments than in exploring them. They prefer thinking around ideas rather than thinking through them. Rather than take readers on a clearly marked journey from point A through point B to point C, they often invite readers to accompany them on an excursion into thought. This is not to suggest that a speculative essay makes no point. In fact it may make multiple points as the essayist plays with ideas and explores them. E. B. White's "The Ring of Time" (page 9) is one speculative essay that makes any number of points. But it does not have a single, clear-cut thesis as narrative and expository essays often do.

ARGUMENTATIVE ESSAYS

Unlike speculative essays, which are loose in structure and informal in tone, *argumentative essays* make their claims directly and explicitly. Though argumentative essays assume various patterns of organization, they share a basic concern: to establish a point by providing evidence to support it. The support may take the form of examples, analogies, facts, statistics, anecdote, and evidence. In addition, argumentative essayists may present counterviews and counterarguments either to dismiss or demolish them. Counterpositions in an essay may include the competing claims of a pro and con structure such as the one Francis Bacon employs in "Of Love" (page 109). Or the form may be a debate as in E. M. Forster's "Our Graves in Gallipoli" (page 122). Whatever structure argumentative essayists employ and whatever methods they use to discredit opposing viewpoints, their intentions are clearly and consistently persuasive.

NARRATIVE ESSAYS

Midway between the formality of the argumentative essay and the informality of the speculative essay are narrative and expository essays. *Narrative essays* include stories, sometimes a single incident, as in George Orwell's "Shooting an Elephant" (page 125). The stories in narrative essays are almost always autobiographical: they form a part of the writer's experience. But even in cases where the story in such an essay is fictional rather than factual, it is used to make a point. Idea is primary. This distinguishes a narrative essay from a short story in which an idea may be inherent in the work, but where the fictional story *per se* takes precedence over any idea we may derive from it. Orwell's "Shooting an Elephant," for example, consists largely of the story of how Orwell (or a fictional narrator) shot an elephant. Although the incident possesses considerable interest as a story, its primary purpose is to advance an idea about imperialism, an idea which is presented explicitly midway through the essay and is referred to again at the end.

EXPOSITORY ESSAYS

Expository essays also advance ideas, but with less insistence than argumentative essays. Although expository writing may contain narrative elements (anecdote for instance), these elements are usually less developed and less central than in narrative writing. The purpose of most expository essays is explanation, to make something clear for readers. They put forth some idea or insight, some fact or experience so readers can better understand it. Although it is important to remember that nearly all essays contain some element of persuasion, their argumentative edge may be dull or sharp. In some expository prose, moreover, the persuasive dimension nearly disappears.

We have suggested that essays can be helpfully categorized with respect to their differing purposes, tones, and patterns of organization. But we should also note that essays rarely appear in such pure forms. More often than not, essayists mix modes, combining narration with exposition, or using exposition and narration in the service of argument. Knowing how writers shift strategies like this will help us read essays more confidently, particularly when we confront experiments in nonfictional prose.

One such development has been the marriage of fact and fiction pioneered by writers dubbed "new journalists." One of the most widely read of the new journalists is Tom Wolfe, who has experimented more fully perhaps than anyone else with the possibilities of the form. Wolfe himself singled out four techniques that have special importance for the new essay style. These include scene-by-scene construction, with a consequent reduction of straight narrative and explanation; a heavy reliance on dialogue, for as Wolfe has noted, "realistic dialogue involves the reader more completely than any other single device;" a manipulation of point of view to "give the reader the feeling of being inside a character's mind and experiencing the emotional reality of the scene as he experiences it;" and the use of symbolic details derived from everyday experience such as gestures, habits, manners, glances, poses, and styles of dress.★ Wolfe has deployed all of these techniques in his first novel, *The Bonfire of the Vanities*.

This brief overview of different types of essays is not meant to be an exhaustive catalogue of essay forms. Essayists don't choose a form from a menu. Rather, they design their essays and discover their form, making use of whatever strategies of organization suit their various purposes, audiences, and occasions. It is the sense the essay makes, the ideas it advances that matter in the end. Whatever our experience of an essay, and whatever its purpose, ultimately an essay attempts to formulate a thought, explore it, work out its implications, and communicate all this to readers.

★Tom Wolfe, ed., *The New Journalism* (New York: Harper and Row, 1973), pp. 31–32.

CHAPTER THREE

Elements of the Essay

An essay, like a poem, play, or story, can be studied from a number of perspectives: we can consider voice, style, structure, and thought—the elements of the essay as a literary form. To clarify our understanding of how essayists say what they mean, we begin by analyzing the essay's voice.

VOICE

When we read an essay we hear a writer's voice, someone speaking to us person to person. The essayist's voice may be commanding or cajoling, intimate or reserved, urgent and insistent, witty and charming—to suggest a few possibilities. The writer's voice is our key to his *tone,* his attitude toward his subject. Consider George Orwell's voice in the third paragraph of "Marrakech," reprinted here for convenience:

When you walk through a town like this—two hundred thousand inhabitants, of whom at least twenty thousand own literally nothing except the rags they stand up in—when you see how the people live, and still more how easily they die, it is always difficult to believe that you are walking among human beings. All colonial empires are in reality founded upon that fact. The people have brown faces—besides, there are so many of them! Are they really the same flesh as yourself? Do they even have names? Or are they merely a kind of undifferentiated brown stuff, about as individual as bees or coral insects? They rise out of the earth, they sweat and starve for a few years, and then they sink back into the nameless mounds of the graveyard and nobody notices that they are gone. And even the graves themselves soon fade back into the soil. Sometimes, out for a walk, as you break your way through the prickly pear, you notice that it is rather bumpy underfoot, and only a certain regularity in the bumps tells you that you are walking over skeletons.

Perhaps the first thing we hear is the writer speaking directly to us, calling us "you." As our eyes and ears, the narrator shares with us what he sees, hears, and more importantly, what he thinks and feels about these things. He also invites our response. When he asks, for example, whether the Moroccans even have names, our response is complex. On the one hand, we may answer "no," for they are unknown, obscure, anonymous; on the other hand, we may answer "yes, of course they have names." And when he asks "are they merely an undifferentiated brown stuff, about as individual as bees or coral insects?" our answer is more complex still. From one perspective the implied argument is that they are no more individual than bees or "brown stuff." But clearly this is not Orwell's view. In fact, it is this inhuman, exploitative view that his essay criticizes. Orwell attacks a viewpoint that many of his readers would subscribe to. They, of course, would not see imperialism as responsible for causing or even contributing to the problems he describes. Orwell, however, aims to make clear that colonialism, founded on a view of human beings as material to be exploited, perpetuates the misery he describes.

Another thing to note about the voice of this passage is its tone at the end and how it is achieved. The final sentence of this paragraph is a statement rather than a question. Like the first sentence, it conveys a sense of the starkness of life for the poor. They "rise" and "sink," "sweat" and "starve." That's it; it can hardly be called *living* in the sense that Orwell's readers would think of life. Balancing the phrases to create a rising and falling rhythm, Orwell communicates the heaviness of life for these people. The tone is compassionate rather than angry. The voice is quiet and controlled with emotion held in check.

To develop your ability to hear an essayist's voice, read the following essay by Joan Didion.

J O A N   D I D I O N

[*b. 1934*]

Los Angeles Notebook

There is something uneasy in the Los Angeles air this afternoon, some unnatural stillness, some tension. What it means is that tonight a Santa Ana will begin to blow, a hot wind from the northeast whining down through the Cajon and San Gorgonio Passes, blowing up sandstorms out along Route 66, drying the hills and the nerves to the flash point. For a few days now we will see smoke back in the canyons, and hear sirens in the night. I have neither heard nor read that a Santa Ana is due, but I know it, and almost everyone I have seen today knows it too. We know it because we feel it. The baby frets. The maid sulks. I rekindle a waning argument with the telephone company, then cut my losses and lie down, given over to whatever it is in the air. To live with the Santa Ana is to accept, consciously or unconsciously, a deeply mechanistic view of human behavior.

I recall being told, when I first moved to Los Angeles and was living on an isolated beach, that the Indians would throw themselves into the sea when the bad wind blew. I could see why. The Pacific turned ominously glossy during a Santa Ana period, and one woke in the night troubled not only by the peacocks screaming in the olive trees but by the eerie absence of surf. The heat was surreal. The sky had a yellow cast, the kind of light sometimes called "earthquake weather." My only neighbor would not come out of her house for days, and there were no lights at night, and her husband roamed the place with a machete. One day he would tell me that he had heard a trespasser, the next a rattlesnake.

"On nights like that," Raymond Chandler once wrote about the Santa Ana, "every booze party ends in a fight. Meek little wives feel the edge of the carving knife and study their husbands' necks. Anything can happen." That was the kind of wind it was. I did not know then that there was any basis for the effect it had on all of us, but it turns out to be another of those cases in which science bears out folk wisdom. The Santa Ana, which is named for one of the canyons it rushes through, is a *foehn* wind, like the *foehn* of Austria and Switzerland and the *hamsin* of Israel. There are a number of persistent malevolent winds, perhaps the best known of which are the mistral of France and the Mediterranean sirocco, but a *foehn* wind has distinct characteristics: it occurs on the leeward slope of a mountain range and, although the air begins as a cold mass, it is warmed as it comes down the mountain and appears finally as a hot dry wind. Whenever and wherever a *foehn* blows, doctors hear about headaches and nausea and allergies, about "nervousness," about "depression." In Los Angeles some teachers do not attempt to conduct formal classes during a Santa Ana, because the children become unmanageable. In Switzerland the suicide rate goes up during the *foehn,* and in the courts of some Swiss cantons the wind is considered a mitigating circumstance for crime. Surgeons are said to watch the wind, because blood does not clot normally during a *foehn*. A few years ago an Israeli physicist discovered that not only during such winds, but for the ten or twelve hours which precede them, the air carries an unusually high ratio of positive to negative ions. No one seems to know exactly why that should be; some talk about friction and others suggest solar disturbances. In any case the positive ions are there, and what an excess of positive ions does, in the simplest terms, is make people unhappy. One cannot get much more mechanistic than that.

Easterners commonly complain that there is no "weather" at all in Southern California, that the days and the seasons slip by relentlessly, numbingly bland. That is quite misleading. In fact the climate is characterized by infrequent but violent extremes: two periods of torrential subtropical rains which continue for weeks and wash out the hills and send subdivisions sliding toward the sea; about twenty scattered days a year of the Santa Ana, which, with its incendiary dryness, invariably means fire. At the first prediction of a Santa Ana, the Forest Service flies men and equipment from northern Cal-

ifornia into the southern forests, and the Los Angeles Fire Department cancels its ordinary non-firefighting routines. The Santa Ana caused Malibu to burn the way it did
in 1956, and Bel Air in 1961, and Santa Barbara in 1964. In the winter of 1966–67
eleven men were killed fighting a Santa Ana fire that spread through the San Gabriel
Mountains.

Just to watch the front-page news out of Los Angeles during a Santa Ana is to get
very close to what it is about the place. The longest single Santa Ana period in recent
years was in 1957, and it lasted not the usual three or four days but fourteen days, from
November 21 until December 4. On the first day 25,000 acres of the San Gabriel Mountains were burning, with gusts reaching 100 miles an hour. In town, the wind reached
Force 12, or hurricane force, on the Beaufort Scale; oil derricks were toppled and people ordered off the downtown streets to avoid injury from flying objects. On November
22 the fire in the San Gabriels was out of control. On November 24 six people were
killed in automobile accidents, and by the end of the week the Los Angeles *Times* was
keeping a box score of traffic deaths. On November 26 a prominent Pasadena attor-
ney, depressed about money, shot and killed his wife, their two sons, and himself. On
November 27 a South Gate divorcée, twenty-two, was murdered and thrown from a
moving car. On November 30 the San Gabriel fire was still out of control, and the
wind in town was blowing eighty miles an hour. On the first day of December four
people died violently, and on the third the wind began to break.

It is hard for people who have not lived in Los Angeles to realize how radically the
Santa Ana figures in the local imagination. The city burning is Los Angeles's deepest
image of itself: Nathanael West perceived that, in *The Day of the Locust;* and at the time
of the 1965 Watts riots what struck the imagination most indelibly were the fires. For
days one could drive the Harbor Freeway and see the city on fire, just as we had always known it would be in the end. Los Angeles weather is the weather of catastro-
phe, of apocalypse, and, just as the reliably long and bitter winters of New England determine the way life is lived there, so the violence and the unpredictability of the Santa
Ana affect the entire quality of life in Los Angeles, accentuate its impermanence, its
unreliability. The wind shows us how close to the edge we are.

(1967)

QUESTIONS

1. How urgent is Didion's tone? How insistent is she about what she is saying? How
   personal is her voice?
2. What does her relentless accumulation of facts contribute to the essay's tone?

STYLE

A writer's style in an essay derives from choices he or she makes in diction, syntax, and figurative language. Notice how James Baldwin uses these aspects of
style in this passage from "Notes of a Native Son" (page 136) in which he describes his father:

He was, I think, very handsome. I gather this from photographs and from my own memories of him, dressed in his Sunday best and on his way to preach a sermon some-where, when I was little. Handsome, proud, and ingrown, "like a toe-nail," some-body said. But he looked to me, as I grew older, like pictures I had seen of African tribal chieftains: he really should have been naked, with war-paint on and barbaric mementos, standing among spears. He could be chilling in the pulpit and indescrib-ably cruel in his personal life and he was certainly the most bitter man I have ever met; yet it must be said that there was something else in him, buried in him, which lent him his tremendous power and, even, a rather crushing charm. It had something to do with his blackness, I think—he was very black—with his blackness and his beauty, and with the fact that he knew that he was black but did not know that he was beautiful. He claimed to be proud of his blackness but it had also been the cause of much humiliation and it had fixed bleak boundaries to his life. He was not a young man when we were growing up and he had already suffered many kinds of ruin; in his outrageously demanding and protective way he loved his children, who were black like him and menaced, like him; and all these things sometimes showed in his face when he tried, never to my knowledge with any success, to establish contact with any of us. When he took one of his children on his knee to play, the child always became fretful and began to cry; when he tried to help one of us with our home-work the absolutely unabating tension which emanated from him caused our minds and our tongues to become paralyzed, so that he, scarcely knowing why, flew into a rage and the child, not knowing why, was punished. If it ever entered his head to bring a surprise home for his children, it was, almost unfailingly, the wrong surprise and even the big watermelons he often brought home on his back in the summer-time led to the most appalling scenes. I do not remember, in all those years, that one of his children was ever glad to see him come home. From what I was able to gather of his early life, it seemed that this inability to establish contact with other people had always marked him and had been one of the things which had driven him out of New Orleans. There was something in him, therefore, groping and tentative, which was never expressed and which was buried with him. One saw it most clearly when he was facing new people and hoping to impress them. But he never did, not for long.

The style here is formal, dignified, elegant, allusive. Baldwin writes about his father, about their relationship, and about the environment in which they lived. He writes personally but not informally. Even though he writes in the first per-son, using *I* and *we, me* and *mine,* he treats his subject with a solemnity achieved by careful control of diction. Baldwin consistently elevates his diction: "con-temptuous," "apprehensive," "unabating," "emanated;" and he includes ab-stractions: "injustice," "hatred," "bitterness," "pride." Such elevated diction contributes to the serious tone of the essay.

Another element that contributes to the solemnity of Baldwin's style is its rhythm. Baldwin tends to interrupt the linear movement of his sentences by embedding or interpolating words and phrases that create a stop-and-go move-ment, a rising and falling sound. The rise and fall of the rhythm adds to the dig-nity of Baldwin's style. Consider the following pair of his sentences and more ordinary alternative versions.

He was, I think, very handsome. (Baldwin)
I think he was very handsome. (alternative)

I do not remember, in all those years, that one of his children
was ever glad to see him come home. (Baldwin)
In all those years, I do not remember that one of his children
was ever glad to see him come home. (alternative)

Baldwin's repeated use of balance and parallelism contributes to his formal style: "He loved his children, who were black like him and menaced like him. . . . When he took one of his children on his knee to play, the child always became fretful and began to cry; when he tried to help one of us with our homework the absolutely unabating tension which emanated from him caused our minds and our tongues to become paralyzed, so that he, scarcely knowing why, flew into a rage and the child, not knowing why, was punished." Baldwin also employs parallel sentences: "It seemed to me that. . . . And it seemed to me, too, that. . . ." Again: "When he was dead I. . . . When he had been dead a long time I. . . ." Such repetitions of sentence structure and repetitions of words ("black," "blackness," and "beauty;" "bitter," "bitterness," and "pride") reinforce Baldwin's formal and solemn tone.

We hear a different tone as Alice Walker describes her mother in this passage from her essay "In Search of Our Mothers' Gardens" (page 159).

Five children later, I was born. And this is how I came to know my mother: she seemed a large, soft, loving-eyed woman who was rarely impatient in our home. Her quick, violent temper was on view only a few times a year, when she battled with the white landlord who had the misfortune to suggest to her that her children did not need to go to school.

She made all the clothes we wore, even my brothers' overalls. She made all the towels and sheets we used. She spent the summers canning vegetables and fruits. She spent the winter evenings making quilts enough to cover all our beds.

During the "working" day, she labored beside—not behind—my father in the fields. Her day began before sunup, and did not end until late at night. There was never a moment for her to sit down, undisturbed, to unravel her own private thoughts; never a time free from interruption—by work or the noisy inquiries of her many children. And yet, it is to my mother—and all our mothers who were not famous—that I went in search of the secret of what has fed that muzzled and often mutilated, but vibrant, creative spirit that the black woman has inherited, and that pops out in wild and unlikely places to this day.

Like Mem, a character in *The Third Life of Grange Copeland,* my mother adorned with flowers whatever shabby house we were forced to live in. And not just your typical straggly country stand of zinnias, either. She planted ambitious gardens—and still does—with over fifty different varieties of plants that bloom profusely from early March until late November. Before she left home for the fields, she watered her flowers, chopped up the grass, and laid out new beds. When she returned from the fields she might divide clumps of bulbs, dig a cold pit, uproot and replant roses, or prune branches from her taller bushes or trees—until night came and it was too dark to see.

Whatever she planted grew as if by magic, and her fame as a grower of flowers spread over three counties. Because of her creativity with her flowers, even my memories of poverty are seen through a screen of blooms—sunflowers, petunias, roses, dahlias, forsythia, spirea, delphiniums, verbena . . . and on and on.

And I remember people coming to my mother's yard to be given cuttings from her flowers; I hear again the praise showered on her because whatever rocky soil she landed on, she turned into a garden. A garden so brilliant with colors, so original in its design, so magnificent with life and creativity, that to this day people drive by our house in Georgia—perfect strangers and imperfect strangers—and ask to stand or walk among my mother's art.

I notice that it is only when my mother is working in her flowers that she is radiant, almost to the point of being invisible—except as Creator: hand and eye. She is involved in work her soul must have. Ordering the universe in the image of her personal conception of Beauty.

Walker, like Baldwin, writes in the first person and about a parent. Her tone differs from his largely because her subject and attitude differ. Walker's appreciation of her mother shines through her prose and is evident in her selection of details. (Compare the details Baldwin includes to describe his father.) Walker's style is lighter, more informal than Baldwin's. Describing her mother's temper as being "on view" and saying that she "battled" with the landlord, Walker uses everyday speech rather than formal diction. Her sentences are simple and short as in the second paragraph, which begins "She made all the clothes we wore, even my brothers' overalls." Walker comments on her mother's skill with flowers in an informal and directly personal way: "And not just your typical straggly country stand of zinnias, either." Further accentuating her informal tone is the way she breaks into sentences with off-hand interruptions, highlighting their casualness by punctuating them with dashes: "—and still does—;" "—and all our mothers who were not famous—." She even trails off at one point: ". . . and on and on."

One additional stylistic feature distinguishes Walker's style from Baldwin's and contributes to her informal tone: her sentence fragments. Twice in the passage quoted above Walker employs sentence fragments, both times at the end of a paragraph: "A garden so brilliant . . . my mother's art;" "Ordering the universe . . . conception of beauty." As a rhetorical strategy for achieving emphasis, the fragment can drive a fact or feeling across with intensity and power. Such features of Walker's prose make her writing more casual and intimate than Baldwin's. Although Walker, like Baldwin, is capable of writing long, intricate sentences, her eloquence is achieved with different stylistic techniques.

Figurative Language

Like poets, dramatists, and fiction writers, essayists use language in literal and nonliteral ways. The kinds of figurative language most prevalent in essays are those that involve comparison, particularly in the forms of *simile* and *metaphor*. Essayists employ simile and metaphor to clarify their thoughts and their feelings. They use these forms of comparison to make one thing clear in terms of another. Sometimes the writer's intention in using the comparison is clear and explicit, as in pointing out young men's faults, Bacon notes that they "will not acknowledge or retract them, like an unready horse that will neither stop nor turn," or Orwell comparing the Marrakech burial ground to a derelict building lot and its lumpy earth to broken brick. Orwell's communicate an image and impression of the place that is the sharper and clearer for the comparisons. Bacon communicates the idea that young men can be stubborn and recalcitrant by illustrating their stubbornness with a simile.

These examples are relatively simple. Both Bacon and Orwell use other less explicit and more complex comparisons when they speak metaphorically of one thing in terms of another. Bacon does this when he suggests that some men are not "ripe for action" until they reach middle age. The implicit comparison is between men and plants, specifically fruit. Like fruit, men come to maturity over time. In the same way that not all fruit ripens at the same time, men do not all become ready for action based on mature decisions at the same time. Some men, like some fruit, ripen faster than others.

Another example of an implicit comparison occurs in Joan Didion's "Los Angeles Notebook" when she talks about *rekindling* an argument with the telephone company. The comparison is carried in her verb, "rekindle," an image of conflagration appropriate to an essay that describes the fiery consequences of the Santa Ana. Moreover, Didion develops the fire imagery much more fully in the final paragraph where she alludes to Nathanael West's novel *The Day of the Locust,* which ends with a vivid depiction of Los Angeles burning. Throughout her essay Didion refers both literally and figuratively to fire.

We can note also in this brief discussion of comparative images that the passages quoted above from Baldwin and Walker also employ comparison in various ways. Walker uses the garden as an image or symbol of her mother's creativity. Elsewhere in her essay, Walker extends the symbolic implications of the garden image to include the creativity of all women, particularly those whose creativity could not find expression in ways available to women today.

In using figurative language, expecially images of comparison, essayists ally themselves with literary artists working in other genres, poetry and fiction, for instance. In fact we might say that the essay's use of figurative language is one element that invites our consideration of it as literature rather than simply as a vehicle for information. Stripped of its comparative figures, of its imagery, the essay becomes less engaging as literature and more strictly a matter of factual reporting. And even though literary essayists such as Orwell and Didion do a good deal of reporting in their essays, they do it by means of linguistic and rhetorical strategies and of formal patterns common to stories and novels. By designing their essays to move us as well as instruct us, Orwell, Didion, Walker, Baldwin, and other writers elevate the factuality of their essays to the status of imaginative literature.

As an exercise in examining aspects of an essayist's style, consider the following selection from Henry David Thoreau's *Walden.*

HENRY DAVID THOREAU

[1817–1862]

The Battle of the Ants

One day when I went out to my wood-pile, or rather my pile of stumps, I observed two large ants, the one red, the other much larger, nearly half an inch long, and black, fiercely contending with one another. Having once got hold they never let go, but struggled and wrestled and rolled on the chips incessantly. Looking farther, I was surprised to find that the chips were covered with such combatants, that it was not a *duellum,* but a *bellum,*° a war between two races of ants, the red always pitted against the black, and frequently two red ones to one black. The legions of these Myrmidons° covered all the hills and vales in my woodyard, and the ground was already strewn with the dead and dying, both red and black. It was the only battle which I have ever witnessed, the only battle-field I ever trod while the battle was raging; internecine war; the red republicans on the one hand, the black imperialists on the other. On every side they were engaged in deadly combat, yet without any noise that I could hear, and human soldiers never fought so resolutely. I watched a couple that were fast locked in each other's embraces, in a little sunny valley amid the chips, now at noonday prepared to fight till the sun went down, or life went out. The smaller red champion had fastened himself like a vise to his adversary's front, and through all the tumblings on that field never for an instant ceased to gnaw at one of his feelers near the root, having already caused the other to go by the board; while the stronger black one dashed him from side to side, and, as I saw on looking nearer, had already divested him of several of his members. They fought with more pertinacity than bulldogs. Neither manifested the least disposition to retreat. It was evident that their battle-cry was "Conquer or die." In the meanwhile there came along a single red ant on the hillside of this valley, evidently full of excitement, who either had dispatched his foe, or had not yet taken part in the battle; probably the latter, for he had lost none of his limbs; whose mother had charged him to return with his shield or upon it.° Or perchance he was some Achilles, who had nourished his wrath apart, and had now come to avenge or rescue his Patroclus.° He saw this unequal combat from afar,—for the blacks were nearly twice the size of the red,—he drew near with rapid pace till he stood on his guard within half an inch of the combatants; then, watching his opportunity, he sprang upon the black warrior, and commenced his operations near the root of his right fore leg, leaving the foe to select among his own members; and so there were three united for life, as if a new kind of attraction had been invented which put all other locks and cements to shame. I should not have wondered by this

---

not a duellum . . . bellum   *not a duel but a war.*   **Myrmidons**   *soldiers who followed the Greek warrior Achilles. Myrmes is the Greek word for ant.*   **to return with his shield . . . upon it**   *Spartan mothers told their sons this as they departed for war.*   **Patroclus**   *Achilles' close friend. When Patroclus was killed, Achilles, who had not been fighting because of wounded pride, returned to battle the Trojans, especially to avenge the death of his friend by killing the Trojan hero, Hector.*

time to find that they had their respective musical bands stationed on some eminent chip, and playing their national airs the while, to excite the slow and cheer the dying combatants. I was myself excited somewhat even as if they had been men. The more you think of it, the less the difference. And certainly there is not the fight recorded in Concord history, at least, if in the history of America, that will bear a moment's comparison with this, whether for the numbers engaged in it, or for the patriotism and heroism displayed. For numbers and for carnage it was an Austerlitz or Dresden.° Concord fight! Two killed on the patriot's side, and Luther Blanchard wounded! Why here every ant was a Buttrick,—"Fire, for God's sake fire!"—and thousands shared the fate of Davis and Hosmer.° There was not one hireling there. I have no doubt that it was a principle they fought for, as much as our ancestors, and not to avoid a three-penny tax on their tea; and the results of this battle will be as important and memorable to those whom it concerns as those of the battle of Bunker Hill, at least.

I took up the chip on which the three I have particularly described were struggling, carried it into my house, and placed it under a tumbler on my window-sill, in order to see the issue. Holding a microscope to the first-mentioned red ant, I saw that, though he was assiduously gnawing at the near fore leg of his enemy, having severed his remaining feeler, his own breast was all torn away, exposing what vitals he had there to the jaws of the black warrior, whose breastplate was apparently too thick for him to pierce; and the dark carbuncles of the sufferer's eyes shone with ferocity such as war only could excite. They struggled half an hour longer under the tumbler, and when I looked again the black soldier had severed the heads of his foes from their bodies, and the still living heads were hanging on either side of him like ghastly trophies at his saddle-bow, still apparently as firmly fastened as ever, and he was endeavoring with feeble struggles, being without feelers and with only the remnant of a leg, and I know not how many other wounds, to divest himself of them; which at length, after half an hour more, he accomplished. I raised the glass, and he went off over the window-sill in that crippled state. Whether he finally survived that combat, and spent the remainder of his days in some Hôtel des Invalides,° I do not know; but I thought that his industry would not be worth much thereafter. I never learned which party was victorious, nor the cause of the war; but I felt for the rest of that day as if I had had my feelings excited and harrowed by witnessing the struggle, the ferocity and carnage of a human battle before my door.

(1854)

QUESTIONS

1. Identify and comment on the effectiveness of Thoreau's comparisons. Consider the small-scale brief similes and the overall analogy between the ant war and the Trojan War.

Austerlitz or Dresden *two fierce battles of the Napoleonic wars.* **Concord fight . . . Hosmer** *The first battle of the American Revolution was fought at Concord Bridge. In that famous fight, Major John Buttrick and his militiamen repelled the British regular army and hired soldiers. Davis and Hosmer were Americans killed, Blanchard an American wounded.* **Hôtel des Invalides** *a veterans' hospital in Paris.*

2. What does Thoreau gain by including the quoted phrases "Conquer or die" and "Fire, for God's sake fire!"?

3. What does Thoreau's Latinate diction contribute to the effects of his prose? Consider especially the following words: *incessantly, internecine, resolutely, divested, pertinacity, dispatched, eminent, carnage, assiduously, industry,* and *ferocity.*

STRUCTURE

The structural features of an essay are not as visible as the stanzas of poems or the acts and scenes of plays. We can gain some sense of the essay's structural variety by considering a few of the essays in this book.

George Orwell's "Shooting an Elephant" (page 125) is largely a chronological account that describes the shooting of an elephant. The sequence of actions, however, is preceded by a two-paragraph introduction, which sets the scene, establishes the tone, and announces the subject. The chronological narrative is then followed by a coda in which Orwell comments on what happened. The narrative portion is thus framed by brief explanations, each of which helps us understand its significance. Moreover, Orwell breaks into the narrative section with an important explanatory paragraph, in which he comments extensively on the meaning the event had for him and on its larger, more generalized political significance.

E. B. White uses an alternating structure in "The Ring of Time" (page 5). He presents a picture of what he sees and then raises questions about it; then he presents more description and again speculates about it. This pattern continues throughout the essay until the final paragraph, which echoes the essay's opening. This gives the essay an alternating structure and a circular one. And that, in part, is an aspect of the the essay's theme—the circular, repetitive ring of time itself.

Some clues for relating the structure of an essay to its meaning include being alert for shifts of focus such as Orwell's shifting scenes in "Marrakech" and Didion's shifts from one type of information to another in "Los Angeles Notebook." In addition, we can look for connections between one part of an essay and another, once we decide what those parts are. Orwell helps us see the parts of "Marrakech" by dividing the five parts with blank space. Didion gives us neither such visual nor such explicit verbal markers; she does, however, shift attention to different kinds of information—historical, literary, scientific, and personal.

Perhaps the most important thing to remember about the structure of essays is this: structure reflects thought and is inextricably connected with it. The form of an essay, its structure of thought, is a clue to how we should read it; its form is an aspect of its meaning. When writers alter the structure of essays, they alter both the meaning of their works and their readers' experience of them. Rearranging the paragraphs of E. B. White's "The Ring of Time," for example, to cluster descriptive paragraphs together and separate them from speculative ones would alter our experience of the essay. Rewriting Orwell's "Shooting an Elephant" to keep the entire story together without the intrusion of narrative commentary would alter the effects the essay creates. In short, if we change the form of a literary work, we change its meaning and effect.

Consider the structure of the following brief essay by Virginia Woolf.

VIRGINIA WOOLF

[1882–1941]

The Death of the Moth

Moths that fly by day are not properly to be called moths; they do not excite that pleasant sense of dark autumn nights and ivy-blossom which the commonest yellow-underwing asleep in the shadow of the curtain never fails to rouse in us. They are hybrid creatures, neither gay like butterflies nor sombre like their own species. Nevertheless the present specimen, with his narrow hay-coloured wings, fringed with a tassel of the same colour, seemed to be content with life. It was a pleasant morning, mid-September, mild, benignant, yet with a keener breath than that of the summer months. The plough was already scoring the field opposite the window, and where the share had been, the earth was pressed flat and gleamed with moisture. Such vigour came rolling in from the fields and the down beyond that it was difficult to keep the eyes strictly turned upon the book. The rooks too were keeping one of their annual festivities; soaring round the tree tops until it looked as if a vast net with thousands of black knots in it had been cast up into the air; which, after a few moments, sank slowly down upon the trees until every twig seemed to have a knot at the end of it. Then, suddenly, the net would be thrown into the air again in a wider circle this time, with the utmost clamour and vociferation, as though to be thrown into the air and settle slowly down upon the tree tops were a tremendously exciting experience.

The same energy which inspired the rooks, the ploughmen, the horses, and even, it seemed, the lean bare-backed downs, sent the moth fluttering from side to side of his square of the window-pane. One could not help watching him. One was, indeed, conscious of a queer feeling of pity for him. The possibilities of pleasure seemed that morning so enormous and so various that to have only a moth's part in life, and a day moth's at that, appeared a hard fate, and his zest in enjoying his meagre opportunities to the full, pathetic. He flew vigorously to one corner of his compartment, and, after waiting there a second, flew across to the other. What remained for him but to fly to a third corner and then to a fourth? That was all he could do, in spite of the size of the downs, the width of the sky, the far-off smoke of houses, and the romantic voice, now and then, of a steamer out at sea. What he could do he did. Watching him, it seemed as if a fibre, very thin but pure, of the enormous energy of the world had been thrust into his frail and diminutive body. As often as he crossed the pane, I could fancy that a thread of vital light became visible. He was little or nothing but life.

Yet, because he was so small, and so simple a form of the energy that was rolling in at the open window and driving its way through so many narrow and intricate corridors in my own brain and in those of other human beings, there was something marvelous as well as pathetic about him. It was as if someone had taken a tiny bead of pure life and decking it as lightly as possible with down and feathers, had set it dancing and zigzagging to show us the true nature of life. Thus displayed one could not get over the strangeness of it. One is apt to forget all about life, seeing it humped and bossed and garnished and cumbered so that it has to move with the greatest circumspection and dignity. Again, the thought of all that life might have been had he been born in any other shape caused one to view his simple activities with a kind of pity.

After a time, tired by his dancing apparently, he settled on the window ledge in the sun, and, the queer spectacle being at an end, I forgot about him. Then, looking up, my eye was caught by him. He was trying to resume his dancing, but seemed either so stiff or so awkward that he could only flutter to the bottom of the window-pane; and when he tried to fly across it he failed. Being intent on other matters I watched these futile attempts for a time without thinking, unconsciously waiting for him to resume his flight, as one waits for a machine, that has stopped momentarily, to start again without considering the reason of its failure. After perhaps a seventh attempt he slipped from the wooden ledge and fell, fluttering his wings, onto his back on the window sill. The helplessness of his attitude roused me. It flashed upon me he was in difficulties; he could no longer raise himself; his legs struggled vainly. But, as I stretched out a pencil, meaning to help him to right himself, it came over me that the failure and awkwardness were the approach of death. I laid the pencil down again.

The legs agitated themselves once more. I looked as if for the enemy against which he struggled. I looked out of doors. What had happened there? Presumably it was midday, and work in the fields had stopped. Stillness and quiet had replaced the previous animation. The birds had taken themselves off to feed in the brooks. The horses stood still. Yet the power was there all the same, massed outside indifferent, impersonal, not attending to anything in particular. Somehow it was opposed to the little hay-coloured moth. It was useless to try to do anything. One could only watch the extraordinary efforts made by those tiny legs against an oncoming doom which could, had it chosen, have submerged an entire city, not merely a city, but masses of human beings; nothing, I knew, had any chance against death. Nevertheless after a pause of exhaustion the legs fluttered again. It was superb this last protest, and so frantic that he succeeded at last in righting himself. One's sympathies, of course, were all on the side of life. Also, when there was nobody to care or to know, this gigantic effort on the part of an insignificant little moth, against a power of such magnitude, to retain what no one else valued or desired to keep, moved one strangely. Again, somehow, one saw life a pure bead. I lifted the pencil again, useless though I knew it to be. But even as I did so, the unmistakable tokens of death showed themselves. The body relaxed, and instantly grew stiff. The struggle was over. The insignificant little creature now knew death. As I looked at the dead moth, this minute wayside triumph of so great a force over so mean an antagonist filled me with wonder. Just as life had been strange a few minutes before, so death was now as strange. The moth having righted himself now lay most decently and uncomplainingly composed. O yes, he seemed to say, death is stronger than I am.

(1942)

QUESTIONS

1. The essay is divided into five paragraphs. What is the focus of each? How is each paragraph related to the one that precedes and follows it?
2. Woolf gives the essay a narrative structure: it recounts an incident—the death of the moth. How, where, and why does she modify the linear chronology of the narrative?
3. What details recur in the essay? What does Woolf accomplish by including them?

THOUGHT

Edward Hoagland, a contemporary American essayist, has described the essay as a work that "hangs somewhere on a line between two sturdy poles: this is what I think, and this is what I am."★ The sense of self and selves provided by essayists is manifested in their styles and voices—Hoagland's "what I am." This we have discussed in the sections on voice and style above. Here we will consider the essayist's "what I think," the way he or she speaks to us, as Hoagland says, "mind to mind."

When writers choose to write an essay rather than a poem, play, or story, it is because, presumably, they have something on their minds. The very choice of factual rather than fictional discourse testifies to the essayist's concern for expressing an idea. Even when essayists rely heavily on narrative to tell stories or description to convey feelings and attitudes, their emphasis ultimately is most often on an idea. It is this primacy of idea, in fact, that makes an essay what it is.

Let us consider the way idea is explored and illustrated in Joan Didion's "Los Angeles Notebook." Although Didion uses many concrete details in building up an impression of Los Angeles, her primary concern is to clarify the nature and effects of the Santa Ana wind. Allied with this is a persuasive intention: to argue for a causal connection between climate and human behavior. Didion enforces a proposition—that climate strongly influences people's behavior, that it determines how they act and react. How far she pushes this idea is a matter for discussion; so is our own sense of how far the idea should be taken. But propose it Didion certainly does. In fact, everything about her six-paragraph discourse is directed toward this single idea.

In a similar way we can see that George Orwell has an idea to advance in "Shooting an Elephant" (page 125). Like the descriptive details of "Marrakech," those of "Shooting an Elephant" illustrate a point. That point surfaces most clearly in the following paragraph—the seventh of the essay.

But at that moment I glanced round at the crowd that had followed me. It was an immense crowd, two thousand at the least and growing every minute. It blocked the road for a long distance on either side. I looked at the sea of yellow faces above the garish clothes—faces all happy and excited over this bit of fun, all certain that the elephant was going to be shot. They were watching me as they would watch a conjurer

★*The Tugman's Passage* (New York: Random House, 1982), p. 25.

about to perform a trick. They did not like me, but with the magical rifle in my hands I was momentarily worth watching. And suddenly I realized that I should have to shoot the elephant after all. The people expected it of me and I had got to do it; I could feel their two thousand wills pressing me forward, irresistibly. And it was at this moment, as I stood there with the rifle in my hands, that I first grasped the hollowness, the futility of the white man's dominion in the East. Here was I, the white man with his gun, standing in front of the unarmed native crowd—seemingly the leading actor of the piece; but in reality I was only an absurd puppet pushed to and fro by the will of those yellow faces behind. I perceived in this moment that when the white man turns tyrant it is his own freedom that he destroys. He becomes a sort of hollow, posing dummy, the conventionalized figure of a sahib. For it is the condition of his rule that he shall spend his life in trying to impress the "natives," and so in every crisis he has got to do what the "natives" expect of him. He wears a mask, and his face grows to fit it. I had got to shoot the elephant. I had committed myself to doing it when I sent for the rifle. A sahib has got to act like a sahib; he has got to appear resolute, to know his own mind and do definite things. To come all that way, rifle in hand, with two thousand people marching at my heels, and then to trail feebly away, having done nothing—no, that was impossible. The crowd would laugh at me. And my whole life, every white man's life in the East, was one long struggle not to be laughed at.

In this paragraph, Orwell interrupts his story about the elephant to specify the significance of the experience. His political point is clear: imperialism is evil; it is destructive of both the oppressed and the oppressors. Orwell does not make this point abstractly or generally. Instead, he presents it within a specific context of time, place, and action: the shooting of an elephant in Burma in the 1930s by a British colonial. To increase the impact of his idea, Orwell uses irony and imagery. The discrepancy between appearances (that the narrator, an authority figure, is in charge) and reality (that he is at the mercy of the unarmed natives, whose will he is following) is ironic. This ironic contrast is underscored by the images of the narrator as the "leading actor" and as an "absurd puppet," with *actor* indicating his role playing and *puppet* his lack of control. Orwell further establishes his point with the image of the mask, which extends the theatrical imagery prevalent in this passage and in the essay overall. This image suggests that although a person may originally keep himself distinct from a role he performs, at some point he may actually become what he initially pretends to be. Orwell suggests that what was initially a part in a drama can become an aspect of an identity.

This complex idea leads forcefully into his statement that "when the white man turns tyrant it is his own freedom that he destroys." The last section of the paragraph explains this point. It is, of course, ironic that in gaining control over others, in assuming power, one loses one's freedom. That paradoxical idea is the heart of both this central explanatory paragraph and the essay overall. It is emphasized, moreover, in the last paragraph, where Orwell confesses that he shot the elephant "to avoid looking the fool."

A final point about idea in essays: thought does not exist independently of feeling. The ideas we discover in essays are felt, not merely thought out. They derive from the writer's emotions; they have their basis in feeling. Feeling, in fact, is mixed with all thought given expression in language. So much so that we might say there is no thinking without feeling. In essays such as Alice Walker's and James Baldwin's, especially, we can discover powerful examples of thought felt with passion, of feeling conveyed with incisive intelligence.

The essay that follows expresses some thoughts about revenge. Consider both what these thoughts are and how strongly they are felt.

FRANCIS BACON

[1561–1626]

Of Revenge

Revenge is a kind of wild justice, which the more man's nature runs to, the more ought law to weed it out. For as for the first wrong, it doth but offend the law, but the revenge of that wrong putteth the law out of office. Certainly in taking revenge, a man is but even with his enemy, but in passing it over, he is superior, for it is a prince's part to pardon. And Solomon, I am sure, saith, "It is the glory of a man to pass by an offense." That which is past is gone and irrevocable, and wise men have enough to do with things present and to come; therefore they do but trifle with themselves that labor in past matters. There is no man doth a wrong for the wrong's sake, but thereby to purchase himself profit, or pleasure, or honor, or the like. Therefore why should I be angry with a man for loving himself better than me? And if any man should do wrong merely out of ill nature, why, yet it is but like the thorn or briar, which prick and scratch because they can do no other. The most tolerable sort of revenge is for those wrongs which there is no law to remedy, but then let a man take heed the revenge be such as there is no law to punish; else a man's enemy is still beforehand, and it is two for one. Some, when they take revenge, are desirous the party should know whence it cometh. This the more generous. For the delight seemeth to not be so much in doing the hurt as in making the party repent. But base and crafty cowards are like the arrow that flieth in the dark. Cosmus, duke of Florence, had a desperate saying against perfidious or neglecting friends, as if those wrongs were unpardonable: "You shall read," saith he, "that we are commanded to forgive our enemies; but you never read that we are commanded to forgive our friends." But yet the spirit of Job was in better tune: "Shall we," saith he, "take good at God's hands, and not be content to take evil also?" And so of friends in a proportion. This is certain, that a man that studieth revenge keeps his own wounds green, which otherwise would heal and do well. Public revenges are for the most part fortunate, as that for the death of Caesar, for the death of Pertinax, for the death of Henry the Third of France, and many more. But in private revenges it is not so. Nay rather, vindictive persons live the life of witches, who, as they are mischievous, so end they unfortunate.

(1612)

QUESTIONS

1. Why can revenge be defined as "a kind of wild justice"? What is wild about revenge? What about it is just?
2. What arguments does Bacon make against revenge? Are his objections primarily moral or practical?
3. What do Bacon's historical and biblical allusions contribute to his ideas about revenge? Why do you think he includes these allusions?

CHAPTER FOUR

Approaching an Essay: Guides for Reading and Writing

The guidelines that follow summarize our discussion of reading essays; we will use them to guide our analysis of an essay by Annie Dillard.

Guidelines for Reading

1. Read through the entire essay to get a feel for what it is about. Center on subject and idea. During this initial reading, be alert to your responses to the work. Jot down your thoughts and feelings in the margins or at the end of the piece. Consider the essay in light of your own experience.
2. Make your second reading more analytical. Zero in on the structure and the development of the argument. Consider how the structure orders the ideas. Be alert for shifts of direction, for changes of language and tone, example and image, scene and point of view. Determine your sense of the writer's tone.
3. During your second reading—or possibly a third—concentrate on language and style. Notice diction and syntax; be alert for imagery and figurative

language. Consider what the style reveals about the writer's purpose and
the audience for which the essay seems to be intended.

4. Be alert for connections both within the essay and beyond it. Single out
passages that highlight the central idea.

5. Consider, in addition, whether the essay shares features with one or more
other literary genres, and what use the author makes of techniques associated with those genres.

6. Consider the values the author expresses in the essay, as well as the essay's
main assumptions.

ANNIE DILLARD

[b. 1945]

Living Like Weasels

A weasel is wild. Who knows what he thinks? He sleeps in his underground den, his
tail draped over his nose. Sometimes he lives in his den for two days without leaving.
Outside, he stalks rabbits, mice, muskrats, and birds, killing more bodies than he can
eat warm, and often dragging the carcasses home. Obedient to instinct, he bites his prey
at the neck, either splitting the jugular vein at the throat or crunching the brain at the
base of the skull, and he does not let go. One naturalist refused to kill a weasel who
was socketed into his hand deeply as a rattlesnake. The man could in no way pry the
tiny weasel off, and he had to walk half a mile to water, the weasel dangling from his
palm, and soak him off like a stubborn label.

And once, says Ernest Thompson Seton—once, a man shot an eagle out of the sky.
He examined the eagle and found the dry skull of a weasel fixed by the jaws to his
throat. The supposition is that the eagle had pounced on the weasel and the weasel
swiveled and bit as instinct taught him, tooth to neck, and nearly won. I would like to
have seen that eagle from the air a few weeks or months before he was shot: was the
whole weasel still attached to his feathered throat, a fur pendant? Or did the eagle eat
what he could reach, gutting the living weasel with his talons before his breast, bending his beak, cleaning the beautiful airborne bones?

I have been reading about weasels because I saw one last week. I startled a weasel who
startled me, and we exchanged a long glance.

Twenty minutes from my house, through the woods by the quarry and across the
highway, is Hollins Pond, a remarkable piece of shallowness, where I like to go at sunset and sit on a tree trunk. Hollins Pond is also called Murray's Pond; it covers two
acres of bottomland near Tinker Creek with six inches of water and six thousand lily
pads. In winter, brown-and-white steers stand in the middle of it, merely dampening
their hooves; from the distant shore they look like miracle itself, complete with mira-

cle's nonchalance. Now, in summer, the steers are gone. The water lilies have blossomed and spread to a green horizontal plane that is terra firma to plodding blackbirds, and tremulous ceiling to black leeches, crayfish, and carp.

This is, mind you, suburbia. It is a five-minute walk in three directions to rows of houses, though none is visible here. There's a 55 mph highway at one end of the pond, and a nesting pair of wood ducks at the other. Under every bush is a muskrat hole or a beer can. The far end is an alternating series of fields and woods, fields and woods, threaded everywhere with motorcycle tracks—in whose bare clay wild turtles lay eggs.

So. I had crossed the highway, stepped over two low barbed-wire fences, and traced the motorcycle path in all gratitude through the wild rose and poison ivy of the pond's shoreline up into high grassy fields. Then I cut down through the woods to the mossy fallen tree where I sit. This tree is excellent. It makes a dry, upholstered bench at the upper, marshy end of the pond, a plush jetty raised from the thorny shore between a shallow blue body of water and a deep blue body of sky.

The sun had just set. I was relaxed on the tree trunk, ensconced in the lap of lichen, watching the lily pads at my feet tremble and part dreamily over the thrusting path of a carp. A yellow bird appeared to my right and flew behind me. It caught my eye; I swiveled around—and the next instant, inexplicably, I was looking down at a weasel, who was looking up at me.

Weasel! I'd never seen one wild before. He was ten inches long, thin as a curve, a muscled ribbon, brown as fruitwood, soft-furred, alert. His face was fierce, small and pointed as a lizard's; he would have made a good arrowhead. There was just a dot of chin, maybe two brown hairs' worth, and then the pure white fur began that spread down his underside. He had two black eyes I didn't see, any more than you see a window.

The weasel was stunned into stillness as he was emerging from beneath an enormous shaggy wild rose bush four feet away. I was stunned into stillness twisted backward on the tree trunk. Our eyes locked, and someone threw away the key.

Our look was as if two lovers, or deadly enemies, met unexpectedly on an overgrown path when each had been thinking of something else: a clearing blow to the gut. It was also a bright blow to the brain, or a sudden beating of brains, with all the charge and intimate grate of rubbed balloons. It emptied our lungs. It felled the forest, moved the fields, and drained the pond; the world dismantled and tumbled into that black hole of eyes. If you and I looked at each other that way, our skulls would split and drop to our shoulders. But we don't. We keep our skulls. So.

He disappeared. This was only last week, and already I don't remember what shattered the enchantment. I think I blinked, I think I retrieved my brain from the weasel's brain, and tried to memorize what I was seeing, and the weasel felt the yank of separation, the careening splashdown into real life and the urgent current of instinct. He vanished under the wild rose. I waited motionless, my mind suddenly full of data and my spirit with pleadings, but he didn't return.

Please do not tell me about "approach-avoidance conflicts." I tell you I've been in that weasel's brain for sixty seconds, and he was in mine. Brains are private places, muttering through unique and secret tapes—but the weasel and I both plugged into another tape simultaneously, for a sweet and shocking time. Can I help it if it was a blank?

What goes on in his brain the rest of the time? What does a weasel think about? He won't say. His journal is tracks in clay, a spray of feathers, mouse blood and bone: uncollected, unconnected, loose-leaf, and blown.

I would like to learn, or remember, how to live. I come to Hollins Pond not so much to learn how to live as, frankly, to forget about it. That is, I don't think I can learn from a wild animal how to live in particular—shall I suck warm blood, hold my tail high, walk with my footprints precisely over the prints of my hands?—but I might learn something of mindlessness, something of the purity of living in the physical senses and the dignity of living without bias or motive. The weasel lives in necessity and we live in choice, hating necessity and dying at the last ignobly in its talons. I would like to live as I should, as the weasel lives as he should. And I suspect that for me the way is like the weasel's: open to time and death painlessly, noticing everything, remembering nothing, choosing the given with a fierce and pointed will.

I missed my chance. I should have gone for the throat. I should have lunged for that streak of white under the weasel's chin and held on, held on through mud and into the wild rose, held on for a dearer life. We could live under the wild rose wild as weasels, mute and uncomprehending. I could very calmly go wild. I could live two days in the den, curled, leaning on mouse fur, sniffing bird bones, blinking, licking, breathing musk, my hair tangled in the roots of grasses. Down is a good place to go, where the mind is single. Down is out, out of your ever-loving mind and back to your careless senses. I remember muteness as a prolonged and giddy fast, where every moment is a feast of utterance received. Time and events are merely poured, unremarked, and ingested directly, like blood pulsed into my gut through a jugular vein. Could two live that way? Could two live under the wild rose, and explore by the pond, so that the smooth mind of each is as everywhere present to the other, and as received and as unchallenged, as falling snow?

We could, you know. We can live any way we want. People take vows of poverty, chastity, and obedience—even of silence—by choice. The thing is to stalk your calling in a certain skilled and supple way, to locate the most tender and live spot and plug into that pulse. This is yielding, not fighting. A weasel doesn't "attack" anything; a weasel lives as he's meant to, yielding at every moment to the perfect freedom of single necessity.

I think it would be well, and proper, and obedient, and pure, to grasp your one necessity and not let it go, to dangle from it limp wherever it takes you. Then even death, where you're going no matter how you live, cannot you part. Seize it and let it seize you up aloft even, till your eyes burn out and drop; let your musky flesh fall off in shreds, and let your very bones unhinge and scatter, loosened over fields, over fields and woods, lightly, thoughtless, from any height at all, from as high as eagles.

(1982)

Voice   Dillard's voice is informal. She speaks to us in the first person, casually, directly: "I tell you I've been in that weasel's brain for sixty seconds. . . ." In advancing the proposition that we live like weasels, Dillard reassures us with "we could, you know." She is thus both confident and authoritative while being personal, even informal. As a result we feel obliged to hear her out, to respond to her passionate insistence; we feel obliged to try to understand even when her explanation grazes mystery.

Style Dillard's voice is part of her style. Her sentences are short—they speak to the point whether that point is factual or mystical. There are few connectives, almost no coordinative *ands, buts,* and *fors;* and there is no subordination through the use of *because, although, if,* and *whenever.* The lack of formal syntactic links contributes to the force and authority of Dillard's style. "A weasel is wild," she tells us, announcing her theme. Before long we learn just how wild. Later she notes that "a weasel lives as he's meant to," concisely summing up both the weasel and the essay.

Dillard seems fond of questions. Her questions engage us, stimulate our responses, spur our thinking: "What goes on in his brain the rest of the time? What does a weasel think about?" Like her assertions, Dillard's questions are clear and direct. Some of her questions are simultaneously speculative and provocative as when she writes, "Could two live that way? Could two live under the wild rose, and explore by the pond?" These questions she answers: "We could, you know," a somewhat frightening kind of assurance. Beyond her authoritative declarations and her frequent startling questions is a single exclamation: "Weasel!" which catches us by surprise and captures Dillard's surprise in encountering it. We shouldn't miss the imperative of her final sentence, which startles as much by its commanding tone as by its startling advice.

A further stylistic observation: Dillard leans heavily on verbs, especially verbs of action, often violent action. She stacks verbs up, which results in a driving, relentless prose. Here are two examples:

> Obedient to instinct, he bites his prey at the neck, either splitting the jugular vein at the throat or crunching the brain at the base of the skull, and he does not let go.

> It emptied our lungs. It felled the forest, moved the fields, and drained the pond; the world dismantled and tumbled into that black hole of eyes.

We should also note her fondness for and skill in using figures of comparison. Describing the weasel, Dillard compares him to "a muscled ribbon," and an "arrowhead" with a color "brown as fruitwood." Describing the impact of her encounter she reaches even further into analogy: "Our look was as if two lovers, or deadly enemies, met unexpectedly." The effect of this look, which she describes in another place as eyes locked together, is "a clearing blow to the gut." The energy of her style, moreover, is captured in the physical imagery and the taut syntax of this phrase.

Structure The structure of the essay can be mapped like this:

1. Paragraphs 1–2: facts about weasels, especially their wildness and their ability to hang on and not let go; two stunning examples (the naturalist and the eagle), one for each of the first two paragraphs.

2. Paragraphs 3–7: This second, longer chunk of the essay depicts Dillard encountering the weasel, exchanging glances with it. The middle paragraphs (4–6) set the scene, with paragraphs 3 and 7 framing the section with the repeated mention of Dillard and the weasel's locked glances. Paragraph 5 mixes details as it contrasts wilderness and civilization. The two exist side-by-side, one within the other: beer cans coexist with muskrat holes; turtle eggs sit in motorcycle tracks; a highway runs alongside a duck pond.

3. Paragraphs 8–13: The crescendo and climax of the essay. Here Dillard describes in detail the weasel (paragraph 8); the shock of their locked looks (9 and 10); and the shattering of the spell (11). She also laments her unsuccessful attempt to reforge the link with the weasel after it had been snapped. The section ends with Dillard (and us) pondering the mystery she has experienced.

4. Paragraphs 14–17: Dillard speculates about the meaning of the encounter with the weasel. She contemplates living like a weasel—what it means, why it appeals (to her) and perhaps appalls (us). She explores the implications of what a weasel's life is like—how it relates to human life, especially her own. She concludes with an image from the opening: an eagle carrying something that is clinging fiercely to it, not letting go, holding on into and beyond death. The image brings the essay full circle—but with one significant difference: we have taken the weasel's place.

Thought   What begins as an expository essay detailing facts about weasels, especially their wildness and tenacity, turns into a meditation on the value and necessity of wildness, instinct, and tenacity in human life. By the end of the essay Dillard has made the weasel a symbol, a model of how we should live. Her tone changes from the factual declaration of the opening into speculative wonder and then into admonition.

But what does she mean? How can we live like weasels? How can we imitate and appropriate the weasel's wildness and tenacity? Dillard doesn't say, exactly. She only exhorts us to seize necessity, to lock on to what is essential and not let go for anything. She seems to invite us to decide for ourselves what our necessity is and then relentlessly catch and hold it.

Another idea surfaces in the essay: that man and animal can indeed communicate and understand one another. Dillard opts for a mystical communion between man and beast, by necessity a brief communion, one beyond the power of words to describe (though Dillard seems to have pulled it off). The experience for woman and weasel "stuns into stillness," stops time, empties one consciousness into another. In linking her mind even momentarily with the weasel, Dillard undergoes an extraordinary experience, a transforming one. It's something she would like to repeat, to get more of, find out more about. The experience prompts her to read up on weasels, reading she turns to good account in using memorable details to launch her essay. She wants not just to learn more about weasels but to know a weasel in this mystical way again. But she can't because her own consciousness, the distinctive human quality of her thinking mind, prevents her from being at one and staying at one with an animal.

There seems to be, thus, in Dillard's essay, a pull in two directions. On the one hand, there is the suggestion that we can link ourselves with the weasel and like him live in necessity instinctively, opening ourselves to time and death, noticing everything and remembering nothing. On the other hand sits a counter idea: that we cannot stay linked with the weasel or with any animal, primarily because our minds prohibit it. We are creatures for whom remembering is necessary, vital. Dillard, in fact, could never have savored her experience and shared it with us without the capacity of remembering. The weasel's mindlessness, its purity of living, cannot be wholly hers or ours, for we are mindful creatures, not mindless ones. Our living as we should is necessarily different from the weasel's living as it should. Although we can learn from the weasel's instinct, its pure living, its tenacity, we can follow it only so far on the way to wildness.

Our consideration of the thought of "Living Like Weasels" brings us to its values. Dillard privileges wildness over civilization, mystical communion over separateness, instinct and tenacity over intellectuality. She prizes the majesty and mystery of nature, and she values the weasel's relentlessness, along with its consistency, predictability, and reliance on instinct. She implies that the simplicity, purity, and elementary fierceness of nature have been lost to man with the advent and development of civilization. We might agree, or we might not, choosing instead to value civilization's laws and directives over the instincts and appetites of the natural world. Whereas Dillard seems to lament her and our inability to keep ourselves joined to nature/weasel in the intense manner of her encounter, some readers may find such a disjunction not only necessary but far happier for human beings. Those readers might see Dillard's mystical union as a dangerous drifting away from human responsibility and obligation. Our reactions both to what Dillard describes directly—the weasel's and eagle's instinct to kill for survival—and what she implies about the relationship between the human and natural worlds will differ markedly depending on our own moral and cultural attitudes. Dillard's essay opens up questions about our relationship to nature, and it leads to questions about our own nature. It strikes to the heart of our values, inviting us by implication to consider what, for us, is necessary and essential. What we decide about this may be very different from what Dillard has decided for herself. And the attitude we take toward our "necessity," as she calls it, may also differ. We may believe, for example, that nothing has to be held with the weasel's tenaciousness, that it is better sometimes to let go rather than hang on.

In raising such questions, we move beyond interpreting Dillard's essay to evaluating it. Our evaluation of its implied and expressed values is an act of judgment or criticism. This judgment extends beyond the moral and cultural values of the essay to our appraisal of it as a literary work. To make such an appraisal, we rely on our experience of the work, on its power to move us. We judge it also according to its power to make us think, to instruct us. And finally, we consider whether or not it pleases us. But all of these considerations cause us to bring our minds to bear on Dillard's essay: on its images, on her style and her literary techniques, on her voice, her values and her attitudes, on the essay's subtle, internal connections, on meaning. Finally, we must consider our own ideas and values against Dillard's. We must make our own judgments, formulate our own beliefs.

Suggestions for Writing
The Experience of Essays

1. Write a paper in which you recount your experience reading a particular essay or series of essays by the same author. You may want to compare your initial experience with your experience in subsequent readings.
2. Compare reading a narrative essay with reading a fictional story. Consider how the experience is different; consider how it is similar.
3. Discuss how any essay can be related to your personal experience. Consider how the ideas of the essay can be linked with your life.

The Interpretation of Essays

4. Explicate the opening paragraph or sentences of any essay. Explain the significance of this opening.
5. Explicate the closing sentences or paragraph of an essay. Explain its success or lack thereof as an ending to the work.
6. Select two or three brief passages from an essay, passages that are significant in both what they say outright and what they implicitly suggest. Explain how the passages are related in thought and style.
7. Analyze the figurative language of an essay. Consider how particular linguistic choices enable the essayist to express an idea more effectively and memorably than could be done without figurative language. Some possibilities: Jonathan Swift's "A Modest Proposal"; Henry David Thoreau's "Battle of the Ants"; Virginia Woolf's "Death of the Moth"; John Donne's "Meditation XVII"; James Baldwin's "Notes of a Native Son."
8. Analyze the ironic dimensions of any essay. Consider why the writer may have used irony in the first place. Consider how effective the irony is and what would be gained or lost without it. Some possibilities: Jonathan Swift's "A Modest Proposal"; E. M. Forster's "Our Graves in Gallipoli"; Mark Twain's "Cub Wants to Be a Pilot."
9. Analyze the symbolism of any essay. Identify the symbols included in the essay, and explain their significance: White's "Ring of Time" and his lake in "Once More to the Lake"; Donne's tolling bell in "Meditation XVII"; Orwell's elephant in "Shooting an Elephant."
10. Analyze the structure of any essay. Consider its major parts or sections and explain what each part contributes to the essay overall and how the parts are related.
11. Discuss the thesis or main idea of any essay. Consider how well the writer presents the main idea and why you are or are not persuaded by it.

The Evaluation of Essays

12. Discuss the values the author expresses in any essay. Identify those values, measure them against your own, and comment on their significance.
13. Write a paper in which you discuss the same subject as the author of an essay. In your discussion of the topic, include references to and direct quotations from the essay.
14. Write a paper in which you explain how a writer's essays relate to the cultural, social, or moral environment of his or her time.

To Research or Imagine

15. Develop an alternate ending for an essay. Change its conclusion in any way you see fit. Be prepared to explain the rationale of your conclusion.
16. Write a paper in which you consider how the essay might be rewritten as a poem, play, or short story. Consider the advantages or disadvantages of such a transformation.
17. Read some letters by an essayist. Consider how the writer appears in the letters compared with the sense of the writer you obtain from reading his or her essays.
18. Read a full-length biography of an essayist. Write a paper explaining how reading the writer's life story increases your understanding or appreciation of the essays.
19. Read a critical study of an essayist or a general critical study of the essay as a literary form. Write a paper explaining how the book aids your understanding or increases your appreciation of what any particular essayist has accomplished with the form.
20. Compare two essayists who write largely or frequently about the same subjects (women's issues or nature, for example). Discuss what the essayists have in common and how they differ.

CHAPTER FIVE

Writing About Essays

REASONS FOR WRITING ABOUT ESSAYS

Why write about essays? One reason is to find out what you think about an essay. Another is to induce yourself to read it more carefully. You may write about a work of nonfiction because it engages you, and you may wish to celebrate it or to argue with its implied ideas and values. Still another reason is that you may simply be required to do so as a course assignment.

Whatever your reasons for writing about essays, a number of things happen when you do. First, in writing about an essay you tend to read it more attentively, noticing things you might overlook in a more casual reading. Second, since writing stimulates thinking, when you write about essays you find yourself thinking more about what a particular work means and why you respond to it as you do. And third, you begin to acquire power over the works you write about, making them more meaningful to you.

INFORMAL WAYS OF WRITING ABOUT ESSAYS

When you write about an essay, you may write for yourself or you may write for others. Writing for yourself, to discover what you think, often takes casual forms such as annotation and freewriting. These less formal kinds of writing help you focus on your reading of essays. They are also helpful in studying for tests.

54

They can serve as preliminary forms of writing when you write more formal papers.

When you annotate a text, you make notes about it, usually in the margins or at the top and bottom of pages—or both. Annotations can also be made within the text, as underlined words, circled phrases, and bracketed sentences or paragraphs. Annotations may also assume the form of arrows, question marks, and various other marks—anything that helps you.

Annotating a literary work offers a convenient and relatively painless way to begin writing about it. Annotating can get you started zeroing in on what you think interesting or important. You can also annotate to signal details that puzzle or disconcert you, so you can follow up on them.

Your annotations serve to focus your attention and clarify your understanding of an essay. Your annotations can save you time when you reread or study a work and when you write a more formal paper.

FORMAL WAYS OF WRITING ABOUT ESSAYS

Among the more common ways of writing about essays is analysis. In writing an analytical essay about an essay or section of an essay, your goal is to explain how one or more particular aspects or issues in the work contribute to its overall meaning. You might analyze the dialogue in a scene from an essay such as "Our Graves in Gallipoli." Your goal would be to explain what the verbal exchanges between characters contribute to the essay's meaning. You might analyze the imagery of Walker's "In Search of Our Mothers' Gardens" or the diction (word choice) of Didion's "Los Angeles Notebook" to see what that imagery and diction suggest about the authors' attitude toward the characters or the action described. Or you might analyze how Woolf's style in "The Death of the Moth" or Thoreau's allusions in "Battle of the Ants" convey attitudes toward their respective subjects that enhance their themes and enrich the meanings of their works overall.

In addition to analyzing these and other literary elements in an essay, you might also compare two essays or passages, perhaps by focusing on two writers' presentations of the same or similar subjects. Or, instead of focusing on literary elements per se, you might write to see how a particular critical perspective illuminates an essay. For example, you might consider the ways reader response criticism or new historicism contributes to your understanding of Kingston's "No Name Woman" or Orwell's "Shooting an Elephant."

WRITING TO INTERPRET AN ESSAY

When we write to explain a literary work our concern is largely to make our understanding of it clear to others. Such writing is based not only on our impressions of the work, but on our interpretation or considered understanding of it. In this section we explore ways to write about literature that are less personal, less informal, and less subjective than those described in the previous section. We describe ways to develop your responses into interpretations. And we illustrate some forms of explanation that your writing about literary works may assume. Our purpose is to show how ideas about literary works can be developed into thoughtful interpretations.

Because the art of interpretation is crucial for literary study and essential for persuasive writing about literature, we illustrate the process more extensively now with a step-by-step explanation of the interpretive process as it leads through a series of notes to an interpretive summary. Exactly how do we arrive at an interpretation of any literary text? How do we go about the process of interpretation and analysis? We can outline the steps to forming an interpretation as follows:

1. We *make observations* about textual details—of information, action, and language.
2. We *establish connections* among our observations, looking for patterns and relationships among them.
3. We *develop inferences* (informed interpretive guesses) based on the connections we make.
4. We *formulate a conclusion* or interpretation, however tentative or provisional, from our inferences.

So that you can participate fully in the interpretive process from beginning to end, we provide you with a fresh text, one that does not appear elsewhere in this book. We invite you to begin by annotating Zora Neale Hurston's essay, "How It Feels to Be Colored Me."

ZORA NEALE HURSTON

[1903–1960]

How It Feels to Be Colored Me

I

I am colored but I offer nothing in the way of extenuating circumstances except the fact that I am the only Negro in the United States whose grandfather on the mother's side was *not* an Indian chief.

2   I remember the very day that I became colored. Up to my thirteenth year I lived in the little Negro town of Eatonville, Florida. It is exclusively a colored town. The only white people I knew passed through the town going to or coming from Orlando. The native whites rode dusty horses, the Northern tourists chugged down the sandy village road in automobiles. The town knew the Southerners and never stopped cane chewing when they passed. But the Northerners were something else again. They were peered at cautiously from behind curtains by the timid. The more venturesome would come out on the porch to watch them go past and got just as much pleasure out of the tourists as the tourists got out of the village.

3   The front porch might seem a daring place for the rest of the town, but it was a gallery seat for me. My favorite place was atop the gate-post. Proscenium box for a born first-nighter. Not only did I enjoy the show, but I didn't mind the actors knowing that I liked it. I usually spoke to them in passing. I'd wave at them and when they returned my salute, I would say something like this: "Howdy-do-well-I-thank-you-where-you-goin'?" Usually the automobile or the horse paused at this, and after a queer exchange of compliments, I would probably "go a piece of the way" with them, as we say in farthest Florida. If one of my family happened to come to the front in time to see me, of course negotiations would be rudely broken off. But even so, it is clear that I was the first "welcome-to-our-state" Floridian, and I hope the Miami Chamber of Commerce will please take notice.

4   During this period, white people differed from colored to me only in that they rode through town and never lived there. They liked to hear me "speak pieces" and sing and wanted to see me dance the parse-me-la, and gave me generously of their small silver for doing these things, which seemed strange to me for I wanted to do them so much that I needed bribing to stop. Only they didn't know it. The colored people gave no dimes. They deplored any joyful tendencies in me, but I was their Zora nevertheless. I belonged to them, to the nearby hotels, to the county—everybody's Zora.

5   But changes came in the family when I was thirteen, and I was sent to school in Jacksonville. I left Eatonville, the town of the oleanders, as Zora. When I disembarked from the river-boat at Jacksonville, she was no more. It seemed that I had suffered a sea change. I was not Zora of Orange County any more. I was now a little colored girl. I found it out in certain ways. In my heart as well as in the mirror. I became a fast brown—warranted not to rub nor run.

II

6   But I am not tragically colored. There is no great sorrow dammed up in my soul, nor lurking behind my eyes. I do not mind at all. I do not belong to the sobbing school of Negrohood who hold that nature somehow has given them a lowdown dirty deal and whose feelings are all hurt about it. Even in the helter-skelter skirmish that is my life, I have seen that the world is to the strong regardless of a little pigmentation more or less. No, I do not weep at the world—I am too busy sharpening my oyster knife.

7   Someone is always at my elbow reminding me that I am the granddaughter of slaves. It fails to register depression with me. Slavery is sixty years in the past. The operation was successful and the patient is doing well, thank you. The terrible struggle that made me an American out of a potential slave said "On the line!" The Reconstruction said "Get set!": and the generation before said "Go!" I am off to a flying start and I must not halt in the stretch to look behind and weep. Slavery is the price I paid for civilization, and the choice was not with me. It is a bully adventure and worth all that I have paid through any ancestors for it. No one on earth ever had a greater chance for glory. The world to be won and nothing to be lost. It is thrilling to think—to know that for any act of mine, I shall get twice as much praise or twice as much blame. It is quite exciting to hold the center of the national stage, with the spectators not knowing whether to laugh or to weep.

8   The position of my white neighbors is much more difficult. No brown specter pulls up a chair beside me when I am down to eat. No dark ghost thrusts its leg against mine in bed. The game of keeping what one has is never so exciting as the game of getting.

III

9   Sometimes it is the other way around. A white person is set down in our midst, but the contrast is just as sharp for me. For instance, when I sit in the drafty basement that is The New World Cabaret with a white person, my color comes. We enter chatting about any little nothing that we have in common and are seated by the jazz waiters. In the abrupt way that jazz orchestras have, this one plunges into a number. It loses no time in circumlocutions, but gets right down to business. It constricts the thorax and splits the heart with its tempo and narcotic harmonies. This orchestra grows rambunctious, rears on its hind legs and attacks the tonal veil with primitive fury, rending it, clawing it until it breaks through to the jungle beyond. I follow those heathen—follow them exultingly. I dance wildly inside myself; I yell within, I whoop; I shake my assegai above my head. I hurl it true to the mark *yeeeeoouw!* I am in the jungle and living in the jungle way. My face is painted red and yellow and my body is painted blue. My pulse is throbbing like a war drum. I want to slaughter something—give pain, give death to what, I do not know. But the piece ends. The men of the orchestra wipe their lips and rest their fingers. I creep back slowly to the veneer we call civilization with the last tone and find the white friend sitting motionless in his seat, smoking calmly.

10   "Good music they have here," he remarks, drumming the table with his fingertips.

11   Music. The great blobs of purple and red emotions have not touched him. He has only heard what I felt. He is far away and I see him but dimly across the ocean and the continent that have fallen between us. He is so pale with his whiteness then and I am *so* colored.

12   I do not always feel colored. Even now I often achieve the unconscious Zora of Eatonville before the Hegira. I feel most colored when I am thrown against a sharp white background.

13   For instance at Barnard. "Beside the waters of the Hudson" I feel my race. Among the thousand white persons, I am a dark rock surged upon, and overswept, but through it all, I remain myself. When covered by the waters, I am; and the ebb but reveals me again.

IV

14   At certain times I have no race, I am *me*. When I set my hat at a certain angle and saunter down Seventh Avenue, Harlem City, feeling as snooty as the lions in front of the Forty-Second Street Library, for instance. So far as my feelings are concerned, Peggy Hopkins Joyce on the Boule Mich with her gorgeous raiment, stately carriage, knees knocking together in a most aristocratic manner, has nothing on me. The cosmic Zora emerges. I belong to no race nor time. I am the eternal feminine with its string of beads.

15   I have no separate feeling about being an American citizen and colored. I am merely a fragment of the Great Soul that surges within the boundaries. My country, right or wrong.

16 Sometimes, I feel discriminated against, but it does not make me angry. It merely astonishes me. How *can* any deny themselves the pleasure of my company? It's beyond me.

17 But in the main, I feel like a brown bag of miscellany propped against a wall. Against a wall in company with other bags, white, red and yellow. Pour out the contents, and there is discovered a jumble of small things priceless and worthless. A first-water diamond, an empty spool, bits of broken glass, lengths of string, a key to a door long since crumbled away, a rusty knife-blade, old shoes saved for a road that never was and never will be, a nail bent under the weight of things too heavy for any nail, a dried flower or two still a little fragrant. In your hand is the brown bag. On the ground before you is the jumble it held—so much like the jumble in the bags, could they be emptied, that all might be dumped in a single heap and the bags refilled without altering the content of any greatly. A bit of colored glass more or less would not matter. Perhaps that is how the Great Stuffer of Bags filled them in the first place—who knows?

(1928)

1. Make Observations

The first thing we do in interpreting Hurston's essay is to record our observations about it. The following list provides a sampling of such observations.

- Hurston writes as an adult looking back on her childhood and adolescence as well as at her adult experiences.
- She describes her experience of living in two places—Eatonville and Jacksonville.
- She refers to the historical past, particularly to slavery and Reconstruction.
- She describes scenes that include white and black people together: welcoming visitors to Eatonville; the jazz club.
- She uses comparisons in describing how she thinks about herself:
  as a patient after an operation (7)
  as an actress on center stage (7)
  as a player in a game of "getting" (8)
  as a "dark rock surged upon and covered by waters" (13)
  as a stone statue of a lion (14)
  as a fragment of the Great Soul (15)
  as a brown bag of miscellany containing both priceless and worthless things (17).
- She divides the essay into four sections.
- She mentions changes and contrasting states of affairs:
  the day she "became colored" (2)
  her "sea change" (5)
  different responses to cabaret music (9)
  the priceless and worthless stuff she is made of (17).
- She chronicles her feelings:
  she does not always feel colored (12)

she feels most colored against a white background (12)
she sometimes feels astonished (16)
she doesn't feel angry about her situation (16)
she has no separate feeling about being American and colored (15)
she feels discriminated against (somehow) (16).

2. Establish Connections

Once we have recorded these and similar observations—or as we do so—we begin making connections between them. The business of making connections is a very personal one. There is no one way of making an interpretation and no predictable conclusion which you must reach. Consequently, we present the interpretive process as a series of questions. The questions are meant to stimulate your thinking and to suggest that the connections you form are only part of the interpretive process.

- What is the relationship between the two scenes Hurston describes? How, for example, does she feel serving as an unofficial welcoming committee of one for Eatonville? How does she feel while listening to music in the cabaret? What, in each case, is her relationship to the white people she is with?
- What significant differences exist for her between Eatonville and Jacksonville? How do you account for her differences in feeling about the two places?
- What common features do her comparisons about herself suggest? How are these comparisons related to the feeling she describes elsewhere?
- What is the focus of each of the four parts of the essay, and how are the parts related?

3. Develop Inferences

On the basis of connections you form, you can make inferences. When we infer something, we reasonably conclude that something is the case based on evidence, on what we know. But be careful, for your inferences are not necessarily true. In the process of drawing inferences, we refer to our own experiences and to what we know about a writer and his or her subject, and we react emotionally as well as rationally. Furthermore, we might see connections between events that other readers do not. Let's say, for example, that we make the following inferences from the information we have.

- Hurston writes about her blackness without bitterness.
- Seeing benefits in being black, possibilities unavailable to whites, she seems to prefer her color.
- She seems proud of her race.
- She values herself, is confident in her abilities, and secure in her sense of selfhood.
- She sees herself as a performer, on center stage, with an opportunity to make a strong impression as a woman, as a black, and as an artist.

- She experiences pain in discovering that she was black ("I found it out . . . in my heart as well as in the mirror.")
- She possesses an irrepressible gaiety, refusing to be depressed about the fact that she is the granddaughter of slaves.
- She is patient, tolerant, and understanding.
- She sees white people as bearing the weight of the race problem in America.

4. Draw Conclusions

As we think about these and other inferences, we might develop a short interpretation or set of conclusions based on our inferences, such as this one:

In "How It Feels to Be Colored Me," Zora Neale Hurston reveals a black woman's confidence in her color, her talent, and her femininity. She sees the issue of color as intrinsically skin-deep and primarily a white problem, which need not result in tragic consequences for blacks. In the first part of the essay, Hurston indicates the significant change that took place in her self-perception when she moved from Eatonville to Jacksonville. She learned there what it meant to be "a little colored girl." In the second part she makes clear that although she felt the sting of discrimination, she doesn't wallow in self-pity, but instead looks hopefully to her opportunities as a human being and as an artist, seeing the world as her oyster. Part three reveals the differences she feels between herself and her white friend. It also includes her important revelation that she feels most black when she is with white people. In the fourth and final section, Hurston describes her paradoxical sense of being a small part of a complex and multifaceted cosmic whole, all the while retaining a distinctive and significant sense of selfhood. In exploring the implied question in Hurston's title (How does it feel to be Black?) Hurston provides an answer: that for her, at least, it feels fine.

If you write a still more elaborate interpretation of Hurston's essay, you would provide evidence in the form of textual detail to support your thinking. You would return to the observations and questions that led you to your interpretation. One way to do this is simply to explain in greater detail what Hurston accomplishes in each of her four sections. The first part, for example, concerns Hurston's growing perception of herself as "colored," while the second focuses on her optimism. You could devote one paragraph to each of these topics, exploring in more depth and detail your understanding of why these are important. You could then do the same for Hurston's third and fourth concerns: her sense of being different from white people, and her sense of individuality. Your expanded essay would have five paragraphs: an introductory paragraph, which appears above as our interpretation, and four additional paragraphs, each of which explains one aspect of Hurston's argument. Then you could decide whether or not you need to add a concluding paragraph.

Another way to expand on your opening paragraph would be to consider what you think of Hurston's ideas and argument. You might ask yourself, for example, whether Hurston's description is accurate or persuasive, or whether it reflects the views of contemporary blacks generally. You might also consider whether Hurston convinces you that her experience illustrates any truths about racial prejudice or about the resilience and resources of human character. You need to decide whether you believe Hurston, and then whether you agree with her—and why.

THREE STUDENT ESSAYS

The following essays analyze the writing of Maxine Hong Kingston, E. B. White, and Virginia Woolf. In the first essay, Suyin So analyzes Kingston's "No Name Woman," the opening segment of her book *The Woman Warrior*. One of the notable features of Ms. So's analysis is the way she begins—with personal experience, which she then relates to a central concern of Kingston's piece.

In the second essay, Betsy Gates analyzes one of White's most famous and popular essays, "Once More to the Lake." Her focus is on White's response to time and change. In the last essay included here Ruth Chung analyzes Virginia Woolf's sketch "Old Mrs. Grey," largely by focusing on its imagery. Toward the end of her essay, Ms. Chung makes a judgment about what Woolf implies about the title character, Old Mrs. Grey, and about humanity's responsibility for her.

Suyin So

On Kingston's "No Name Woman"

In fifth grade, the object of my affections reacted with scornful laughter when informed of my romantic interests in him. Mortified, I ran home to what I considered my source of comfort and advice, my mother. She too was mortified, but more out of rage than sympathy. Her "advice" was a command. She told me, "You're only ten. Don't like anyone." I protested, asking her how I could just "not like anyone." Her wrath grew exponentially, and I realized I was touching on an exceedingly hot subject. The question lingers with me, though. I wonder that a woman could expect a human being to put a cap on her affection, to tell themselves "No, don't like anyone."

This Victorian attitude toward male-female relations is detectable in Maxine Hong Kingston's "No Name Woman," where we are presented with the image of her long-dead, long-forgotten aunt, who throws herself and her illegitimate child into a well the same night her entire village raids their home to terrorize her family. Kingston also introduces us to her Chinese family, who buries the aunt deep in an unmarked grave and even deeper in their memory, denying she ever existed. Kingston herself is included in the introductions, as a girl, watching her father count his remaining change after she and her siblings are indulged in the extravagance of a single carnival ride. This tapestry of life, so heavily dyed with the color of the Chinese heritage and culture, is woven with many threads, each an entire tale in itself. Yet the primary image is that of the cheating aunt, the adulterer, whose story is artfully recounted by her niece, Kingston.

In this sole character of the aunt, too, there are countless facets, many of them products of Kingston's imagination and curiosity. She wonders what this formerly unknown aunt was like, what clothes she wore. Yet she is refused any answers to her questions, for, as her mother tells her, "She has never been born." Her father has no sisters, only brothers. There was never a bastard child in the family, only the legitimate products of safe, regulated, dowried, planned marriages. This denial, however, does not stop Kingston from thinking about this woman, from hazarding guesses about her nature and her ordeal. The aunt, then, becomes the central point of the story, the focus of Kingston's account.

The first part of the essay is the aunt's tale as told by Kingston's mother. In a typically Chinese fashion, the mother

coldly, almost scientifically, recounts the discovery of her
husband's sister, the demented attack of the village on their
child, "plugging up the well." The mother ends the story with
a warning: "what happened to her could happen to you. Don't
humiliate us." No sympathy is shown for the woman; but to them
she was evil defined, a harlot who caused the honor of her
family to be tainted, her family harassed and humiliated.

Kingston, her curiosity piqued, is both awed and impressed
by her aunt. She wonders about her aunt, painting her in
various lights. At one point, she is the victim of rape,
forced to have sex with some man, for "women in the old China
did not choose." At another, she is portrayed as a woman in
control of herself, making herself pretty so as to lure a
lover. There is a similarity between Kingston's musings and
her mother's account of the story in that Kingston rather
imitates her mother's concise manner of speaking. She allows
no romantic conjecture to enter her thoughts. There is no
mention of unrequited love or lustful fantasies. She prefers
only to theorize on the nature of her aunt, the circumstances
surrounding the situation. She does, however, allow a small
amount of romanticization into her descriptions of the woman,
placing her in a most feminine light, examining her face for
sunspots, in the market hoping for a second glance from the
man. It is also of value to note that Kingston rejects her
earlier image of her aunt as a rape victim in favor of a less
helpless, stronger idea of the woman as one making her own
decisions. We see the aunt as a normal woman with normal wants
and desires. Kingston uses this image of her aunt as the
oppressed romantic to make clear her sympathy for her. It is,
albeit, only a limited sympathy, but it is the most the aunt
will receive.

Here more than anywhere, the essence of Kingston's piece
emerges, in the way that mother and daughter treat the same
subject. One, the product of no-nonsense Chinese tradition,
uses the tale as a warning to her just-pubescent daughter. The
daughter, still somewhat no-nonsense yet imbued with America's
culture, dreamily wonders what her aunt was like, how she wore
her hair. The "culture shock" of the first generation, the
clash between old and new, tradition and change is exemplified
here, as Kingston and her mother are at ideological odds about
the treatment of this subject.

"Chinese-Americans, . . . how do you separate what is
peculiar to childhood, to poverty, insanities, one family,
your mother who marked your growing with stories, from what is
Chinese?" Kingston demands an answer to her question, one
asked out of confusion and bewilderment. She echoes a
generation of children of immigrants, one that wonders aloud

the same question. She is unable to answer herself directly. Yet in her own work, she draws lines that define what is Chinese and what is not. To her mother, who emphatically states, "She could not have been pregnant, you see, because her husband had been gone for years," adultery is distinctly *not Chinese*. To the women of the village, who looked like "great sea snails," paying too much attention to your looks was distinctly *not Chinese*. Sex, as the author maintains, was distinctly *not Chinese*.

At the heart of the essay, underneath the tale of the unfortunate aunt, is the answer to her question, an exploration of Chinese culture. Kingston mixes story with explanation, interspersing her aunt's tale with broader details about the Chinese. It is subtle but effective in educating the reader about her culture. Rather than including an outright definition of all things Chinese, she illustrates certain aspects of the culture's characteristics. The almost practical sexism—the "waste" of having a daughter in starvation time, the bartering of a woman as an object only slightly more valuable than a rooster, the slavish obeisance expected from every woman—all this is inherent in understanding Kingston. Without this foregone conclusion, one cannot comprehend the drastic double standard placed upon women, where men were allowed to wander off and abandon their traditions and women were expected to uphold them. One cannot comprehend how an entire village could destroy a home, slaughter livestock, torture the woman and her family until she kills herself, yet not even attempt to seek and punish the man who certainly played his role in the drama.

Also paramount to understanding this essay is the extreme Victorian attitude so pervasive in the Chinese. Like my mother, who expected me to control my immature affections as though emotion were an on/off switch, society in China expected women to live without passion or desire. Sex was not a pleasure, but rather a duty, a responsibility to produce someone to take care of you in old age, to fold paper into houses and clothing after your death. To indulge in anything more than the absolutely vital was a sin, to indulge in something as volatile as sex was considered a double sin.

Yet even these seemingly despicable traits are born out of Necessity, something so important to Kingston's mother it is capitalized. If a girl baby is less worthy than a boy baby, it is only because the boy will work longer and harder, will carry on the family name and produce heirs. If sex is a vile activity, it is only because a population of such huge proportions is fragile, starvation all too frequent, and food too scarce for a couple to entertain hopes of a very large family. Necessity was omnipotent, truly the river that guided their lives as it did with Kingston's mother. I do not excuse boorish behavior, but I must find and explain the practical reasons for it.

Kingston's aunt, the no name woman, without identity or persona, was unfortunate in that she was discovered violating these traditions. She dared to step out from the safe, secure confines of society's rules, to venture out into the vague unknown. In doing so, she risked persecution from society, being shoved into non-existence forever, haunting her family as a ghost, not as a spirit. She serves as a reminder to young women of the terrible consequences of hasty decisions, as a tragic character in a compelling and dramatic tale and, finally, as an illustration that teaches reader and author alike what it truly means to be Chinese.

Betsy Gates
Essay #3
Expos-17
R. DiYanni

An Analysis of White's "Once More to the Lake"

In his essay "Once More to the Lake," E. B. White tells the story of summer as he has known it. He went to a lake in Maine as a boy each August and now, having a son of his own, he compares his present experience there to his experiences in the past. Seemingly unchanging, the lake appears a constant place that shows no years and holds all life to be the same. White believes that his visit to the lake will make him the boy that he was. However, nothing can stop living things from aging and eventually passing away. Time and change serve to link White's life to his son's as well as to confirm his role as the father in the chain of youth and old age.

Almost immediately, White shows the lake as a haven from the "restlessness of the tides" in his adult life. Despite having become a "salt-water man" since his boyhood summers, he once again seeks the "placidity of a lake in the woods." In this first section before White actually arrives at the lake, he speculates about how it will be different from his past vacations. He wonders how "time would have marred this unique, this holy spot." He speaks of time as the enemy, remembering how the lake was so pleasant, containing the stillness of a cathedral. While preparing himself for the desolation, he marvels at how strange it is that "you remember one thing, and that suddenly reminds you of another."

Once he settles in with his boy at a camp and into the kind of summertime he had known, White could tell "that it was going to be pretty much the same as it had been before." He describes hearing his boy quietly sneak out to the lake in early morning as he once did. The sensation that his boy was he and he was his father persists. White seems to be confused in his role with his son. The memories and his present actions are alike and thus reverse his place in his own mind. He would say something and suddenly it would be not he but his father who was saying the words or making the gesture. It gave White "a creepy sensation."

The lake represents youth and leads White to the conclusion that "there had been no years." The arrival of a dragonfly at his end of the fishing rod convinces him that "everything was as it always had been." The small waves were the same, the boat was the same boat, and under the floorboards were the same fresh-water leavings and debris. Watching his dragonfly, "there had been no years between the ducking of this dragonfly and the other one," the one that was part of his memory. He looked at the boy, who was silently watching his fly, and it was White's hands that held the boy's rod, White's eyes watching. This scenario further convinces White and the reader that the lake keeps everything the same. So far, the descriptions of White's feeling that he is his son keep the reader content. Like White, one finds it encouraging that a place such as the lake can be found as a respite from change and time.

Nothing can change the lake. They caught two bass and killed them swiftly. Later, as they returned for a swim, the lake was exactly as they had left it. It "seemed an utterly enchanted sea, this lake you could leave to its own devices for a few hours and come back to, and find that it had not stirred, this constant and trustworthy body of water." The stillness of the lake is something for White to hold on to, and to prove to himself that there "had been no years." White wants to believe that he can leave the lake again and upon his return he will be the same. The lake makes him the same by haunting him with the memories of the past.

White, however, is fooling himself. Things change, like the middle path that he describes as having "the marks of the hooves, and the splotches of dried, flaky manure." That path is gone, and an old way of doing things with it. Although White mentions these changes nonchalantly because the lake still functions in the same way, the reader remembers that these changes signify something more. The waitresses are different in that they wash their hair, caring more about appearance in a visual world. Values are changing, but this seems insignificant compared to the fact that the same diner is still standing and its waitresses, though different, are still fifteen. The reader begins to feel sorry for White as he is still under the illusion that time has stopped at the lake. He is merely an aging father who continues to believe that he can experience youth once again.

White finally begins to show his unhappiness at some changes as he describes the arrival at the lake. The summers had "been infinitely precious and worth saving." The ritual of a big arrival, "a business in itself," was of great importance. "There had been jollity and peace and goodness." "Arrival was less exciting nowadays, when you sneaked up in your car and parked it under a tree near the camp and took out the bags and in five minutes it was all over, no fuss, no loud wonderful fuss about trunks."

White's perception has changed dramatically. As a boy, the times did not need to be saved. They were the present. The most important thing was fun. Now, to White, the important things are "peace and goodness and jollity." Another thing that was wrong was the sound of outboard motors. It jarred, unlike the peaceful hum of the inboard motors he had used as a boy. The most disturbing fact about these motors was that his son enjoyed them. The change was not missed a bit on his part. The differences between White and his son are slowly creeping in.

White says that they "had a good week at the camp. The bass were biting well and the sun shone endlessly, day after day." However, this description has none of the zest that his childhood memories do. White talks about the sweet mornings lying in bed and the girls singing and the boys playing their mandolins. While the store is in the same place, there is a tar road and cars in front of it. Yet White still says that everywhere he went he had trouble making out which was him, the one walking by his side or the one walking in his pants.

In the last section of his essay, White describes a thunderstorm as it occurs at the lake. He describes it as a revival of an old melodrama that he had seen long ago with childish awe. "The whole thing was so familiar," and all of the stages of the storm were the same. However, his feelings were not. White lacks the enthusiasm that he had as a boy. As the calm sets in, he watches all of the children run out and cry with joy and relief at the prospect of going swimming in the rain.

White is reduced to a mere observer, and the realization that he is no longer the boy that he once was begins to present itself. White describes this feeling as he languidly watches his son, who says he's going swimming without any thought of going in himself. He saw "his hard little body, skinny and bare, . . . wince slightly as he pulled up around his vitals the small, soggy, icy garment." Suddenly, his own groin felt the chill of death.

The ending is effective as it sums up the point that the essay leans toward. Nothing can stop time: everything must change. White's reaction to the thunderstorm brings to mind the title of the essay. "Once More to the Lake" suggests a finality that this "chill of death" has a strong connection to. Where is White's father during this visit with his son? Inevitably, he has passed away. It seemed as if White had found the cure for middle age, but the lake only served to remind him what had once been. White has finally realized that his fate is to be the same as his father's. He cannot change the reality of life and death.

Ruth Chung

Woolf's Old Mrs. Grey

   In her essay "Old Mrs. Grey," Virginia Woolf paints a
picture of a ninety-two-year old woman whose supreme desire is
to die. There is no action or movement in this portrait; Mrs.
Grey merely sits alone in a corner of her house. Woolf's page-
long description of her not only depicts the sufferings of a
single individual but of the old and the grey in general. And
yet it is clear that the purpose of this piece is more than
the extraction of sympathy. Woolf's purpose is to express her
view that a life of such suffering is not worth living. She
asserts that the physical and mental agonies of old age should
not be prolonged on humanitarian grounds.

   Throughout the essay, Woolf uses Mrs. Grey's house and the
landscape outside to metaphorically describe her mental state.
Woolf's description of the house and the rolling fields and
hills seems to be just another picturesque view of England's
countryside. From the context of Mrs. Grey's pain and her
desire to die, however, the house, with its door wide open,
may represent her body on the verge of death. The metaphor may
run still deeper, describing her mind, open and ready to be
enveloped and swallowed by death's rays. It also follows that
the image of the fields and hills, described as places of
"stainless and boundless rest; space unlimited; untrodden
grass; wild birds flying" comes to represent the pure,
unblemished paradise, the haven from pain for which Mrs. Grey
yearns. It could also simply be a representation of death, a
state of being (or of not being) that everyone must eventually
face, a time when "even the busiest, most contented suddenly
let fall what they hold."

   Woolf further describes Mrs. Grey's longing for death using
light as a symbol to enhance her metaphor. Through the seven
by four foot opening of Mrs. Grey's front door, sunshine
pours in from outside, putting "embarrassing pressure" on the
fire burning in the grate, which appears only as "a small
spot of dusty light feebly trying to escape. . . ." Here, the
fire burning in the grate may represent the appeals and
delights of life, which have become dreary to Mrs. Grey when
compared to the lure of the after-life, the sweet respite of
death, as represented by the streaming sunshine from outside.
Mrs. Grey is so enamored by the prospect of going to such a
paradise of rest and relief, that living for the present
becomes pointless; it seems silly to do the week's wash "when

out there over the fields over the hills, there is no washing; no pinning of clotheslines; mangling and ironing; no work at all."

The idea of a new life dawning is also represented by "morning spreading seven foot by four green and sunny," which tries to infiltrate the house and beckons to Mrs. Grey through the front door. Mrs. Grey welcomes this light as much as she welcomes death, but the light has not yet been able to permeate the whole house. She has put so much hope into this state of rest, that "when the colour went out of the doorway, she could not see the other page which is then lit up." This "other page" represents Mrs. Grey's present chapter of life, which has potential, even in her pain, to be enjoyable and fulfilling. But Mrs. Grey can only see this life as she sees the fire burning in the grate, which becomes dim in the light of her suffering and pain. She is so weary of her life that "her eyes had ceased to focus themselves . . . they could see but without looking." It isn't that she is physically blind, but that her pain is so great that it is all she can see. It could also be that nothing in her present life seems to be worth looking at because she cannot appreciate the little pleasures of life: "She had never used her eyes on anything minute and difficult; merely upon faces, and dishes and fields."

However, it is not fair to take Mrs. Grey's suffering lightly either, for she suffers excruciating pain. Woolf compares her pain to a sadistic snake: "a zigzag of pain, wriggling across the door, pain that twisted her legs as it wriggled; jerked her body to and fro like a marionette." Woolf also speaks of a sharp, cutting pain by describing Mrs. Grey's body as being "wrapped around the pain as a damp sheet is folded over a wire . . . spasmodically jerked by a cruel invisible hand." The startling image of Mrs. Grey that these comparisons create, of her body writhing, twisting like a live wire shows the sufferings the elderly must endure and explains Mrs. Grey's state of mind, her abnormal eagerness for death.

Woolf gives the reader further insight into Mrs. Grey's mental state by taking us into her mind as well as allowing us to hear what she has to say. She looks back to her active childhood, her entrance into the adult world, and the time spent with her eleven brothers and sisters. But these memories can only bring her sorrow and loneliness when she compares those times to the present. She is literally jerked back to its reality by a convulsion: "The line jerked. She was thrown forward in her chair." Her old body is sick and deteriorating and all of her siblings have died; she has even survived her husband and her children.

The tone of Mrs. Grey's voice as she mumbles is not bitter, for she has no energy in her weary body or soul to complain. Woolf's fragmented sentences also reflect Mrs. Grey's tiredness as though she doesn't have even enough energy to speak: " 'All dead. All dead . . . My brothers and sisters. And my husband gone. My daughter too. But I go on.' ". Her words also have an almost Mother Goose-rhyme quality to them: " 'I'm an ignorant old woman. I can't read or write and every morning when I crawls downstairs, I say I wish it were night. . . .' " This suggests a regression into a childish state, into senility, but the words are coherent, expressing her feelings of debilitation and inadequacy. While her words have no hint of bitterness in them they serve to evoke pity. Her daily supplications to God: "O let me pass" show how desperately she yearns to be relieved of her suffering. The thought of Mrs. Grey crawling downstairs and crawling into bed by herself every day is especially poignant and helps the reader to understand her fatigue and loneliness.

In the last paragraph, Woolf concludes by seeming to lay the blame for Mrs. Grey's suffering on humanity, again using metaphor. She asserts that it is the hand of humanity that jerks so cruelly on the wire of pain, that "puts out the eyes and the ears," that "pinions" the bodies of the elderly on those wires of pain by trying to keep them alive. They are like tortured birds, pinned to a barn door, like "a rook that still lives, even with a nail through it." Woolf suggests that we, humanity, are responsible for prolonging their sufferings by caring for them and by trying to ameliorate their lives "with a bottle of medicine, a cup of tea, a dying fire." In a way, it seems as if Woolf is not really blaming humanity for the sufferings of the elderly but merely reprimanding us for not being aware of them. Or perhaps she is merely voicing her own ambivalence about the issue of euthanasia. And yet her strong language in the last paragraph and in other parts of the essay accuses us of being the active perpetrators of a crime, a crime that we could not help. If Woolf's intention for this essay was, indeed, to lay the blame on us for Mrs. Grey's pain, it is an invalid and unfair indictment, for Woolf demands that we be selfish and inhumane in order to be humane, to help the elderly by turning our backs on them. Woolf does not realize that even we, who accept the suffering of our parents and grandparents, accept it for our own futures as well as an immutable fact of life.

QUESTIONS FOR WRITING ABOUT ESSAYS

The following questions can help you focus your thinking about the elements of essays, in preparation for writing analytical papers. Use the questions as a checklist to guide you to important aspects of any essay or extended work of nonfiction you read.

Voice and Tone

1. How would you characterize the voice of the essayist? Does the essayist speak in his or her own voice? To what extent does the essayist create imaginary voices in the piece?
2. What is the essayist's attitude toward his or her subject? What is the essayist's tone? What details of language—diction, syntax, imagery, rhythm—convey the writer's tone?

Style

3. Is the writer's style direct or indirect? Formal or informal? High or low? Familiar or detached? Easy or hard to read? Something in between each of these opposite pairs?
4. What is the effect of the writer's stylistic choices—of the degree of formality of the prose, of its directness or obliqueness?
5. What kinds of diction does the writer employ? What kinds of sentences does he or she write? How reliant upon image and metaphor is the essayist? With what effects?

Structure

6. How is the essay organized? Where are its introduction, body, and conclusion?
7. How are the parts of the essay related? To what extent does the writer make use of comparison and contrast? Of classification and causal analysis?
8. How do the individual paragraphs of the essay follow from and relate to one another?

Thought

9. What is the essayist's central idea? Where is that idea most evident? Is the idea directly implied or directly stated?
10. What kinds of evidence does the essayist use to support the central idea? Are you persuaded by the arguments? Why or why not?

CHAPTER SIX

Two Essayists in Context

READING E. B. WHITE AND MAXINE HONG KINGSTON IN DEPTH

Reading the essays of E. B. White is a somewhat different experience from reading the nonfiction of Maxine Hong Kingston for several reasons. Not only are the writers' backgrounds and generations different, White an east coast born and bred white male who came into adulthood between the First and Second World Wars, Kingston a Chinese-American west coast woman who grew up in California in the 1950s and 1960s. Kingston's work mixes fact and fiction in a unique blend of quasi-autobiographical writing. Kingston essays included in this chapter form parts of two books that possess an artistic unity and integrity. White's essays, on the other hand, were written at different times, in different places, for different audiences of readers, as reflected in their varied places of original publication. The White essays gathered here, thus, were originally published as just that—as essays rather than as parts of a larger artistic whole.

These contextual differences are accentuated by others. White's thematic interests differ dramatically from Kingston's. White writes about vacation trips to a New England lake, about visits to the circus, about raising geese—and about sailing, Model-T cars, the moon landing, and a widely ranging host of topics beyond the three selections included here. Kingston mines a narrower vein, focusing almost exclusively on facets of her Chinese ancestry, dramatizing thereby ways her Chinese-American cultural context is at odds with the Chinese cultural context of previous generations.

White and Kingston offer readers additional contexts for reading their nonfiction. Both have also written fiction, though the most extensive and best known of White's fiction was written explicitly for children. Both have also written about writing. And both have attracted sufficient critical attention for there to be some disagreement about the nature and quality of their work—though this is more an issue for Kingston's prose than for White's.

It is one of the wonderful paradoxes of literary experience, however, that as much as the works of White and Kingston differ, both writers, in their highly individualistic particularity, nonetheless transcend their local selves in reflecting universal needs and concerns. One doesn't have to be a white eastern male to appreciate White's essays any more than one has to be a contemporary Asian-American woman to understand and value Kingston's prose. While reflecting the local particulars of their experience, White and Kingston speak to the broadest of human concerns—of living through time and change, of balancing conflicting cultural loyalties, of relating to the larger social and natural worlds of which we are all a part.

The essays and materials collected in this chapter provide a hint of this compelling unity and rich diversity.

QUESTIONS FOR IN-DEPTH READING

1. What general or overall thematic connections can you make between different works?
2. What stylistic similarities do you notice between and among different works?
3. How do the works differ in emphasis, tone, and style?
4. Once you have identified a writer's major preoccupations, place each work on a spectrum or a grid that represents the range of the writer's concerns.
5. What connections and disjunctions do you find between the following literary elements as they are embodied in different essays by the same writer?
   a. voice and tone
   b. language and style
   c. structure and organization
   d. theme and thought
6. To what extent are your responses to and perceptions of different works by the same writer shared by others—by critics, by classmates, and by the writers themselves?
7. What relationships and differences do you see between the work of one writer and that of another who shares similar thematic interests, stylistic proclivities, or cultural, religious, or social values?

INTRODUCTION TO E. B. WHITE

[*1899–1985*]

E. B. White is generally recognized as one of America's finest writers. Long associated with *The New Yorker,* for which he wrote stories, sketches, essays, and editorials, White also contributed to another prominent magazine, *Harper's,* writing a monthly column, "One Man's Meat," from 1938 to 1943. These columns were collected and published with a few additional pieces from *The New Yorker* as *One Man's Meat* (1944). This book was followed by two other collections of miscellany, *The Second Tree from the Corner* (1954) and *The Points of My Compass* (1962). Besides these collections, White published, over a slightly longer span of years, three children's books: *Stuart Little* (1945), *Charlotte's Web* (1952), and *The Trumpet of the Swan* (1970). In 1976, White published a selection of his best essays, those, as he says, which had "an odor of durability clinging to them." *The Essays of E. B. White* was followed a year later by a selection of White's letters, titled simply enough, *Letters of E. B. White. Poems and Sketches of E. B. White* appeared in 1981.

Although not a complete bibliography of White's published work, this list does suggest something of White's range and versatility, as well as something about the way writing has been for him steady work over a long stretch of time. And the steadiest of White's work, in both senses of the word, has been his essays. In fact, it is as an essayist that White is best known and most highly acclaimed. It is as an essayist that he identifies himself, defining an essayist as "a self-liberated man sustained by the childish belief that everything he thinks about, everything that happens to him, is of general interest." And again, as one who is "content with living a free life and enjoying the satisfactions of a somewhat undisciplined existence."

Edward Hoagland has noted that White's name has become almost synonymous with *essay.* And for good reason, since it is the form most congenial to his temperament, a form that allows him the latitude he needs to roam freely in thought, a form that he has been able to stamp with his own imprint. This imprint is reflected in the following elements: a scrupulous respect for his readers; an uncanny accuracy in the use of language; and an uncommon delight in common, everyday things. White sees the extraordinary in the ordinary, noticing and valuing what most of us either overlook or take for granted. And from his repeated and respectful acts of attention flow reminiscences, speculations, explorations, and questions about our common humanity, about our relationships with one another, with the past, with the worlds of technology and nature.

White is a writer whose insights derive directly from his literal observations, from what he sees. Thoreau, one of White's favorite writers—and one with whom White has much in common—once remarked that "you can't say more than you can see." White's writing bears this out. The relationship between sight and insight, between observation and speculation, is evident in essays such as "The Ring of Time," which begins with a description of a circus act and ends with speculations about time and change, and "Once More to the Lake," in which White reminisces about his boyhood summer holidays in Maine, both describing the place with startling vividness and offering unsettling speculations about the meaning of his memories. In these and other essays, White's writing is rooted in the crucial act of vision, a vision which sees into and beyond the surface of his subjects.

White's best writing, however, is more than a record of what he has seen and thought. It is also art, literature. His best work is crafted, shaped, formed with the same attention to details of structure, texture, image, and tone that poets or painters, sculptors or novelists give their work. In "The Ring of Time," "Once More to the Lake," and "The Geese," matters of fact, details of time, place, and circumstance give way to larger concerns. The circus is more than a circus ring: it becomes an emblem of time and change; the lake is more than a summer vacation place: it becomes an image of serenity and a reminder of time, change, even death; the old gander's plight becomes White's. The images of light and water, the symbolism of circus ring and lake, along with a concern for understanding the present in relation to the past and the future, the emblematic nature of the geese—these emphases lift their respective essays beyond the merely personal and reminiscent, beyond the ordinary and the everyday into the extraordinary universality of art.

About writing itself, White has said a good deal, and said it well. In the chapter he contributed to the now famous *Elements of Style,* White notes that when we speak of a writer's style we mean "the sound his words make on paper." The voice that we hear is what distinguishes one writer from another; and it is one good reason why, to get a good sense of a writer's style, we should read his or her work aloud. Beyond this concern for hearing what language can do, White notes that a writer's style "reveals something of his spirit, his habits, his capacities, his bias . . . it is the Self escaping into the open." And, as White suggests, this Self cannot be hidden, for a writer's style "reveals his identity as surely as would his fingerprints."

Recognizing that writing is hard work requiring endurance, thought, and revision ("revising is part of writing"), White advises that beginning writers let their ears be their guide, that they avoid all tricks and mannerisms, that they see writing as "one way to go about thinking," and, finally, that they achieve style both by affecting none and by believing "in the truth and worth of the scrawl."

Throughout his years as a writer, White has often been asked for advice about writing. To one seeker he wrote: "Remember that writing is translation, and the opus to be translated is yourself." On another occasion he responded to a seventeen-year-old girl this way:

> You asked me about writing—how I did it. There is no trick to it. If you like to write and want to write, you write, no matter where you are or what else you are doing or whether anyone pays any heed. . . . If you want to write about feelings, about the end of summer, about growing, write about it. A great deal of writing is not "plotted"—most of my essays have no plot structure, they are a ramble in the woods, or a ramble in the basement of my mind.

There is a naturalness, an ease about White's writing, both in these offhand remarks from his letters and in his more elaborately plotted essays. It is an ease that derives in part from a refusal to be either pompous or pedantic; it is an ease that derives also from a consistent attempt to be honest, to achieve the candor he admires in Montaigne; and it is a naturalness that is reflected in his style, a style that mingles the high subject and the low, the big word and the small, without flamboyance or ostentation. White's style, in short, is a badge of his character—intelligent, honest, witty, exact, and fundamentally endearing.

WHITE ON WRITING

E. B. WHITE

The Essayist

The essayist is a self-liberated man, sustained by the childish belief that everything he thinks about, everything that happens to him, is of general interest. He is a fellow who thoroughly enjoys his work, just as people who take bird walks enjoy theirs. Each new excursion of the essayist, each new "attempt," differs from the last and takes him into new country. This delights him. Only a person who is congenitally self-centered has the effrontery and the stamina to write essays.

There are as many kinds of essays as there are human attitudes or poses, as many essay flavors as there are Howard Johnson ice creams. The essayist arises in the morning and, if he has work to do, selects his garb from an unusually extensive wardrobe: he can pull on any sort of shirt, be any sort of person, according to his mood or his subject matter—philosopher, scold, jester, raconteur, confidant, pundit, devil's advocate, enthusiast. I like the essay, have always liked it, and even as a child was at work, attempting to inflict my young thoughts and experiences on others by putting them on paper. I early broke into print in the pages of *St. Nicholas*. I tend still to fall back on the essay form (or lack of form) when an idea strikes me, but I am not fooled about the place of the essay in twentieth-century American letters—it stands a short distance down the line. The essayist, unlike the novelist, the poet, and the playwright, must be content in his self-imposed role of second-class citizen. A writer who has his sights trained on the Nobel Prize or other earthly triumphs had best write a novel, a poem, or a play, and leave the essayist to ramble about, content with living a free life and enjoying the satisfactions of a somewhat undisciplined existence. (Dr. Johnson called the essay "an irregular, undigested piece"; this happy practitioner has no wish to quarrel with the good doctor's characterization.)

There is one thing the essayist cannot do, though—he cannot indulge himself in deceit or in concealment, for he will be found out in no time. Desmond MacCarthy, in his introductory remarks to the 1928 E. P. Dutton & Company edition of Montaigne, observes that Montaigne "had the gift of natural candour. . . ." It is the basic ingredient. And even the essayist's escape from discipline is only a partial escape: the essay, although a relaxed form, imposes its own disciplines, raises its own problems, and these disciplines and problems soon become apparent and (we all hope) act as a deterrent to anyone wielding a pen merely because he entertains random thoughts or is in a happy or wandering mood.

I think some people find the essay the last resort of the egoist, a much too self-conscious and self-serving form for their taste; they feel that it is presumptuous of a writer to assume that his little excursions or his small observations will interest the reader. There is some justice in their complaint. I have always been aware that I am by nature self-absorbed and egotistical; to write of myself to the extent I have done indicates a too great attention to my own life, not enough to the lives of others. I have worn many shirts, and not all of them have been a good fit. But when I am discouraged or downcast I need only fling open the door of my closet, and there, hidden behind everything else, hangs the mantle of Michel de Montaigne, smelling slightly of camphor.

from Essays of E. B. White

CRITICS ON WHITE

KEN SMITH

On *"The Ring of Time"*

In this essay White describes a chance encounter at the circus. When he visited the winter training headquarters of the Ringling circus, in Sarasota, Florida, he and other paying spectators came upon a practice session of a young, bareback rider. In this session an enchanting incident took place, and in the first half of the essay White struggles to describe it. In drawing our attention to his struggle as a writer, White sympathizes with the bareback rider's own struggle for artistry. He argues that the richest moments of life, the grace notes of its daily melodies, are personal and elusive, and he sketches some of the ensuing concerns of the artist. He tries to show, by analogy at least, what (he believes) the rider's efforts must mean to her. But he also tries to evoke two very different senses of time, one that White argues is common to the young and one that he holds in his later years. The first of these White believes the bareback rider feels as she takes her practice ride, since she is "too young to know that time does not really move in a circle at all. . . . She is at that enviable moment in life when she believes that she can go once around the ring, make one complete circuit, and at the end be exactly the same age as at the start." In her bodily grace and ease White feels her confidence in time's enduring circuits.

This illusion is sustained by several things: the girl's youthfulness, her common sentiment of youthful immortality, the light generated by her own graceful and casual artistry, which creates the lovely circuit that time follows here; White's own artistry in recreating the circuit; and additionally, the fact that many human experiences are circular rather than linear, or at least they feel that way to us as we experience them in our bodies. As in "Once More to the Lake," the richness of physical experience as the seasons circle and move us through their displays is very seductive. This sense of time is made up of circuits that return each day and year, enveloping the body and teaching the mind what the body has known. But we commonly know time in another way as well, as a linear progression leading us into age. The first half of "The Ring of Time" evokes the charm of the first of these two senses of time and sustains it as long as possible, only to withdraw in the end and admit that the enchanting ride, the seemingly timeless event, has ended and the rider has left the arena. While the artist seeks to make something of her own artistry, to improve the golden moment, the present, and occasionally succeeds, time marches on relentlessly and sweeps away the youth's faith in the ring of time, the protected circle.

from Critical Essays on E. B. White, *Robert L. Rout, Jr., ed.*

EDWARD SAMPSON

On "Once More to the Lake"

Then, as the rhythm of the essay asserts itself, the blend again of past and present, and again White's sense of duality with his son. The unity, the circularity, of time is epitomized by the thunderstorm that comes up over the lake: the same rumbles, the same rain afterwards, the same swimmers in the rain, and the same jokes about getting wet, "linking the generations in a strong indestructible chain."

But at the end, beautifully worked out, the tone suddenly shifts. White's son, going in swimming during the rain, gets his dripping trunks from the line and puts them on: "I watched him, his hard little body, skinny and bare, saw him wince slightly as he pulled up around his vitals the small, soggy, icy garment. As he buckled the swollen belt suddenly my groin felt the chill of death." Age and death are present with frightening vividness, and time suddenly seems to reverse itself, for White is no longer young and in the past. Because the aura of death surrounds his son as well as himself, the generations are linked again, but in mortality, not in life.

We find in this essay much of the credo of E. B. White. Here is his simple love of nature; his nostalgia for the past, and along with that his inclination (never quite given in to) to reject the present (the tarred road, the outboard motors) in favor of the past; his preference for doing rather than thinking (the walking, the fishing, the boating); his feeling for the mystery outside the church, not inside it ("this holy spot," "cathedral stillness"); his vivid language, with his liking for the simple, natural figures of speech ("the boat would leap ahead, charging bullfashion at the dock"); his love for people, for his son, and his sense of identity with the young (which made him such a good writer, later on, of children's stories); and the everpresent sense of death that with White was sometimes whimsical—Thurber said, "He expects every day of his life that something will kill him: a bit of mold, a small bug, a piece of huckleberry pie" and sometimes intensely serious: his poem "The Cornfield" ends with these lines:

> And being present at the birth
> Of my child's wonderment at earth,
> I felt my own life stir again
> By the still graveyard of the grain.

Above all, we find here White's sense of reality, a sense so deceptively off-hand at times that many readers could be misled and think of White as a pale modern Thoreau who is revisiting Walden, echoing his master, and escaping from the world with a happy phrase or two.

from E. B. White

E. B. WHITE: ESSAYS

Once More to the Lake

One summer, along about 1904, my father rented a camp on a lake in Maine and took us all there for the month of August. We all got ringworm from some kittens and had to rub Pond's Extract on our arms and legs night and morning, and my father rolled over in a canoe with all his clothes on; but outside of that the vacation was a success and from then on none of us ever thought there was any place in the world like that lake in Maine. We returned summer after summer—always on August 1 for one month. I have since become a salt-water man, but sometimes in summer there are days when the restlessness of the tides and the fearful cold of the sea water and the incessant wind that blows across the afternoon and into the evening make me wish for the placidity of a lake in the woods. A few weeks ago this feeling got so strong I bought myself a couple of bass hooks and a spinner and returned to the lake where we used to go, for a week's fishing and to revisit old haunts.

I took along my son, who had never had any fresh water up his nose and who had seen lily pads only from train windows. On the journey over to the lake I began to wonder what it would be like. I wondered how time would have marred this unique, this holy spot—the coves and streams, the hills that the sun set behind, the camps and the paths behind the camps. I was sure that the tarred road would have found it out, and I wondered in what other ways it would be desolated. It is strange how much you can remember about places like that once you allow your mind to return into the grooves that lead back. You remember one thing, and that suddenly reminds you of another thing. I guess I remembered clearest of all the early mornings, when the lake was cool and motionless, remembered how the bedroom smelled of the lumber it was made of and of the wet woods whose scent entered through the screen. The partitions in the camp were thin and did not extend clear to the top of the rooms, and as I was always the first up I would dress softly so as not to wake the others, and sneak out into the sweet outdoors and start out in the canoe, keeping close along the shore in the long shadows of the pines. I remembered being very careful never to rub my paddle against the gunwale for fear of disturbing the stillness of the cathedral.

The lake had never been what you would call a wild lake. There were cottages sprinkled around the shores, and it was in farming country although the shores of the lake were quite heavily wooded. Some of the cottages were owned by nearby farmers, and you would live at the shore and eat your meals at the farmhouse. That's what our family did. But although it wasn't wild, it was a fairly large and undisturbed lake and there were places in it that, to a child at least, seemed infinitely remote and primeval.

I was right about the tar: it led to within half a mile of the shore. But when I got back there, with my boy, and we settled into a camp near a farmhouse and into the kind of summertime I had known, I could tell that it was going to be pretty much the same as it had been before—I knew it, lying in bed the first morning, smelling the bedroom and hearing the boy sneak quietly out and go off along the shore in a boat. I began to sustain the illusion that he was I, and therefore, by simple transposition, that I was my father. This sensation persisted, kept cropping up all the time we were there. It was not an entirely new feeling, but in this setting it grew much stronger. I seemed to be living a dual existence. I would be in the middle of some simple act, I would be picking up a bait box or laying down a table fork, or I would be saying something, and suddenly it would be not I but my father who was saying the words or making the gesture. It gave me a creepy sensation.

We went fishing the first morning. I felt the same damp moss covering the worms in the bait can, and saw the dragonfly alight on the the tip of my rod as it hovered a few inches from the surface of the water. It was the arrival of this fly that convinced me beyond any doubt that everything was as it always had been, that the years were a mirage and that there had been no years. The small waves were the same, chucking the rowboat under the chin as we fished at anchor, and the boat was the same boat, the same color green and the ribs broken in the same places, and under the floorboards the same fresh-water leavings and débris—the dead helgramite, the wisps of moss, the rusty discarded fishhook, the dried blood from yesterday's catch. We stared silently at the tips of our rods, at the dragonflies that came and went. I lowered the tip of mine into the water, tentatively, pensively dislodging the fly, which darted two feet away, poised, darted two feet back, and came to rest again a little farther up the rod. There had been no years between the ducking of this dragonfly and the other one—the one that was part of memory. I looked at the boy, who was silently watching his fly, and it was my hands that held his rod, my eyes watching. I felt dizzy and didn't know which rod I was at the end of.

We caught two bass, hauling them in briskly as though they were mackerel, pulling them over the side of the boat in a businesslike manner without any landing net, and stunning them with a blow on the back of the head. When we got back for a swim before lunch, the lake was exactly where we had left it, the same number of inches from the dock, and there was only the merest suggestion of a breeze. This seemed an utterly enchanted sea, this lake you could leave to its own devices for a few hours and come back to, and find that it had not stirred, this constant and trustworthy body of water. In the shallows, the dark, water-soaked sticks and twigs, smooth and old, were undulating in clusters on the bottom against the clean ribbed sand, and the track of the mussel was plain. A school of minnows swam by, each minnow with its small individual shadow, doubling the attendance, so clear and sharp in the sunlight. Some of the other campers were in swimming, along the shore, one of them with a cake of soap, and the water felt thin and clear and unsubstantial. Over the years there had been this person with the cake of soap, this cultist, and here he was. There had been no years.

Up to the farmhouse to dinner through the teeming, dusty field, the road under our sneakers was only a two-track road. The middle track was missing, the one with the marks of the hooves and the splotches of dried, flaky manure. There had always been three tracks to choose from in choosing which track to walk in; now the choice was narrowed down to two. For a moment I missed terribly the middle alternative. But the way led past the tennis court, and something about the way it lay there in the sun reassured me; the tape had loosened along the backline, the alleys were green with plantains and other weeds, and the net (installed in June and removed in September) sagged in the dry noon, and the whole place steamed with midday heat and hunger and emptiness. There was a choice of pie for dessert, and one was blueberry and one was apple, and the waitresses were the same country girls, there having been no passage of time, only the illusion of it as in a dropped curtain—the waitresses were still fifteen; their hair had been washed, that was the only difference—they had been to the movies and seen the pretty girls with the clean hair.

Summertime, oh, summertime, pattern of life indelible, the fadeproof lake, the woods unshatterable, the pasture with the sweetfern and the juniper forever and ever, summer without end; this was the background, and the life along the shore was the design, the cottagers with their innocent and tranquil design, their tiny docks with the flagpole and the American flag floating against the white clouds in the blue sky, the little paths over the roots of the trees leading from camp to camp and the paths leading back to the outhouses and the can of lime for sprinkling, and at the souvenir counters at the store the miniature birchbark canoes and the postcards that showed things looking a little better than they looked. This was the American family at play, escaping the city heat, wondering whether the newcomers in the camp at the head of the cove were "common" or "nice," wondering whether it was true that the people who drove up for Sunday dinner at the farmhouse were turned away because there wasn't enough chicken.

It seemed to me, as I kept remembering all this, that those times and those summers had been infinitely precious and worth saving. There had been jollity and peace and goodness. The arriving (at the beginning of August) had been so big a business in itself, at the railway station the farm wagon drawn up, the first smell of the pine-laden air, the first glimpse of the smiling farmer, and the great importance of the trunks and your father's enormous authority in such matters, and the feel of the wagon under you for the long ten-mile haul, and at the top of the last long hill catching the first view of the lake after eleven months of not seeing this cherished body of water. The shouts and cries of the other campers when they saw you, and the trunks to be unpacked, to give up their rich burden. (Arriving was less exciting nowadays, when you sneaked up in your car and parked it under a tree near the camp and took out the bags and in five minutes it was all over, no fuss, no loud wonderful fuss about trunks.)

Peace and goodness and jollity. The only thing that was wrong now, really, was the sound of the place, an unfamiliar nervous sound of the outboard motors. This was the note that jarred, the one thing that would sometimes break the illusion and set the years moving. In those other summertimes all motors were inboard; and when they were at a little distance, the noise they made was a sedative, an ingredient of summer sleep. They were one-cylinder and two-cylinder engines, and some were make-and-break and some were jump-spark, but they all made a sleepy sound across the lake. The one-lungers throbbed and fluttered, and the twin-cylinder ones purred and purred, and that was a quiet sound, too. But now the campers all had outboards. In the daytime, in the hot mornings, these motors made a petulant, irritable sound; at night, in the still evening when the afterglow lit the water, they whined about one's ears like mosquitoes. My boy loved our rented outboard, and his great desire was to achieve single-handed mastery over it, and authority, and he soon learned the trick of choking it a little (but not too much), and the adjustment of the needle valve. Watching him I would remember the things you could do with the old one-cylinder engine with the heavy flywheel, how you could have it eating out of your hand if you got really close to it spiritually. Motorboats in those days didn't have clutches, and you would make a landing by shutting off the motor at the proper time and coasting in with a dead rudder. But there was a way of reversing them, if you learned the trick, by cutting the switch and putting it on again exactly on the final dying revolution of the flywheel, so that it would kick back against compression and begin reversing. Approaching a dock in a strong following breeze, it was difficult to slow up sufficiently by the ordinary coasting method, and if a boy felt he had complete mastery over his motor, he was tempted to keep it running beyond its time and then reverse it a few feet from the dock. It took a cool nerve, because if you threw the switch a twentieth of a second too soon you would catch the flywheel when it still had speed enough to go up past center, and the boat would leap ahead, charging bull-fashion at the dock.

We had a good week at the camp. The bass were biting well and the sun shone endlessly, day after day. We would be tired at night and lie down in the accumulated heat of the little bedrooms after the long hot day and the breeze would stir almost imperceptibly outside and the smell of the swamp drift in through the rusty screens. Sleep would come easily and in the morning the red squirrel would be on the roof, tapping out his gay routine. I kept remembering everything, lying in bed in the mornings—the small steamboat that had a long rounded stern like the lip of a Ubangi, and how quietly she ran on the moonlight sails, when the older boys played their mandolins and the girls sang and we ate doughnuts dipped in sugar, and how sweet the music was on the water in the shining night, and what it had felt like to think about girls then. After breakfast we would go up to the store and the things were in the same place—the minnows in a bottle, the plugs and spinners disarranged and pawed over by the youngsters from the boys' camp, the Fig Newtons and the Beeman's gum. Outside, the road was tarred and cars stood in front of the store. Inside, all was just as it had always been, except there was more Coca-Cola and not so much Moxie and root beer and birch beer and sarsaparilla. We would walk out with the bottle of pop apiece and sometimes the pop would backfire up our noses and hurt. We explored the streams, quietly, where the turtles slid off the sunny logs and dug their way into the soft bottom; and we lay on the town wharf and fed worms to the tame bass. Everywhere we went I had trouble making out which was I, the one walking at my side, the one walking in my pants.

One afternoon while we were there at that lake a thunderstorm came up. It was like the revival of an old melodrama that I had seen long ago with childish awe. The second-act climax of the drama of the electrical disturbance over a lake in America had not changed in any important respect. This was the big scene, still the big scene. The whole thing was so familiar, the first feeling of oppression and heat and a general air around camp of not wanting to go very far away. In mid-afternoon (it was all the same) a curious darkening of the sky, and a lull in everything that had made life tick; and then the way the boats suddenly swung the other way at their moorings with the coming of a breeze out of the new quarter, and the premonitory rumble. Then the kettle drum, then the snare, then the bass drum and cymbals, then crackling light against the dark, and the gods grinning and licking their chops in the hills. Afterward the calm, the rain steadily rustling in the calm lake, the return of light and hope and spirits, and the campers running out in joy and relief to go swimming in the rain, their bright cries perpetuating the deathless joke about how they were getting simply drenched, and the children screaming with delight at the new sensation of bathing in the rain, and the joke about getting drenched linking the generations in a strong indestructible chain. And the comedian who waded in carrying an umbrella.

When the others went swimming, my son said he was going in, too. He pulled his dripping trunks from the line where they had hung all through the shower and wrung them out. Languidly, and with no thought of going in, I watched him, his hard little body, skinny and bare, saw him wince slightly as he pulled up around his vitals the small, soggy, icy garment. As he buckled the swollen belt, suddenly my groin felt the chill of death.

(1941)

The Geese

Allen Cove, July 9, 1971

To give a clear account of what took place in the barnyard early in the morning on that last Sunday in June, I will have to go back more than a year in time, but a year is nothing to me these days. Besides, I intend to be quick about it, and not dawdle.

I have had a pair of elderly gray geese—a goose and a gander—living on this place for a number of years, and they have been my friends. "Companions" would be a better word; geese are friends with no one, they badmouth everybody and everything. But they are companionable once you get used to their ingratitude and their false accusations. Early in the spring, a year ago, as soon as the ice went out of the pond, my goose started to lay. She laid three eggs in about a week's time and then died. I found her halfway down the lane that connects the barnyard with the pasture. There were no marks on her—she lay with wings partly outspread, and with her neck forward in the grass, pointing downhill. Geese are rarely sick, and I think this goose's time had come and she had simply died of old age. I had noticed that her step had slowed on her trips back from the pond to the barn where her nest was. I had never known her age, and so had nothing else to go on. We buried her in our private graveyard, and I felt sad at losing an acquaintance of such long standing—long standing and loud shouting.

Her legacy, of course, was the three eggs. I knew they were good eggs and did not like to pitch them out. It seemed to me that the least I could do for my departed companion was to see that the eggs she had left in my care were hatched. I checked my hen pen to find out whether we had a broody, but there was none. During the next few days, I scoured the neighborhood for a broody hen, with no success. Years ago, if you needed a broody hen, almost any barn or henhouse would yield one. But today broodiness is considered unacceptable in a hen; the modern hen is an egg-laying machine, and her natural tendency to sit on eggs in springtime has been bred out of her. Besides, not many people keep hens anymore—when they want a dozen eggs, they don't go to the barn, they go to the First National.

Days went by. My gander, the widower, lived a solitary life—nobody to swap gossip with, nobody to protect. He seemed dazed. The three eggs were not getting any younger, and I myself felt dazed—restless and unfulfilled. I had stored the eggs down cellar in the arch where it is cool, and every time I went down there for something they seemed silently to reproach me. My plight had become known around town, and one day a friend phoned and said he would lend me an incubator designed for hatching the eggs of waterfowl. I brought the thing home, cleaned it up, plugged it in, and sat down to read the directions. After studying them, I realized that if I were to tend eggs in that incubator, I would have to withdraw from the world for thirty days—give up everything, just as a broody goose does. Obsessed though I was with the notion of bringing life into three eggs, I wasn't quite prepared to pay the price.

Instead, I abandoned the idea of incubation and decided to settle the matter by acquiring three ready-made goslings, as a memorial to the goose and a gift for the lonely gander. I drove up the road about five miles and dropped in on Irving Closson. I knew Irving had geese; he has everything—even a sawmill. I found him shoeing a very old horse in the doorway of his barn, and I stood and watched for a while. Hens and geese wandered about the yard, and a turkey tom circled me, wings adroop, strutting. The horse, with one forefoot between the man's knees, seemed to have difficulty balancing himself on three legs but was quiet and sober, almost asleep. When I asked Irving if he planned to put shoes on the horse's hind feet, too, he said, "No, it's hard work for me, and he doesn't use those hind legs much anyway." Then I brought up the question of goslings, and he took me into the barn and showed me a sitting goose. He said he thought she was covering more than twenty eggs and should bring off her goslings in a couple of weeks and I could buy a few if I wanted. I said I would like three.

I took to calling at Irving's every few days—it is about the pleasantest place to visit anywhere around. At last, I was rewarded: I pulled into the driveway one morning and saw a goose surrounded by green goslings. She had been staked out like a cow. Irving had simply tied a piece of string to one leg and fastened the other end to a peg in the ground. She was a pretty goose—not as large as my old one had been, and with a more slender neck. She appeared to be a cross-bred bird, two-toned gray, with white markings—a sort of particolored goose. The goslings had the cheerful, bright, innocent look that all baby geese have. We scooped up three and tossed them into a box, and I paid Irving and carried them home.

My next concern was how to introduce these small creatures to their foster father, my old gander. I thought about this all the way home. I've had just enough experience with domesticated animals and birds to know that they are a bundle of eccentricities and crotchets, and I was not at all sure what sort of reception three strange youngsters would get from a gander who was full of sorrows and suspicions. (I once saw a gander, taken by surprise, seize a newly hatched gosling and hurl it the length of the barn floor.) I had an uneasy feeling that my three little charges might be dead within the hour, victims of a grief-crazed old fool. I decided to go slow. I fixed a makeshift pen for the goslings in the barn, arranged so that they would be separated from the gander but visible to him, and he would be visible to them. The old fellow, when he heard youthful voices, hustled right in to find out what was going on. He studied the scene in silence and with the greatest attention. I could not tell whether the look in his eye was one of malice or affection—a goose's eye is a small round enigma. After observing this introductory scene for a while, I left and went into the house.

Half an hour later, I heard a commotion in the barnyard: the gander was in full cry. I hustled out. The goslings, impatient with life indoors, had escaped from their hastily constructed enclosure in the barn and had joined their foster father in the barnyard. The cries I had heard were his screams of welcome—the old bird was delighted with the turn that events had taken. His period of mourning was over, he now had interesting and useful work to do, and he threw himself into the role of father with immense satisfaction and zeal, hissing at me with renewed malevolence, shepherding the three children here and there, and running interference against real and imaginary enemies. My fears were laid to rest. In the rush of emotion that seized him at finding himself the head of a family, his thoughts turned immediately to the pond, and I watched admiringly as he guided the goslings down the long, tortuous course through the weedy land and on down across the rough pasture between blueberry knolls and granite boulders. It was a sight to see him hold the heifers at bay so the procession could pass safely. Summer was upon us, the pond was alive again. I brought the three eggs up from the cellar and dispatched them to the town dump.

At first, I did not know the sex of my three goslings. But nothing on two legs grows any faster than a young goose, and by early fall it was obvious that I had drawn one male and two females. You tell the sex of a goose by its demeanor and its stance—the way it holds itself, its general approach to life. A gander carries his head high and affects a threatening attitude. Females go about with necks in a graceful arch and are less aggressive. My two young females looked like their mother, particolored. The young male was quite different. He feathered out white all over except for his wings, which were a very light, pearly gray. Afloat on the pond, he looked almost like a swan, with his tall, thin white neck and his cocked-up white tail—a real dandy, full of pompous thoughts and surly gestures.

Winter is a time of waiting, for man and goose. Last winter was a long wait, the pasture deep in drifts, the lane barricaded, the pond inaccessible and frozen. Life centered in the barn and the barnyard. When the time for mating came, conditions were unfavorable, and this was upsetting to the old gander. Geese like a body of water for their coupling; it doesn't have to be a large body of water—just any wet place in which a goose can become partly submerged. My old gander, studying the calendar, inflamed

by passion, unable to get to the pond, showed signs of desperation. On several occasions, he tried to manage with a ten-quart pail of water that stood in the barnyard. He
would chivvy one of his young foster daughters over to the pail, seize her by the nape,
and hold her head under water while he made his attempt. It was never a success and
usually ended up looking more like a comedy tumbling act than like coitus. One got
the feeling during the water-pail routine that the gander had been consulting one of
the modern sex manuals describing peculiar positions. Anyway, I noticed two things:
the old fellow confined his attentions to one of the two young geese and let the other
alone, and he never allowed his foster son to approach either of the girls—he was very
strict about that, and the handsome young male lived all spring in a state of ostracism.

Eventually, the pond opened up, the happy band wended its way down across the
melting snows, and the breeding season was officially opened. My pond is visible from
the house, but it is at quite a distance. I am not a voyeur and do not spend my time
watching the sex antics of geese or anything else. But I try to keep reasonably well posted
on all the creatures around the place, and it was apparent that the young gander was
not allowed by his foster father to enjoy the privileges of the pond and that the old
gander's attentions continued to be directed to just one of the young geese. I shall call
her Liz to make this tale easier to tell.

Both geese were soon laying. Liz made her nest in the barn cellar; her sister, Apathy, made hers in the tie-ups on the main floor of the barn. It was the end of April or
the beginning of May. Still awfully cold—a reluctant spring.

Apathy laid three eggs, then quit. I marked them with a pencil and left them for the
time being in the nest she had constructed. I made a mental note that they were in-
fertile. Liz, unlike her sister, went right on laying, and became a laying fool. She dal-
lied each morning at the pond with her foster father, and she laid and laid and laid, like
a commercial hen. I dutifully marked the eggs as they arrived—1, 2, 3, and so on. When
she had accumulated a clutch of fifteen, I decided she had all she could cover. From
then on, I took to removing the oldest egg from the nest each time a new egg was de-
posited. I also removed Apathy's three eggs from *her* next, discarded them, and began
substituting the purloined eggs from the barn cellar—the ones that rightfully belonged
to Liz. Thus I gradually contrived to assemble a nest of fertile eggs for each bird, all of
them laid by the fanatical Liz.

During the last week in May, Apathy, having produced only three eggs of her own
but having acquired ten through the kind offices of her sister and me, became broody
and began to sit. Liz, with a tally of twenty-five eggs, ten of them stolen, showed not
the slightest desire to sit. Laying was her thing. She laid and laid, while the other goose
sat and sat. The old gander, marveling at what he had wrought, showed a great deal of
interest in both nests. The young gander was impressed but subdued. I continued to
remove the early eggs from Liz's nest, holding her to a clutch of fifteen and discarding
the extras. In late June, having produced forty-one eggs, ten of which were under Apathy, she at last sat down.

I had marked Apathy's hatching date on my desk calendar. On the night before the
goslings were due to arrive, when I made my rounds before going to bed, I looked in
on her. She hissed, as usual, and ran her neck out. When I shone my light at her, two
tiny green heads were visible, thrusting their way through her feathers. The goslings
were here—a few hours ahead of schedule. My heart leapt up. Outside, in the barnyard, both ganders stood vigil. They knew very well what was up: ganders take an enor-

mous interest in family affairs and are deeply impressed by the miracle of the egg-that-becomes-goose. I shut the door against them and went to bed.

Next morning, Sunday, I rose early and went straight to the barn to see what the night had brought. Apathy was sitting quietly while five goslings teetered about on the slopes of the nest. One of them, as I watched, strayed from the others, and, not being able to find his way back, began sending out cries for help. They were the kind of distress signal any anxious father would instantly respond to. Suddenly, I heard sounds of a rumble outside in the barnyard where the ganders were—loud sounds of scuffling. I ran out. A fierce fight was in progress—it was no mere skirmish, it was the real thing. The young gander had grabbed the old one by the stern, his white head buried in feathers right where it would hurt the most, and was running him around the yard, punishing him at every turn—thrusting him on ahead and beating him unmercifully with his wings. It was an awesome sight, these two great male birds locked in combat, slugging it out—not for the favors of a female but for the dubious privilege of assuming the responsibilities of parenthood. The young male had suffered all spring the indignities of a restricted life at the pond; now he had turned, at last, against the old one, as though to get even. Round and round, over rocks and through weeds, they raced, struggling and tripping, the old one in full retreat and in apparent pain. It was a beautiful late-June morning, with fair-weather clouds and a light wind going, the grasses long in the orchard—the kind of morning that always carries for me overtones of summer sadness, I don't know why. Overhead, three swallows circled at low altitude, pursuing one white feather, the coveted trophy of nesting time. They were like three tiny fighter planes giving air support to the battle that raged below. For a moment, I thought of climbing the fence and trying to separate the combatants, but instead I just watched. The engagement was soon over. Plunging desperately down the lane, the old gander sank to the ground. The young one let go, turned, and walked back, screaming in triumph, to the door behind which his newly won family were waiting: a strange family indeed—the sister who was not even the mother of the babies, and the babies who were not even his own get.

When I was sure the fight was over, I climbed the fence and closed the barnyard gate, effectively separating victor from vanquished. The old gander had risen to his feet. He was in almost the same spot in the lane where his first wife had died mysteriously more than a year ago. I watched as he threaded his way slowly down the narrow path between clumps of thistles and daisies. His head was barely visible above the grasses, but his broken spirit was plain to any eye. When he reached the pasture bars, he hesitated, then painfully squatted and eased himself under the bottom bar and into the pasture, where he sat down on the cropped sward in the bright sun. I felt very deeply his sorrow and his defeat. As things go in the animal kingdom, he is about my age, and when he lowered himself to creep under the bar, I could feel in my own bones his pain at bending down so far. Two hours later, he was still sitting there, the sun by this time quite hot. I had seen his likes often enough on the benches of the treeless main street of a Florida city—spent old males, motionless in the glare of the day.

Toward the end of the morning, he walked back up the lane as far as the gate, and there he stood all afternoon, his head and orange bill looking like the head of a great snake. The goose and her goslings had emerged into the barnyard. Through the space between the boards of the gate, the old fellow watched the enchanting scene: the goslings taking their frequent drinks of water, climbing in and out of the shallow pan for their first swim, closely guarded by the handsome young gander, shepherded by the pretty young goose.

After supper, I went into the tie-ups and pulled the five remaining, unhatched eggs from the nest and thought about the five lifeless chicks inside the eggs—the unlucky ones, the ones that lacked what it takes to break out of an egg into the light of a fine June morning. I put the eggs in a basket and set the basket with some other miscellany consigned to the dump. I don't know anything sadder than a summer's day.

(1971)

INTRODUCTION TO MAXINE HONG KINGSTON

[b. 1940]

Although she had a novel published in 1989 *(Tripmaster Monkey: His Fake Book)*, Maxine Hong Kingston is best known for her earlier mixed-genre works, *The Woman Warrior* (1976) and *China Men* (1980), winner of the American Book Award. Kingston has described the earlier work as the book of her mother since it is filled with stories her mother told her, stories about Chinese women, her Asian ancestors whom Kingston describes as the ghosts of her girlhood. *China Men,* by contrast, is her father book since it tells the stories of her male ancestors, including her father and grandfathers—though she learned these male stories too from women, especially from her mother. Both books are filled with stories. Both mix fact and fiction, autobiography and legend, combining in imaginative ways family history with fictional invention.

Kingston's books are, thus, difficult to classify. They refuse to sit still and accept the tidy categories we devise for prose narrative. The selections excerpted here from these two family chronicles reflect the curious and striking effects Kingston achieves throughout them with her blending of myth and legend with autobiography and family history. Moreover, in addition to their provocative combinations of fact and fiction, the two books possess another striking quality: their compelling voices. Kingston's narratives retell heard stories, stories told *by* her and stories told *to* her. Her stories derive from an oral tradition—the "talk story"—sustained largely by Chinese women. Kingston thus simultaneously inherits this oral narrative tradition and participates in it. Perhaps even more importantly, however, by inscribing her mother's stories and imagining her own variants of them, Kingston marks that tradition with her own distinctive imaginative imprint. In doing so, she demonstrates the power of these stories to enthrall readers outside the Chinese cultural tradition.

Maxine Hong Kingston was born and raised in Stockton, California, where her immigrant parents operated a laundry. She graduated from the University of California at Berkeley in 1962, and she has taught high school and college English, primarily in Hawaii, where she lived for seventeen years before moving to Oakland, California.

Kingston's autobiographical impulse appears strongly in "Silence," an excerpt from *The Woman Warrior.* In "Silence," we see Kingston begin to negotiate the struggle between the Chinese culture she inherited and the American culture she was born into. Her silence powerfully illustrates her uncertainty about how to invoke one cultural perspective without revoking or violating the other.

Kingston's versatility in letting the voices of others speak through her is powerfully manifested in "No Name Woman," the opening section of *The Woman Warrior.* As Esther Schor has pointed out in *Women's Voices,* the first voice we hear in "No Name Woman" is the voice of her mother, who "ironically . . . admonishes the daughter to silence even as she nourishes her with stories." Kingston's instincts as a writer are revealed not only in the stories she chooses to tell, but in the voices she creates to tell them. This is as true for the multiple voices we hear in "No Name Woman" as for the singularly different voices that sound in the other tales Kingston narrates in both books, including the brief parable, "On Discovery," which turns gender role and power inside out.

To some extent, Kingston is a woman's writer precisely because she gives public voice to what women had spoken only in private or what they had to keep silent. To some extent, she is also an ethnic writer, one who transmits stories of her Cantonese heritage. Her artistry and imaginative sympathy, however, transcend the limits of both gender and culture, as Kingston invents a world and constructs a self that appear both strange and familiar, at once "other" and recognizably our own.

KINGSTON ON WRITING

MAXINE HONG KINGSTON

Excerpts from "Imagined Life"

All right. To make your mother and your scandalous friends read about themselves and still like you, you have to be very cunning, very crafty. Don't commit yourself. Don't be pinned down. Give many versions of events. Tell the most flattering motives. Say: "Of course, it couldn't have been money that she was after." In *The Woman Warrior,* my mother-book, the No Name Woman might have been raped; she might have had a love affair; she might have been "a wild woman, and kept rollicking company. Imagining her free with sex . . ." Imagining many lives for her made me feel free. I have so much freedom in telling about her, I'm almost free even from writing itself, and therefore obeying my mother, who said, "Don't tell."
. . . .

My father doesn't say, "Don't tell." He doesn't say much at all. The way to end the silence he gave me was to write this sentence: "I'll tell you what I suppose from your silences and few words, and you can tell me that I'm mistaken." You may use that sentence yourself if you like. Copy it down and see what comes next.

My father is answering me by writing poems and commentary in the margins of my books. The pirated translations have wide margins. Writing commentary is a traditional Chinese literary form. You can break reader's block by writing well.

Yes, the imagined life is so exhilarating that householders go in quest of new lands—the Gold Mountain and China. The Gold Mountain is a land of gold-cobbled streets, and it is also a country with no war and no taxes; it is governed by women. Most of us are here in America today because somebody in our families imagined the Gold Mountain vividly enough to come looking for it. I guess most people think they've found it, and "Gold Mountain" is synonymous with "United States of America." But we aren't peaceful; taxes are due the day after tomorrow; and women aren't in charge. You see how much work we have ahead of us—we still have that country to find, and we still have its stories to tell.

. . . .

I haven't seen China yet. I didn't want to go there before finishing my two books because I was describing the place that we Americans imagine to be China. The mythic China has its own history, smells, flowers, one hundred birds, long-lived people, dialects, music. We can taste its sweetness when our grandmother sends us invisible candy. The place is so real that we talk about it in common, and we get mail from there. As real as the Brontës' childhood cities. As real as Dungeons and Dragons. If I had gotten on a plane and flown to the China that's over there, I might have lost the imagined land.

(1983)

CRITICS ON KINGSTON

ESTHER H. SCHOR

On Maxine Hong Kingston

The first voice we hear in Maxine Hong Kingston's *Woman Warrior* is her mother's: " 'You must not tell anyone,' my mother said, 'what I am about to tell you.' " Ironically, the mother admonishes her daughter to silence even as she nourishes her with stories of her Chinese forebears. This memorable opening signals both the complexity of Kingston's identity as a Chinese-American woman writer and the complexity of the writing itself, a stunning blend of autobiography, history, myth, folklore, and legend.

One cannot read very far in either of Kingston's books without confronting the difficulty of telling fact from fiction. In "No Name Woman," for example, she supposes that her pregnant aunt had been raped, then considers who the rapist might have been. Finally, she wonders "whether he masked himself when he joined the raid on her family." Similarly, in "The Father from China," in *China Men,* Kingston narrates five different versions of her father's entry into the United States. We cannot be sure whether he entered at New York or at San Francisco, as a stowaway or through immigration at Angel Island, illegally or legally. Instead of facts about her family, Kingston recreates for us the spell of the "talk-story," a Cantonese tradition kept alive mainly by women. (Even the stories told in *China Men,* Kingston claims, were told to her by women.) The story-talkers of Kingston's childhood tell stories in multiple versions, sometimes with graphic, startling details, sometimes in whispers. Like the powerful account of her aunt's pregnancy, childbirth, and suicide, the stories contain silences that compel the listener to venture imaginatively into the dangerous world of the story. Kingston's suppositions—"I wonder," "perhaps," "may have"—enable us to witness the writer taking up her voice among the story-talkers of her childhood. . . .

While Kingston has insisted that her two books were written "more or less simultaneously," *China Men* reveals several developments in Kingston's autobiographical art. First, Kingston intersperses brief, stark Chinese legends among lengthy narratives about her father, grandfather, great-grandfather, and brother. In "On Discovery" Kingston renders legendary material in an attenuated, suggestive, parabolic style. We sense an odd kinship between Kingston's impulse to concentrate a story and her impulse to vary a story. She is out to convince us that memorable stories owe as great a debt to the imagination and skill of the teller as they do to experience. "On Discovery" assaults the reader with the knowledge that beautiful women, like beautiful writing, arise by dint of pain and effort. In the extreme world of the parable, even a man can become a woman; Tang Ao, having submitted to the rigors of femininity, becomes disarmingly beautiful. But unlike texts, women suffer when they submit to rigorous standards that are not of their making. While "On Discovery" fantasizes a female revenge, it also probes the irony of using power to recapitulate one's own oppression.

from Women's Voices

KING-KOK CHEUNG

On *The Woman Warrior*

In *The Woman Warrior* we find it in the hushed disappointment attendant upon the birth of girls, in the expunging of the narrator's wayward aunt from family history, in the narrator's inability to speak a second language, in her choked-back anger at sexist maxims, in her impotent words against white bosses, and in her drawn-out illness incurred by self-hatred at being an inarticulate Chinese American. In *China Men* it extends beyond the exclusion of women to signify both the literal silencing of Chinese male laborers in Hawaii and the symbolic erasure of men of Chinese descent from mainstream American history . . . muffled. In fact, her works have all too often been read as factual testimony. As a result, the slippery and variable subject positions that underlie her polyphonic texts often escape the eyes of critics. Leslie W. Rabine and Stephen H. Sumida are notable exceptions. Rabine notes that *The Woman Warrior* is structured in a double and simultaneous movement, containing "the voice of a writer who in a certain sense has already returned to write about her people . . . but who writes as the girl who cannot return." Sumida suggests that Kingston's autobiography is perhaps "a work of 'fiction' in which the author uses a 'naive' if not 'unreliable' narrator . . . whose very misunderstandings or misappropriations . . . of 'Chinese' history and culture are part of the author's critical characterization of her and of a narrow 'American' society which alienates her from seeing truly." We shall see that there is more than one reason for what Sumida calls "misappropriations," and that the narrative strategies themselves contradict the narrator's explicit assertions. . . .

Asian American intellectuals have endlessly debated the "authenticity" of *The Woman Warrior.* Those who attack Kingston for blurring the line between reality and fantasy seem unmindful of the narrator's insistent admissions of her own penchant for fabrication and her inability to discern fact from fiction. Even those on the author's side tend to defend her autobiography on the ethnographic ground that the narrator's experience accords well with their own. Kingston, vexed by the anthropological approach to the book, protests: "After all, I am not writing history or sociology but a 'memoir' like Proust." Subtitled *Memoirs of a Girlhood among Ghosts, The Woman Warrior* is told mostly though not exclusively from the point of view of a confused female adolescent. I believe that the work, insofar as it can be construed as mimetic, mirrors not objective truth but the subjective experience of an imaginative girl growing up as a member of a racial minority amid conflicting imperatives.

from "Provocative Silence," in Articulate Silences

Feminism and History in "On Discovery"

The story of Tang Ao can be read from several feminist angles. As with Maxine's fantasy about Fa Mu Lan and the witch amazons, a first glance yields yet another instance of women's "counterinvestment," their strategy of reversing oppression by aping the oppressors. But the depiction of Tang Ao's excruciating pain—felt, I believe, by male and female readers alike—suggests not so much vindictiveness on the author's part as her attempt to foreground the asymmetrical construction of gender. Whereas Fa Mu Lan ventures into the male arena voluntarily, Tang Ao's crossover, as Donald C. Goellnicht observes, represents a "demotion": "no one, it seems, wants to fill the 'feminine' gender role." In making women the captors of Tang Ao and in inverting masculine and feminine roles, Kingston defamiliarizes patriarchal practices. Like the author of *Flowers in the Mirror,* Kingston contravenes the commonplace acceptance of Chinese women as sex objects by subjecting a man to the tortures suffered for centuries by Chinese women.

To read this fable in a feminist register alone is to obscure its significance as "metahistory." The story concludes as follows: "Some scholars say that that country [the Land of Women] was discovered during the reign of Empress Wu (A.D. 694–705), and some say earlier than that, A.D. 441, and it was in North America." Although others have speculated about a Chinese discovery of America around the fifth century, the association of the Land of Women with North America is to my knowledge purely Kingston's invention. Kingston's reference to invented sources—a ploy she shares with George Eliot, who provides many of the epigraphs that open the chapters of her later novels— is at once a parody of the patriarchal tradition of authorities and a form of self-authorization. In presenting obvious fiction as though it were history, Kingston lays bare the method she is to use throughout the book. She not only challenges the "historical" construction of China Men but presents alternative accounts as "counter-memory."

from "Provocative Silence," in Articulate Silences

MAXINE HONG KINGSTON: PROSE

No Name Woman

"You must not tell anyone," my mother said, "what I am about to tell you. In China your father had a sister who killed herself. She jumped into the family well. We say that your father has all brothers because it is as if she had never been born.

"In 1924 just a few days after our village celebrated seventeen hurry-up weddings— to make sure that every young man who went 'out on the road' would responsibly come home—your father and his brothers and your grandfather and his brothers and your aunt's new husband sailed for America, the Gold Mountain. It was your grandfather's last trip. Those lucky enough to get contracts waved good-bye from the decks. They fed and guarded the stowaways and helped them off in Cuba, New York, Bali, Hawaii. 'We'll meet in California next year,' they said. All of them sent money home.

"I remember looking at your aunt one day when she and I were dressing; I had not noticed before that she had such a protruding melon of a stomach. But I did not think, 'She's pregnant,' until she began to look like other pregnant women, her shirt pulling and the white tops of her black pants showing. She could not have been pregnant, you see, because her husband had been gone for years. No one said anything. We did not discuss it. In early summer she was ready to have the child, long after the time when it could have been possible.

"The village had also been counting. On the night the baby was to be born the villagers raided our house. Some were crying. Like a great saw, teeth strung with lights, files of people walked zigzag across our land, tearing the rice. Their lanterns doubled in the disturbed black water, which drained away through the broken bunds. As the villagers closed in, we could see that some of them, probably men and women we knew well, wore white masks. The people with long hair hung it over their faces. Women with short hair made it stand up on end. Some had tied white bands around their foreheads, arms, and legs.

"At first they threw mud and rocks at the house. Then they threw eggs and began slaughtering our stock. We could hear the animals scream their deaths—the roosters, the pigs, a last great roar from the ox. Familiar wild heads flared in our night windows; the villagers encircled us. Some of the faces stopped to peer at us, their eyes rushing like searchlights. The hands flattened against the panes, framed heads, and left red prints.

"The villagers broke in the front and the back doors at the same time, even though we had not locked the doors against them. Their knives dripped with the blood of our animals. They smeared blood on the doors and walls. One woman swung a chicken, whose throat she had slit, splattering blood in red arcs about her. We stood together in the middle of our house, in the family hall with the pictures and tables of the ancestors around us, and looked straight ahead.

"At that time the house had only two wings. When the men came back, we would build two more to enclose our courtyard and a third one to begin a second courtyard. The villagers pushed through both wings, even your grandparents' rooms, to find your aunt's, which was also mine until the men returned. From this room a new wing for one of the younger families would grow. They ripped up her clothes and shoes and broke her combs, grinding them underfoot. They tore her work from the loom. They scattered the cooking fire and rolled the new weaving in it. We could hear them in the kitchen breaking our bowls and banging the pots. They overturned the great waist-high earthenware jugs; duck eggs, pickled fruits, vegetables burst out and mixed in acrid torrents. The old woman from the next field swept a broom through the air and loosed the spirits-of-the-broom over our heads. 'Pig.' 'Ghost.' 'Pig,' they sobbed and scolded while they ruined our house.

"When they left, they took sugar and oranges to bless themselves. They cut pieces from the dead animals. Some of them took bowls that were not broken and clothes that were not torn. Afterward we swept up the rice and sewed it back up into sacks. But the smells from the spilled preserves lasted. Your aunt gave birth in the pigsty that night. The next morning when I went for the water, I found her and the baby plugging up the family well.

"Don't let your father know that I told you. He denies her. Now that you have started to menstruate, what happened to her could happen to you. Don't humiliate us. You wouldn't like to be forgotten as if you had never been born. The villagers are watchful."

Whenever she had to warn us about life, my mother told stories that ran like this one, a story to grow up on. She tested our strength to establish realities. Those in the emigrant generations who could not reassert brute survival died young and far from home. Those of us in the first American generations have had to figure out how the invisible world the emigrants built around our childhoods fits in solid America.

The emigrants confused the gods by diverting their curses, misleading them with crooked streets and false names. They must try to confuse their offspring as well, who, I suppose, threaten them in similar ways—always trying to get things straight, always trying to name the unspeakable. The Chinese I know hide their names; sojourners take new names when their lives change and guard their real names with silence.

Chinese-Americans, when you try to understand what things in you are Chinese, how do you separate what is peculiar to childhood, to poverty, insanities, one family, your mother who marked your growing with stories, from what is Chinese? What is Chinese tradition and what is the movies?

If I want to learn what clothes my aunt wore, whether flashy or ordinary, I would have to begin, "Remember Father's drowned-in-the-well sister?" I cannot ask that. My mother has told me once and for all the useful parts. She will add nothing unless powered by Necessity, a riverbank that guides her life. She plants vegetable gardens rather than lawns; she carries the odd-shaped tomatoes home from the fields and eats food left for the gods.

Whenever we did frivolous things, we used up energy; we flew high kites. We children came up off the ground over the melting cones our parents brought home from work and the American movie on New Year's Day—*Oh, You Beautiful Doll* with Betty Grable one year, and *She Wore a Yellow Ribbon* with John Wayne another year. After the one carnival ride each, we paid in guilt; our tired father counted his change on the dark walk home.

Adultery is extravagance. Could people who hatch their own chicks and eat the embryos and the heads for delicacies and boil the feet in vinegar for party food, leaving only the gravel, eating even the gizzard lining—could such people engender a prodigal aunt? To be a woman, to have a daughter in starvation time was a waste enough. My aunt could not have been the lone romantic who gave up everything for sex. Women in the old China did not choose. Some man had commanded her to lie with him and be his secret evil. I wonder whether he masked himself when he joined the raid on her family.

Perhaps she had encountered him in the fields or on the mountain where the daughters-in-law collected fuel. Or perhaps he first noticed her in the marketplace. He was not a stranger because the village housed no strangers. She had to have dealings with him other than sex. Perhaps he worked an adjoining field, or he sold her the cloth for the dress she sewed and wore. His demand must have surprised, then terrified her. She obeyed him; she always did as she was told.

When the family found a young man in the next village to be her husband, she had stood tractably beside the best rooster, his proxy, and promised before they met that she would be his forever. She was lucky that he was her age and she would be the first wife, an advantage secure now. The night she first saw him, he had sex with her. Then he left for America. She had almost forgotten what he looked like. When she tried to envision him, she only saw the black and white face in the group photograph the men had had taken before leaving.

The other man was not, after all, much different from her husband. They both gave orders: she followed. "If you tell your family, I'll beat you. I'll kill you. Be here again next week." No one talked sex, ever. And she might have separated the rapes from the rest of living if only she did not have to buy her oil from him or gather wood in the same forest. I want her fear to have lasted just as long as rape lasted so that the fear could have been contained. No drawn-out fear. But women at sex hazarded birth and hence lifetimes. The fear did not stop but permeated everywhere. She told the man, "I think I'm pregnant." He organized the raid against her.

On nights when my mother and father talked about their life back home, sometimes they mentioned an "outcast table" whose business they still seemed to be settling, their voices tight. In a commensal tradition, where food is precious, the powerful older people made wrongdoers eat alone. Instead of letting them start separate new lives like the Japanese, who could become samurais and geishas, the Chinese family, faces averted but eyes glowering sideways, hung on to the offenders and fed them leftovers. My aunt must have lived in the same house as my parents and eaten at an outcast table. My mother spoke about the raid as if she had seen it, when she and my aunt, a daughter-in-law to a different household, should not have been living together at all. Daughters-in-law lived with their husbands' parents, not their own; a synonym for marriage in Chinese is "taking a daughter-in-law." Her husband's parents could have sold her, mortgaged her, stoned her. But they had sent her back to her own mother and father, a mysterious act hinting at disgraces not told me. Perhaps they had thrown her out to deflect the avengers.

She was the only daughter; her four brothers went with her father, husband, and uncles "out on the road" and for some years became western men. When the goods were divided among the family, three of the brothers took land, and the youngest, my father, chose an education. After my grandparents gave their daughter away to her husband's family, they had dispensed all the adventure and all the property. They expected her alone to keep the traditional ways, which her brothers, now among the barbarians, could fumble without detection. The heavy, deep-rooted women were to maintain the past against the flood, safe for returning. But the rare urge west had fixed upon our family, and so my aunt crossed boundaries not delineated in space.

The work of preservation demands that the feelings playing about in one's guts not be turned into action. Just watch their passing like cherry blossoms. But perhaps my aunt, my forerunner, caught in a slow life, let dreams grow and fade and after some months or years went toward what persisted. Fear at the enormities of the forbidden kept her desires delicate, wire and bone. She looked at a man because she liked the way the hair was tucked behind his ears, or she liked the question-mark line of a long torso curving at the shoulder and straight at the hip. For warm eyes or a soft voice or a slow walk— that's all—a few hairs, a line, a brightness, a sound, a pace, she gave up family. She offered us up for a charm that vanished with tiredness, a pigtail that didn't toss when the wind died. Why, the wrong lighting could erase the dearest thing about him.

It could very well have been, however, that my aunt did not take subtle enjoyment of her friend, but, a wild woman, kept rollicking company. Imagining her free with sex doesn't fit, though. I don't know any women like that, or men either. Unless I see her life branching into mine, she gives me no ancestral help.

To sustain her being in love, she often worked at herself in the mirror, guessing at the colors and shapes that would interest him, changing them frequently in order to hit on the right combination. She wanted him to look back.

On a farm near the sea, a woman who tended her appearance reaped a reputation for eccentricity. All the married women blunt-cut their hair in flaps about their ears or pulled it back in tight buns. No nonsense. Neither style blew easily into heart-catching tangles. And at their weddings they displayed themselves in their long hair for the last time. "It brushed the backs of my knees," my mother tells me. "It was braided, and even so, it brushed the backs of my knees."

At the mirror my aunt combed individuality into her bob. A bun could have been contrived to escape into black streamers blowing in the wind or in quiet wisps about her face, but only the older women in our picture album wear buns. She brushed her hair back from her forehead, tucking the flaps behind her ears. She looped a piece of thread, knotted into a circle between her index fingers and thumbs, and ran the double strand across her forehead. When she closed her fingers as if she were making a pair of shadow geese bite, the string twisted together catching the little hairs. Then she pulled the thread away from her skin, ripping the hairs out neatly, her eyes watering from the needles of pain. Opening her fingers, she cleaned the thread, then rolled it along her hairline and the tops of her eyebrows. My mother did the same to me and my sisters and herself. I used to believe that the expression "caught by the short hairs" meant a captive held with a depilatory string. It especially hurt at the temples, but my mother said we were lucky we didn't have to have our feet bound when we were seven. Sisters used to sit on their beds and cry together, she said, as their mothers or their slave removed the bandages for a few minutes each night and let the blood gush back into their veins. I hope that the man my aunt loved appreciated a smooth brow, that he wasn't just a tits-and-ass man.

Once my aunt found a freckle on her chin, at a spot that the almanac said predestined her for unhappiness. She dug it out with a hot needle and washed her wound with peroxide.

More attention to her looks than these pullings of hairs and pickings at spots would have caused gossip among the villagers. They owned work clothes and good clothes, and they wore good clothes for feasting the new seasons. But since a woman combing her hair hexes beginnings, my aunt rarely found an occasion to look her best. Women looked like great sea snails—the corded wood, babies, and laundry they carried were the whorls on their backs. The Chinese did not admire a bent back; goddesses and warriors stood straight. Still there must have been a marvelous freeing of beauty when a worker laid down her burden and stretched and arched.

Such commonplace loveliness, however, was not enough for my aunt. She dreamed of a lover for the fifteen days of New Year's, the time for families to exchange visits, money, and food. She plied her secret comb. And sure enough she cursed the year, the family, the village, and herself.

Even as her hair lured her imminent lover, many other men looked at her. Uncles, cousins, nephews, brothers would have looked, too, had they been home between journeys. Perhaps they had already been restraining their curiosity, and they left, fearful that their glances, like a field of nesting birds, might be startled and caught. Poverty hurt, and that was their first reason for leaving. But another, final reason for leaving the crowded house was the never-said.

She may have been unusually beloved, the precious only daughter, spoiled and mirror gazing because of the affection the family lavished on her. When her husband left, they welcomed the chance to take her back from the in-laws; she could live like the little daughter for just a while longer. There are stories that my grandfather was different from other people, "crazy ever since the little Jap bayoneted him in the head." He used to put his naked penis on the dinner table, laughing. And one day he brought home a baby girl, wrapped up inside his brown western-style greatcoat. He had traded one of his sons, probably my father, the youngest, for her. My grandmother made him trade back. When he finally got a daughter of his own, he doted on her. They must have all loved her, except perhaps my father, the only brother who never went back to China, having once been traded for a girl.

Brothers and sisters, newly men and women, had to efface their sexual color and present plain miens. Disturbing hair and eyes, a smile like no other, threatened the ideal of five generations living under one roof. To focus blurs, people shouted face to face and yelled from room to room. The immigrants I know have loud voices, unmodulated to American tones even after years away from the village where they called their friendships out across the fields. I have not been able to stop my mother's screams in public libraries or over telephones. Walking erect (knees straight, toes pointed forward, not pigeon-toed, which is Chinese-feminine) and speaking in an inaudible voice, I have tried to turn myself American-feminine. Chinese communication was loud, public. Only sick people had to whisper. But at the dinner table, where the family members came nearest one another, no one could talk, not the outcasts nor any eaters. Every word that falls from the mouth is a coin lost. Silently they gave and accepted food with both hands. A preoccupied child who took his bowl with one hand got a sideways glare. A complete moment of total attention is due everyone alike. Children and lovers have no singularity here, but my aunt used a secret voice, a separate attentiveness.

She kept the man's name to herself throughout her labor and dying; she did not accuse him that he be punished with her. To save her inseminator's name she gave silent birth.

He may have been somebody in her own household, but intercourse with a man outside the family would have been no less abhorrent. All the village were kinsmen, and the titles shouted in loud country voices never let kinship be forgotten. Any man within visiting distance would have been neutralized as a lover—"brother," "younger brother," "older brother"—one hundred and fifteen relationship titles. Parents researched birth charts probably not so much to assure good fortune as to circumvent incest in a population that has but one hundred surnames. Everybody has eight million relatives. How useless then sexual mannerisms, how dangerous.

As if it came from an atavism deeper than fear, I used to add "brother" silently to boys' names. It hexed the boys, who would or would not ask me to dance, and made them less scary and as familiar and deserving of benevolence as girls.

But, of course, I hexed myself also—no dates. I should have stood up, both arms waving, and shouted out across libraries, "Hey, you! Love me back." I had no idea, though, how to make attraction selective, how to control its direction and magnitude. If I made myself American-pretty so that the five or six Chinese boys in the class fell in love with me, everyone else—the Caucasian, Negro, and Japanese boys—would too. Sisterliness, dignified and honorable, made much more sense.

Attraction eludes control so stubbornly that whole societies designed to organize relationships among people cannot keep order, not even when they bind people to one another from childhood and raise them together. Among the very poor and the wealthy, brothers married their adopted sisters, like doves. Our family allowed some romance, paying adult brides' prices and providing dowries so that their sons and daughters could marry strangers. Marriage promises to turn strangers into friendly relatives—a nation of siblings.

In the village structure, spirits shimmered among the live creatures, balanced and held in equilibrium by time and land. But one human being flaring up into violence could open up a black hole, a maelstrom that pulled in the sky. The frightened villagers, who depended on one another to maintain the real, went to my aunt to show her a personal, physical representation of the break she had made in the "roundness." Misallying couples snapped off the future, which was to be embodied in true offspring. The villagers punished her for acting as if she could have a private life, secret and apart from them.

If my aunt had betrayed the family at a time of large grain yields and peace, when many boys were born, and wings were being built on many houses, perhaps she might have escaped such severe punishment. But the men—hungry, greedy, tired of planting in dry soil—and had been forced to leave the village in order to send food-money home. There were ghost plagues, bandit plagues, wars with the Japanese, floods. My Chinese brother and sister had died of an unknown sickness. Adultery, perhaps only a mistake during good times, became a crime when the village needed food.

The round moon cakes and round doorways, the round tables of graduated size that fit one roundness inside another, round windows and rice bowls—these talismans had lost their power to warn this family of the law: a family must be whole, faithfully keeping the descent line by having sons to feed the old and the dead, who in turn look after the family. The villagers came to show my aunt and her lover-in-hiding a broken house. The villagers were speeding up the circling of events because she was too shortsighted to see that her infidelity had already harmed the village, that waves of consequences would return unpredictably, sometimes in disguise, as now, to hurt her. This roundness had to be made coin-sized so that she would see its circumference: punish her at the birth of her baby. Awaken her to the inexorable. People who refused fatalism because they could invent small resources insisted on culpability. Deny accidents and wrest fault from the stars.

After the villagers left, their lanterns now scattering in various directions toward home, the family broke their silence and cursed her. "Aiaa, we're going to die. Death is coming. Death is coming. Look what you've done. You've killed us. Ghost! Dead ghost! Ghost! You've never been born." She ran out into the fields, far enough from the house so that she could no longer hear their voices, and pressed herself against the earth, her own land no more. When she felt the birth coming, she thought that she had been hurt. Her body seized together. "They've hurt me too much," she thought. "This is gall, and it will kill me." With forehead and knees against the earth, her body convulsed and then relaxed. She turned on her back, lay on the ground. The black well of sky and stars went out and out and out forever; her body and her complexity seemed to disappear. She was one of the stars, a bright dot in blackness, without home, without a companion, in eternal cold and silence. An agoraphobia rose in her, speeding higher and higher, bigger and bigger; she would not be able to contain it; there would be no end to fear.

Flayed, unprotected against space, she felt pain return, focusing her body. This pain chilled her—a cold, steady kind of surface pain. Inside, spasmodically, the other pain, the pain of the child, heated her. For hours she lay on the ground, alternately body and space. Sometimes a vision of normal comfort obliterated reality: she saw the family in the evening gambling at the dinner table, the young people massaging their elders' backs. She saw them congratulating one another, high joy on the mornings the rice shoots came up. When these pictures burst, the stars drew yet further apart. Black space opened.

She got to her feet to fight better and remembered that old-fashioned women gave birth in their pigsties to fool the jealous, pain-dealing gods, who do not snatch piglets. Before the next spasms could stop her, she ran to the pigsty, each step a rushing out into emptiness. She climbed over the fence and knelt in the dirt. It was good to have a fence enclosing her, a tribal person alone.

Laboring, this woman who had carried her child as a foreign growth that sickened her every day, expelled it at last. She reached down to touch the hot, wet, moving mass, surely smaller than anything human, and could feel that it was human after all—fingers, toes, nails, nose. She pulled it up on to her belly, and it lay curled there, butt in the air, feet precisely tucked one under the other. She opened her loose shirt and buttoned the child inside. After resting, it squirmed and thrashed and she pushed it up to her breast. It turned its head this way and that until it found her nipple. There, it made little snuffling noises. She clenched her teeth at its preciousness, lovely as a young calf, a piglet, a little dog.

She may have gone to the pigsty as a last act of responsibility: she would protect this child as she had protected its father. It would look after her soul, leaving supplies on her grave. But how would this tiny child without family find her grave when there would be no marker for her anywhere, neither in the earth nor the family hall? No one would give her a family hall name. She had taken the child with her into the wastes. At its birth the two of them had felt the same raw pain of separation, a wound that only the family pressing tight could close. A child with no descent line would not soften her life but only trail after her, ghostlike, begging her to give it purpose. At dawn the villagers on their way to the fields would stand around the fence and look.

Full of milk, the little ghost slept. When it awoke, she hardened her breasts against the milk that crying loosens. Toward morning she picked up the baby and walked to the well.

Carrying the baby to the well shows loving. Otherwise abandon it. Turn its face into the mud. Mothers who love their children take them along. It was probably a girl; there is some hope of forgiveness for boys.

"Don't tell anyone you had an aunt. Your father does not want to hear her name. She has never been born." I have believed that sex was unspeakable and words so strong and fathers so frail that "aunt" would do my father mysterious harm. I have thought that my family, having settled among immigrants who had also been their neighbors in the ancestral land, needed to clean their name, and a wrong word would incite the kinspeople even here. But there is more to this silence: they want me to participate in her punishment. And I have.

In the twenty years since I heard this story I have not asked for details nor said my aunt's name; I do not know it. People who can comfort the dead can also chase after them to hurt them further—a reverse ancestor worship. The real punishment was not the raid swiftly inflicted by the villagers, but the family's deliberately forgetting her. Her betrayal so maddened them, they saw to it that she would suffer forever, even after death. Always hungry, always needing, she would have to beg food from other ghosts, snatch and steal it from those whose living descendants give them gifts. She would have to fight the ghosts massed at crossroads for the buns a few thoughtful citizens leave to decoy her away from village and home so that the ancestral spirits could feast unharassed. At peace, they could act like gods, not ghosts, their descent lines providing them with paper suits and dresses, spirit money, paper houses, paper automobiles, chicken, meat, and rice into eternity—essences delivered up in smoke and flames, steam and incense rising from each rice bowl. In an attempt to make the Chinese care for people outside the family, Chairman Mao encourages us now to give our paper replicas to the spirits of outstanding soldiers and workers, no matter whose ancestors they may be. My aunt remains forever hungry. Goods are not distributed evenly among the dead.

My aunt haunts me—her ghost drawn to me because now, after fifty years of neglect, I alone devote pages of paper to her, though not origamied into houses and clothes. I do not think she always means me well. I am telling on her, and she was a spite suicide, drowning herself in the drinking water. The Chinese are always very frightened of the drowned one, whose weeping ghost, wet hair hanging and skin bloated, waits silently by the water to pull down a substitute.

(1976)

Silence

When I went to kindergarten and had to speak English for the first time, I became silent. A dumbness—a shame—still cracks my voice in two, even when I want to say "hello" casually, or ask an easy question in front of the check-out counter, or ask directions of a bus driver. I stand frozen, or I hold up the line with the complete, grammatical sentence that comes squeaking out at impossible length. "What did you say?" says the cab driver, or "Speak up," so I have to perform again, only weaker the second time. A telephone call makes my throat bleed and takes up that day's courage. It spoils my day with self-disgust when I hear my broken voice come skittering out into the open. It makes people wince to hear it. I'm getting better, though. Recently I asked the postman for special-issue stamps; I've waited since childhood for postmen to give me some of their own accord. I am making progress, a little every day.

My silence was thickest—total—during the three years that I covered my school paintings with black paint. I painted layers of black over houses and flowers and suns, and when I drew on the blackboard, I put a layer of chalk on top. I was making a stage curtain, and it was the moment before the curtain parted or rose. The teachers called my parents to school, and I saw they had been saving my pictures, curling and cracking, all alike and black. The teachers pointed to the pictures and looked serious, talked seriously too, but my parents did not understand English. ("The parents and teachers of criminals were executed," said my father.) My parents took the pictures home. I spread them out (so black and full of possibilities) and pretended the curtains were swinging open, flying up, one after another, sunlight underneath, mighty operas.

During the first silent year I spoke to no one at school, did not ask before going to the lavatory, and flunked kindergarten. My sister also said nothing for three years, silent in the playground and silent at lunch. There were other quiet Chinese girls not of our family, but most of them got over it sooner than we did. I enjoyed the silence. At first it did not occur to me I was supposed to talk or to pass kindergarten. I talked at home and to one or two of the Chinese kids in class. I made motions and even made some jokes. I drank out of a toy saucer when the water spilled out of the cup, and everybody laughed, pointing at me, so I did it some more. I didn't know that Americans don't drink out of saucers.

I liked the Negro students (Black Ghosts) best because they laughed the loudest and talked to me as if I were a daring talker too. One of the Negro girls had her mother coil braids over her ears Shanghai-style like mine; we were Shanghai twins except that she was covered with black like my paintings. Two Negro kids enrolled in Chinese school, and the teachers gave them Chinese names. Some Negro kids walked me to school and home, protecting me from the Japanese kids, who hit me and chased me and stuck gum in my ears. The Japanese kids were noisy and tough. They appeared one day in kindergarten, released from concentration camp, which was a tic-tac-toe mark, like barbed wire, on the map.

It was when I found out I had to talk that school become a misery, that the silence became a misery. I did not speak and felt bad each time that I did not speak. I read aloud in first grade, though, and heard the barest whisper with little squeaks come out of my throat. "Louder," said the teacher, who scared the voice away again. The other Chinese girls did not talk either, so I knew the silence had to do with being a Chinese girl.

Reading out loud was easier than speaking because we did not have to make up what to say, but I stopped often, and the teacher would think I'd gone quiet again. I could not understand "I." The Chinese "I" has seven strokes, intricacies. How could the American "I," assuredly wearing a hat like the Chinese, have only three strokes, the middle so straight? Was it out of politeness that this writer left off the strokes the way a Chinese has to write her own name small and crooked? No, it was not politeness; "I" is a capital and "you" is lower-case. I stared at that middle line and waited so long for its black center to resolve into tight strokes and dots that I forgot to pronounce it. The other troublesome word was "here," no strong consonant to hang on to, and so flat, when "here" is two mountainous ideographs. The teacher, who had already told me every day how to read "I" and "here," put me in the low corner under the stairs again, where the noisy boys usually sat.

When my second grade class did a play, the whole class went to the auditorium except the Chinese girls. The teacher, lovely and Hawaiian, should have understood about us, but instead left us behind in the classroom. Our voices were too soft or nonexistent, and our parents never signed the permission slips anyway. They never signed anything unnecessary. We opened the door a crack and peeked out, but closed it again quickly. One of us (not me) won every spelling bee, though.

I remember telling the Hawaiian teacher, "We Chinese can't sing 'land where our fathers died.'" She argued with me about politics, while I meant because of curses. But how can I have that memory when I couldn't talk? My mother says that we, like the ghosts, have no memories.

After American school, we picked up our cigar boxes, in which we had arranged books, brushes, and an inkbox neatly, and went to Chinese school, from 5:00 to 7:30 P.M. There we chanted together, voices rising and falling, loud and soft, some boys shouting, everybody reading together, reciting together and not alone with one voice. When we had a memorization test, the teacher let each of us come to his desk and say the lesson to him privately, while the rest of the class practiced copying or tracing. Most of the teachers were men. The boys who were so well behaved in the American school played tricks on them and talked back to them. The girls were not mute. They screamed and yelled during recess, when there were no rules; they had fistfights. Nobody was afraid of children hurting themselves or of children hurting school property. The glass doors to the red and green balconies with the gold joy symbols were left wide open so that we could run out and climb the fire escapes. We played capture-the-flag in the auditorium, where Sun Yat-sen and Chiang Kai-shek's pictures hung at the back of the stage, the Chinese flag on their left and the American flag on their right. We climbed the teak ceremonial chairs and made flying leaps off the stage. One flag headquarters was behind the glass door and the other on stage right. Our feet drummed on the hollow stage. During recess the teachers locked themselves up in their office with the shelves of books, copybooks, inks from China. They drank tea and warmed their hands at a stove. There was no play supervision. At recess we had the school to ourselves, and also we could roam as far as we could go—downtown, Chinatown stores, home— as long as we returned before the bell rang.

At exactly 7:30 the teacher again picked up the brass bell that sat on his desk and swung it over our heads, while we charged down the stairs, our cheering magnified in the stairwell. Nobody had to line up.

Not all of the children who were silent at American school found voice at Chinese school. One new teacher said each of us had to get up and recite in front of the class, who was to listen. My sister and I had memorized the lesson perfectly. We said it to each other at home, one chanting, one listening. The teacher called on my sister to recite first. It was the first time a teacher had called on the second-born to go first. My sister was scared. She glanced at me and looked away; I looked down at my desk. I hoped that she could do it because if she could, then I would have to. She opened her mouth and a voice came out that wasn't a whisper, but it wasn't a proper voice either. I hoped that she would not cry, fear breaking up her voice like twigs underfoot. She sounded as if she were trying to sing through weeping and strangling. She did not pause or stop to end the embarrassment. She kept going until she said the last word, and then she sat down. When it was my turn, the same voice came out, a cripple animal running on broken legs. You could hear splinters in my voice, bones rubbing jagged against one another. I was loud, though. I was glad I didn't whisper.

How strange that the emigrant villagers are shouters, hollering face to face. My father asks, "Why is it I can hear Chinese from blocks away? Is it that I understand the language? Or is it they talk loud?" They turn the radio up full blast to hear the operas, which do not seem to hurt their ears. And they yell over the singers that wail over the drums, everybody talking at once, big arm gestures, spit flying. You can see the disgust on American faces looking at women like that. It isn't just the loudness. It is the way Chinese sounds, ching-chong ugly, to American ears, not beautiful like Japanese sayonara words with the consonants and vowels as regular as Italian. We make guttural peasant noise and have Ton Duc Thang names you can't remember. And the Chinese can't hear Americans at all; the language is too soft and western music unhearable. I've watched a Chinese audience laugh, visit, talk-story, and holler during a piano recital, as if the musician could not hear them. A Chinese-American, somebody's son, was playing Chopin, which has no punctuation, no cymbals, no gongs. Chinese piano music is five black keys. Normal Chinese women's voices are strong and bossy. We American-Chinese girls had to whisper to make ourselves American-feminine. Apparently we whispered even more softly than the Americans. Once a year the teachers referred my sister and me to speech therapy, but our voices would straighten out, unpredictably normal, for the therapists. Some of us gave up, shook our heads, and said nothing, not one word. Some of us could not even shake our heads. At times shaking my head no is more self-assertion than I can manage. Most of us eventually found some voice, however faltering. We invented an American-feminine speaking personality.

(1976)

On Discovery

Once upon a time, a man, named Tang Ao, looking for the Gold Mountain, crossed an ocean, and came upon the Land of Women. The women immediately captured him, not on guard against ladies. When they asked Tang Ao to come along, he followed; if he had had male companions, he would've winked over his shoulder.

"We have to prepare you to meet the queen," the women said. They locked him in a canopied apartment equipped with pots of makeup, mirrors, and a woman's clothes. "Let us help you off with your armor and boots," said the women. They slipped his coat off his shoulders, pulled it down his arms, and shackled his wrists behind him. The women who kneeled to take off his shoes chained his ankles together.

A door opened, and he expected to meet his match, but it was only two old women with sewing boxes in their hands. "The less you struggle, the less it'll hurt," one said, squinting a bright eye as she threaded her needle. Two captors sat on him while another held his head. He felt an old woman's dry fingers trace his ear; the long nail on her little finger scraped his neck. "What are you doing?" he asked. "Sewing your lips together," she joked, blackening needles in a candle flame. The ones who sat on him bounced with laughter. But the old woman did not sew his lips together. They pulled his earlobes taut and jabbed a needle through each of them. They had to poke and probe before puncturing the layers of skin correctly, the hole in the front of the lobe in line with the one in back, the layers of skin sliding about so. They worked the needle through—a last jerk for the needle's wide eye ("needle's nose" in Chinese). They strung his raw flesh with silk threads; he could feel the fibers.

The women who sat on him turned to direct their attention to his feet. They bent his toes so far backward that his arched foot cracked. The old ladies squeezed each foot and broke many tiny bones along the sides. They gathered his toes, toes over and under one another like a knot of ginger root. Tang Ao wept with pain. As they wound the bandages tight and tighter around his feet, the women sang footbinding songs to distract him: "Use aloe for binding feet and not for scholars."

During the months of a season, they fed him on women's food: the tea was thick with white chrysanthemums and stirred the cool female winds inside his body; chicken wings made his hair shine; vinegar soup improved his womb. They drew the loops of thread through the scabs that grew daily over the holes in his earlobes. One day they inserted gold hoops. Every night they unbound his feet, but his veins had shrunk, and the blood pumping through them hurt so much, he begged to have his feet rewrapped tight. They forced him to wash his used bandages, which were embroidered with flowers and smelled of rot and cheese. He hung the bandages up to dry, streamers that drooped and draped wall to wall. He felt embarrassed; the wrappings were like underwear, and they were his.

One day his attendants changed his gold hoops to jade studs and strapped his feet to shoes that curved like bridges. They plucked out each hair on his face, powdered him white, painted his eyebrows like a moth's wings, painted his cheeks and lips red. He served a meal at the queen's court. His hips swayed and his shoulders swiveled because of his shaped feet. "She's pretty, don't you agree?" the diners said, smacking their lips at his dainty feet as he bent to put dishes before them.

In the Women's Land there are no taxes and no wars. Some scholars say that that country was discovered during the reign of Empress Wu (A.D. 694–705), and some say earlier than that, A.D. 441, and it was in North America.

(1980)

CHAPTER SEVEN

A Collection
of Essays

There are as many kinds of essays as there are human attitudes or poses. . . . The essay, although a relaxed form, imposes its own disciplines, raises its own problems.

E. B. W<small>HITE</small>

The essay can do everything a poem can do, and everything a short story can do— everything but fake it. . . . There's nothing you cannot do with it; no subject matter is forbidden, no structure is proscribed. . . . The material is the world itself, which, so far, keeps on keeping on.

A<small>NNIE</small> D<small>ILLARD</small>

MICHEL DE MONTAIGNE

[1533–1592]

*Of smells**

TRANSLATED BY DONALD FRAME

^AIt is said of some, as of Alexander the Great, that their sweat emitted a sweet odor, owing to some rare and extraordinary constitution of theirs, of which Plutarch and

---

*The superscript letters distinguish the three strata of the essay: A is for material published before 1588, B for writing in 1588, and C for material published after 1588

others seek the cause. But the common make-up of bodies is the opposite, and the best condition they may have is to be free of smell. The sweetness even of the purest breath has nothing more excellent about it than to be without any odor that offends us, as is that of very healthy children. That is why, says Plautus,

> A woman smells good when she does not smell.

The most perfect smell for a woman is to smell of nothing, ^Bas they say that her actions smell best when they are imperceptible and mute. ^AAnd perfumes are rightly considered suspicious in those who use them, and thought to be used to cover up some natural defect in that quarter. Whence arise these nice sayings of the ancient poets: To smell good is to stink:

> You laugh at us because we do not smell.
> I'd rather smell of nothing than smell sweet.
> MARTIAL

And elsewhere:

> Men who smell always sweet, Posthumus, don't smell good.
> MARTIAL

^BHowever, I like very much to be surrounded with good smells, and I hate bad ones beyond measure, and detect them from further off than anyone else:

> My scent will sooner be aware
> Where goat-smells, Polypus, in hairy arm-pits lurk,
> Than keen hounds scent a wild boar's lair.
> HORACE

^CThe simplest and most natural smells seem to me the most agreeable. And this concern chiefly affects the ladies. Amid the densest barbarism, the Scythian women, after washing, powder and plaster their whole body and face with a certain odoriferous drug that is native to their soil; and having removed this paint to approach the men, they find themselves both sleek and perfumed.

^BWhatever the odor is, it is a marvel how it clings to me and how apt my skin is to imbibe it. He who complains of nature that she has left man without an instrument to convey smells to his nose is wrong, for they convey themselves. But in my particular case my mustache, which is thick, performs that service. If I bring my gloves or my handkerchief near it, the smell will stay there a whole day. It betrays the place I come from. The close kisses of youth, savory, greedy, and sticky, once used to adhere to it and stay there for several hours after. And yet, for all that, I find myself little subject to epidemics, which are caught by communication and bred by the contagion of the air; and I have escaped those of my time, of which there have been many sorts in our cities and our armies. ^CWe read of Socrates that though he never left Athens during many recurrences of the plague which so many times tormented that city, he alone never found himself the worse for it.

^BThe doctors might, I believe, derive more use from odors than they do; for I have often noticed that they make a change in me and work upon my spirits according to their properties; which makes me approve of the idea that the use of incense and perfumes in churches, so ancient and widespread in all nations and religions, was intended to delight us and arouse and purify our senses to make us more fit for contemplation.

^CI should like, in order to judge of it, to have shared the art of those cooks who know how to add a seasoning of foreign odors to the savor of foods, as was particularly remarked in the service of the king of Tunis, who in our time landed at Naples to confer with the Emperor Charles. They stuffed his foods with aromatic substances, so sumptuously that one peacock and two pheasants came to a hundred ducats to dress them in that manner; and when they were carved, they filled not only the dining hall but all the rooms in his palace, and even the neighboring houses, with sweet fumes which did not vanish for some time.

^BThe principal care I take in my lodgings is to avoid heavy, stinking air. Those beautiful cities Venice and Paris weaken my fondness for them by the acrid smell of the marshes of the one and of the mud of the other.

(1580)

FRANCIS BACON

[1561–1626]

Of Love

The stage is more beholding to Love than the life of man. For as to the stage, love is ever matter of comedies, and now and then of tragedies, but in life it doth much mischief, sometimes like a syren, sometimes like a fury. You may observe that amongst all the great and worthy persons (whereof the memory remaineth, either ancient or recent) there is not one that hath been transported to the mad degree of love, which shows that great spirits and great business do keep out this weak passion. You must except nevertheless Marcus Antonius, the half partner of the empire of Rome, and Appius Claudius, the decemvir and lawgiver; whereof the former was indeed a voluptuous man, and inordinate, but the latter was an austere and wise man; and therefore it seems (though rarely) that love can find entrance not only into an open heart, but also into a heart well fortified, if watch be not well kept. It is a poor saying of Epicurus, *Satis magnum alter alteri theatrum sumus,*° as if man, made for the contemplation of heaven and all noble objects, should do nothing but kneel before a little idol, and make himself a subject, though not of the mouth (as beasts are), yet of the eye, which was given him for higher purposes. It is a strange thing to note the excess of this passion, and how it braves the nature and value of things, by this: that the speaking in a perpetual

Satis . . . sumus *Each of us is a great enough audience for the other.*

hyperbole is comely in nothing but in love. Neither is it merely in the phrase, for whereas it hath been well said that the arch-flatterer, with whom all the petty flatterers have intelligence, is a man's self, certainly the lover is more. For there was never proud man thought so absurdly well of himself as the lover doth of the person loved; and therefore it was well said, *That it is impossible to love and to be wise.* Neither doth this weakness appear to others only, and not to the party loved, but to the loved most of all, except the love be reciproque. For it is a true rule that love is ever rewarded either with the reciproque or with an inward and secret contempt. By how much the more men ought to beware of this passion, which loseth not only other things but itself. As for the other losses, the poet's relation doth well figure them: that he that preferred Helena quitted the gifts of Juno and Pallas.° For whosoever esteemeth too much of amorous affection quitteth both riches and wisdom. This passion hath his floods in the very times of weakness, which are great prosperity and great adversity, though this latter hath been less observed, both which times kindle love, and make it more fervent, and therefore show it to be the child of folly. They do best who, if they cannot but admit love, yet make it keep quarter and sever it wholly from their serious affairs and actions of life, for if it check once with business, it troubleth men's fortunes, and maketh men that they can no ways be true to their own ends. I know not how, but martial men are given to love; I think it is but as they are given to wine, for perils commonly ask to be paid in pleasures. There is in man's nature a secret inclination and motion towards love of others, which if it be not spent upon some one or a few, doth naturally spread itself towards many, and maketh men become humane and charitable, as it is seen sometime in friars. Nuptial love maketh mankind; friendly love perfecteth it; but wanton love corrupteth and embaseth it.

(1612)

JOHN DONNE

[1572–1631]

Meditation XVII: For Whom the Bell Tolls

Perchance he for whom this bell tolls may be so ill, as that he knows not it tolls for him; and perchance I may think myself so much better than I am, as that they who are about me, and see my state, may have caused it to toll for me, and I know not that. The church is Catholic, universal, so are all her actions; all that she does belongs to all. When she baptizes a child, that action concerns me; for that child is thereby connected to that body which is my head too, and ingrafted into that body whereof I am a mem-

---

Helena . . . Juno . . . Pallas *The Greek goddesses Juno (war), Venus (love), and Pallas Athena (wisdom) asked Paris, prince of Troy, to decide which was most beautiful. Paris chose Venus. She rewarded him with Helen, the most beautiful woman in the world, whose abduction by Paris precipitated the Greek and Trojan war.*

ber. And when she buries a man, that action concerns me: all mankind is of one author, and is one volume; when one man dies, one chapter is not torn out of the book, but translated into a better language; and every chapter must be so translated; God employs several translators; some pieces are translated by age, some by sickness, some by war, some by justice; but God's hand is in every translation, and his hand shall bind up all our scattered leaves again for that library where every book shall lie open to one another. As therefore the bell that rings to a sermon calls not upon the preacher only, but upon the congregation to come, so this bell calls us all; but how much more me, who am brought so near the door by this sickness. There was a contention as far as a suit (in which both piety and dignity, religion and estimation, were mingled), which of the religious orders should ring to prayers first in the morning; and it was determined, that they should ring first that rose earliest. If we understand aright the dignity of this bell that tolls for our evening prayer, we would be glad to make it ours by rising early, in that application, that it might be ours as well as his, whose indeed it is. The bell doth toll for him that thinks it doth; and though it intermit again, yet from that minute that that occasion wrought upon him, he is united to God. Who casts not up his eye to the sun when it rises? but who takes off his eye from a comet when that breaks out? Who bends not his ear to any bell which upon any occasion rings? but who can remove it from that bell which is passing a piece of himself out of this world? No man is an island, entire of itself; every man is a piece of the continent, a part of the main. If a clod be washed away by the sea, Europe is the less, as well as if a promontory were, as well as if a manor of thy friend's or of thine own were: any man's death diminishes me, because I am involved in mankind, and therefore never send to know for whom the bells tolls; it tolls for thee. Neither can we call this a begging of misery, or a borrowing of misery, as though we were not miserable enough of ourselves, but must fetch in more from the next house, in taking upon us the misery of our neighbours. Truly it were an excusable covetousness if we did, for affliction is a treasure, and scarce any man hath enough of it. No man hath affliction enough that is not matured and ripened by it, and made fit for God by that affliction. If a man carry treasure in bullion, or in a wedge of gold, and have none coined into current money, his treasure will not defray him as he travels. Tribulation is treasure in the nature of it, but it is not current money in the use of it, except we get nearer and nearer our home, heaven, by it. Another man may be sick too, and sick to death, and this affliction may lie in his bowels, as gold in a mine, and be of no use to him; but this bell, that tells me of his affliction, digs out and applies that gold to me: if by this consideration of another's danger I take mine own into contemplation, and so secure myself, by making my recourse to my God, who is our only security.

(1624)

JONATHAN SWIFT

[1667–1745]

A Modest Proposal

FOR PREVENTING THE CHILDREN OF POOR PEOPLE
IN IRELAND FROM BEING A BURDEN TO THEIR
PARENTS OR COUNTRY, AND FOR MAKING THEM
BENEFICIAL TO THE PUBLIC

It is a melancholy object to those who walk through this great town or travel in the country, when they see the streets, the roads, and cabin doors crowded with beggars of the female sex, followed by three, four, or six children, all in rags and importuning every passenger for an alms. These mothers, instead of being able to work for their honest livelihood, are forced to employ all their time in strolling to beg sustenance for their helpless infants, who, as they grow up, either turn thieves for want of work, or leave their dear native country to fight for the Pretender in Spain, or sell themselves to the Barbadoes.

I think it is agreed by all parties that this prodigious number of children in the arms, or on the backs, or at the heels of their mothers, and frequently of their fathers, is in the present deplorable state of the kingdom a very great additional grievance; and therefore whoever could find out a fair, cheap, and easy method of making these children sound and useful members of the commonwealth would deserve so well of the public as to have his statue set up for a preserver of the nation.

But my intention is very far from being confined to provide only for the children of professed beggars; it is of a much greater extent, and shall take in the whole number of infants at a certain age who are born of parents in effect as little able to support them as those who demand our charity in the streets.

As to my own part, having turned my thoughts for many years upon this important subject, and maturely weighed the several schemes of other projectors, I have always found them grossly mistaken in their computation. It is true a child just dropped from its dam may be supported by her milk for a solar year with little other nourishment, at most not above the value of two shillings, which the mother may certainly get, or the value in scraps, by her lawful occupation of begging; and it is exactly at one year old that I propose to provide for them in such a manner as instead of being a charge upon their parents or the parish, or wanting food and raiment for the rest of their lives, they shall, on the contrary, contribute to the feeding and partly to the clothing of many thousands.

There is likewise another great advantage in my scheme, that it will prevent those voluntary abortions, and that horrid practice of women murdering their bastard children, alas! too frequent among us, sacrificing the poor innocent babes, I doubt, more to avoid the expense than the shame, which would move tears and pity in the most savage and inhuman breast.

The number of souls in this kingdom being usually reckoned one million and a half, of these I calculate there may be about two hundred thousand couples whose wives are breeders; from which number I subtract thirty thousand couples who are able to maintain their own children, although I apprehend there cannot be so many, under the present distress of the kingdom; but this being granted, there will remain an hundred and seventy thousand breeders. I again subtract fifty thousand for those women who miscarry, or whose children die by accident or disease within the year. There only remain an hundred and twenty thousand children of poor parents annually born. The question therefore is, how this number shall be reared and provided for, which, as I have already said, under the present situation of affairs is utterly impossible by all the methods hitherto proposed. For we can neither employ them in handicraft or agriculture; we neither build houses (I mean in the country) nor cultivate land: they can very seldom pick up a livelihood by stealing till they arrive at six years old, except where they are of towardly parts; although I confess they learn the rudiments much earlier, during which time they can, however, be properly looked upon only as probationers, as I have been informed by a principal gentleman in the county of Cavan, who protested to me that he never knew above one or two instances under the age of six, even in a part of the kingdom so renowned for the quickest proficiency in that art.

I am assured by our merchants that a boy or girl before twelve years old is no salable commodity; and even when they come to this age they will not yield above three pounds or three pounds and half-a-crown at most on the Exchange; which cannot turn to account either to the parents or the kingdom, the charge of nutriment and rags having been at least four times that value.

I shall now therefore humbly propose my own thoughts, which I hope will not be liable to the least objection.

I have been assured by a very knowing American of my acquaintance in London that a young healthy child well nursed is at a year old a most delicious, nourishing, and wholesome food, whether stewed, roasted, baked, or boiled; and I make no doubt that it will equally serve in a fricassee or a ragout.

I do therefore humbly offer it to public consideration that of the hundred and twenty thousand children already computed, twenty thousand may be reserved for breed, whereof only one-fourth part to be males, which is more than we allow to sheep, black cattle or swine; and my reason is that these children are seldom the fruits of marriage, a circumstance not much regarded by our savages; therefore one male will be sufficient to serve four females. That the remaining hundred thousand may at a year old be offered in sale to the persons of quality and fortune through the kingdom, always advising the mother to let them suck plentifully in the last month, so as to render them plump and fat for a good table. A child will make two dishes at an entertainment for friends; and when the family dines alone, the fore or hind quarter will make a reasonable dish, and seasoned with a little pepper or salt will be very good boiled on the fourth day, especially in winter.

I have reckoned upon a medium that a child just born will weigh twelve pounds, and in a solar year if tolerably nursed increaseth to twenty-eight pounds.

I grant this food will be somewhat dear, and therefore very proper for landlords, who, as they have already devoured most of the parents, seem to have the best title to the children.

Infants' flesh will be in season throughout the year, but more plentiful in March, and a little before and after; for we are told by a grave author, an eminent French physician, that fish being a prolific diet, there are more children born in Roman Catholic countries about nine months after Lent than at any other season; therefore reckoning a year after Lent, the markets will be more glutted than usual, because the number of popish infants is at least three to one in this kingdom; and therefore it will have one other collateral advantage, by lessening the number of Papists among us.

I have already computed the charge of nursing a beggar's child (in which list I reckon all cottagers, laborers, and four-fifths of the farmers) to be about two shillings per annum, rags included; and I believe no gentleman would repine to give ten shillings for the carcass of a good fat child, which, as I have said, will make four dishes of excellent nutritive meat, when he hath only some particular friend or his own family to dine with him. Thus the squire will learn to be a good landlord, and grow popular among his tenants; the mother will have eight shillings net profit, and be fit for work till she produces another child.

Those who are more thrifty (as I must confess the times require) may flay the carcass; the skin of which artificially dressed will make admirable gloves for ladies, and summer boots for fine gentlemen.

As to our city of Dublin, shambles may be appointed for this purpose in the most convenient parts of it, and butchers we may be assured will not be wanting; although I rather recommend buying the children alive, and dressing them hot from the knife, as we do roasting pigs.

A very worthy person, a true lover of his country, and whose virtues I highly esteem, was lately pleased, in discoursing on this matter, to offer a refinement upon my scheme. He said that many gentlemen of this kingdom, having of late destroyed their deer, he conceived that the want of venison might be well supplied by the bodies of young lads and maidens, not exceeding fourteen years of age nor under twelve, so great a number of both sexes in every country being now ready to starve for want of work and service: and these to be disposed of by their parents, if alive, or otherwise by their nearest relations. But with due deference to so excellent a friend and so deserving a patriot, I cannot be altogether in his sentiments. For as to the males, my American acquaintance assured me from frequent experience that their flesh was generally tough and lean, like that of our schoolboys, by continual exercise, and their taste disagreeable; and to fatten them would not answer the charge. Then as to the females, it would, I think, with humble submission, be a loss to the public, because they soon would become breeders themselves: and besides, it is not improbable that some scrupulous people might be apt to censure such a practice (although indeed very unjustly) as a little bordering upon cruelty; which, I confess, hath always been with me the strongest objection against any project, how well soever intended.

But in order to justify my friend, he confessed that this expedient was put into his head by the famous Psalmanazar, a native of the island Formosa, who came from thence to London above twenty years ago, and in conversation told my friend that in his country when any young person happened to be put to death, the executioner sold the carcass to persons of quality as a prime dainty, and that in his time the body of a plump girl of fifteen, who was crucified for an attempt to poison the emperor, was sold to his Imperial Majesty's prime minister of state, and other great mandarins of the court, in joints from the gibbet, at four hundred crowns. Neither indeed can I deny that if the same use were made of several plump young girls in this town, who, without one single groat to their fortunes, cannot stir abroad without a chair, and appear at the playhouse and assemblies in foreign fineries, which they never will pay for, the kingdom would not be the worse.

Some persons of a desponding spirit are in great concern about that vast number of poor people, who are aged, diseased, or maimed, and I have been desired to employ my thoughts what course may be taken to ease the nation of so grievous an encumbrance. But I am not in the least pain upon that matter, because it is very well known that they are every day dying and rotting, by cold and famine, and filth and vermin, as fast as can be reasonably expected. And as to the younger laborers, they are now in almost as hopeful a condition. They cannot get work, and consequently pine away for want of nourishment, to a degree that if at any time they are accidentally hired to common labor, they have not strength to perform it; and thus the country and themselves are happily delivered from the evils to come.

I have too long digressed, and therefore shall return to my subject. I think the advantages by the proposal which I have made are obvious and many, as well as of the highest importance.

For first, as I have already observed, it would greatly lessen the number of Papists, with whom we are yearly overrun, being the principal breeders of the nation as well as our most dangerous enemies; and who stay at home on purpose with a design to deliver the kingdom to the Pretender, hoping to take their advantage by the absence of so many good Protestants, who have chosen rather to leave their country than stay at home and pay tithes against their conscience to an Episcopal curate.

Secondly, the poorer tenants will have something valuable of their own, which by law may be made liable to distress, and help to pay their landlord's rent; their corn and cattle being already seized, and money a thing unknown.

Thirdly, whereas the maintenance of an hundred thousand children, from two years old and upwards, cannot be computed at less than ten shillings apiece per annum, the nation's stock will be thereby increased fifty thousand pounds per annum, besides the profit of a new dish introduced to the tables of all gentlemen of fortune in the kingdom who have any refinement in taste. And the money will circulate among ourselves, the goods being entirely of our own growth and manufacture.

Fourthly, the constant breeders, besides the gain of eight shillings sterling per annum by the sale of their children, will be rid of the charge of maintaining them after the first year.

Fifthly, this food would likewise bring great custom to taverns, where the vintners will certainly be so prudent as to procure the best receipts for dressing it to perfection, and consequently have their houses frequented by all the fine gentlemen, who justly value themselves upon their knowledge in good eating; and a skillful cook, who understands how to oblige his guests, will contrive to make it as expensive as they please.

Sixthly, this would be a great inducement to marriage, which all wise nations have either encouraged by rewards or enforced by laws and penalties. It would increase the care and tenderness of mothers toward their children, when they were sure of a settlement for life to the poor babes, provided in some sort by the public, to their annual profit instead of expense. We should see an honest emulation among the married women, which of them could bring the fattest child to the market. Men would become as fond of their wives during the time of their pregnancy as they are now of their _since their wives will be carrying such valuable merchandise_

mares in foal, their cows in calf, or sows when they are ready to farrow; nor offer to beat or kick them (as is too frequent a practice) for fear of miscarriage. _they'll be less to beat their wives._

Many other advantages might be enumerated. For instance, the addition of some thousand carcasses in our exportation of barreled beef, the propagation of swine's flesh, and improvement in the art of making good bacon, so much wanted among us by the great destruction of pigs, too frequent at our tables, and are no way comparable in taste or magnificence to a well-grown, fat yearling child, which roasted whole will make a considerable figure at a lord mayor's feast, or any other public entertainment. But this and many others I omit, being studious of brevity.

Supposing that one thousand families in this city would be constant customers for infants' flesh, besides others who might have it at merry meetings, particularly weddings and christenings, I compute that Dublin would take off annually about twenty thousand carcasses, and the rest of the kingdom (where probably they will be sold somewhat cheaper) the remaining eighty thousand. _—increased economic resource_

I can think of no one objection that will possibly be raised against this proposal, unless it should be urged that the number of people will be thereby much lessened in the kingdom. This I freely own, and it was indeed one principal design in offering it to the world. I desire the reader will observe that I calculate my remedy for this one individual kingdom of Ireland, and for no other that ever was, is, or, I think, ever can be upon earth. Therefore let no man talk to me of other expedients: of taxing our absentees at five shillings a pound; of using neither clothes nor household furniture except what is of our own growth and manufacture; of utterly rejecting the materials and instruments that promote foreign luxury; of curing the expensiveness of pride, vanity, idleness, and gaming in our women; of introducing a vein of parsimony, prudence, and temperance; of learning to love our country, in the want of which we differ even from Laplanders and the inhabitants of Topinamboo; of quitting our animosities and factions, nor act any longer like the Jews, who were murdering one another at the very moment their city was taken; of being a little cautious not to sell our country and consciences for nothing; of teaching landlords to have at least one degree of mercy toward their tenants; lastly, of putting a spirit of honesty, industry, and skill into our shopkeepers, who, if a resolution could now be taken to buy only our native goods, would immediately unite to cheat and exact upon us in the price, the measure, and the goodness, nor could ever yet be brought to make one fair proposal of just dealing, though often and earnestly invited to it.

Therefore I repeat, let no man talk to me of these and the like expedients, till he has at least some glimpse of hope that there will be ever some hearty and sincere attempt to put them in practice. _—don't just talk about what you can do. Do it!_

But as to myself, having been wearied out for many years with offering vain, idle, visionary thoughts, and at length utterly despairing of success, I fortunately fell upon this proposal, which, as it is wholly new, so it has something solid and real, of no expense and little trouble, full in our own power, and whereby we can incur no danger in disobliging England. For this kind of commodity will not bear exportation, the flesh being of too tender a consistence to admit a long continuance in salt, although perhaps I could name a country _—England_ which would be glad to eat up our whole nation without it.

After all, I am not so violently bent upon my own opinion as to reject any offer proposed by wise men, which shall be found equally innocent, cheap, easy, and effectual. But before something of that kind shall be advanced in contradiction to my scheme,

The Real Solutions

he's not another (Thespece solution) out but willing to from) no one listens!!!

and offering a better, I desire the author or authors will be pleased maturely to consider two points. First, as things now stand, how they will be able to find food and raiment for an hundred thousand useless mouths and backs. And secondly, there being a round million of creatures in human figure throughout this kingdom, whose whole subsistence put into a common stock would leave them in debt two millions of pounds sterling, adding those who are beggars by profession to the bulk of farmers, cottagers, and laborers, with their wives and children, who are beggars in effect; I desire those politicians who dislike my overture, and may perhaps be so bold as to attempt an answer, that they will first ask the parents of these mortals whether they would not at this day think it a great happiness to have been sold for food at a year old in the manner I prescribe, and thereby have avoided such a perpetual scene of misfortunes as they have since gone through by the oppression of landlords, the impossibility of paying rent without money or trade, the want of common sustenance, with neither house nor clothes to cover them from the inclemencies of the weather, and the most inevitable prospect of entailing the like or greater miseries upon their breed for ever.

I profess, in the sincerity of my heart, that I have not the least personal interest in endeavoring to promote this necessary work, having no other motive than the public good of my country, by advancing our trade, providing for infants, relieving the poor, and giving some pleasure to the rich. I have no children by which I can propose to get a single penny; the youngest being nine years old, and my wife past child-bearing.

(1729)

MARK TWAIN

[1835–1910]

"Cub" Wants to Be a Pilot

When I was a boy there was but one permanent ambition among my comrades in our village on the west bank of the Mississippi River. That was to be a steamboatman. We had transient ambitions of other sorts but they were only transient. When a circus came and went, it left us all burning to become clowns; the first Negro minstrel show that ever came to our section left us all suffering to try that kind of life; now and then we had a hope that, if we lived and were good, God would permit us to be pirates. These ambitions faded out, each in its turn; but the ambition to be a steamboatman always remained.

Once a day a cheap, gaudy packet arrived upward from St. Louis, and another downward from Keokuk. Before these events, the day was glorious with expectancy; after them, the day was a dead and empty thing. Not only the boys but the whole village felt this. After all these years I can picture that old time to myself now, just as it was then: the white town drowsing in the sunshine of a summer's morning; the streets empty or pretty nearly so; one or two clerks sitting in front of the Water Street stores, with their splint-bottomed chairs tilted back against the walls, chins on breasts, hats slouched over their faces, asleep—with shingle-shavings enough around to show what broke them down; a sow and a litter of pigs loafing along the sidewalk, doing a good business in watermelon rinds and seeds; two or three lonely little freight piles scattered about the "levee"; a pile of "skids" on the slope of the stone-paved wharf, and the fragrant town drunkard asleep in the shadow of them; two or three wood flats at the head of the wharf but nobody to listen to the peaceful lapping of the wavelets against them; the great Mississippi, the majestic, the magnificent Mississippi, rolling its mile-wide tide along, shining in the sun; the dense forest away on the other side; the "point" above the town, and the "point" below, bounding the river-glimpse and turning it into a sort of sea, and withal a very still and brilliant and lonely one. Presently a film of dark smoke appears above one of those remote "points"; instantly a Negro drayman, famous for his quick eye and prodigious voice, lifts up the cry, "S-t-e-a-m-boat a-comin'!" and the scene changes! The town drunkard stirs, the clerks wake up, a furious clatter of drays follows, every house and store pours out a human contribution, and all in a twinkling the dead town is alive and moving. Drays, carts, men, boys, all go hurrying from many quarters to a common center, the wharf. Assembled there, the people fasten their eyes upon the coming boat as upon a wonder they are seeing for the first time. And the boat *is* rather a handsome sight, too. She is long and sharp and trim and pretty; she has two tall, fancy-topped chimneys, with a gilded device of some kind swung between them; a fanciful pilot-house, all glass and "gingerbread," perched on top of the "texas" deck behind them; the paddle-boxes are gorgeous with a picture or with gilded rays above the boat's name; the boiler-deck, the hurricane-deck, and the texas deck are fenced and ornamented with clean white railings; there is a flag gallantly flying from the jack-staff; the furnace doors are open and the fires glaring bravely; the upper decks are black with passengers; the captain stands by the big bell, calm, imposing, the envy of all; great volumes of the blackest smoke are rolling and tumbling out of the chimneys—a husbanded grandeur created with a bit of pitch-pine just before arriving at a town; the crew are grouped on the forecastle; the broad stage is run far out over the port bow and an envied deck-hand stands picturesquely on the end of it with a coil of rope in his hand; the pent steam is screaming through the gauge-cocks; the captain lifts his hand, a bell rings, the wheels stop; then they turn back, churning the water to foam, and the steamer is at rest. Then such a scramble as there is to get aboard and to get ashore, and to take in freight and to discharge freight, all at one and the same time; and such a yelling and cursing as the mates facilitate it all with! Ten minutes later the steamer is under way again, with no flag on the jack-staff and no black smoke issuing from the chimneys. After ten more minutes the town is dead again and the town drunkard asleep by the skids once more.

My father was a justice of the peace and I supposed he possessed the power of life and death over all men and could hang anybody that offended him. This was distinction enough for me as a general thing, but the desire to be a steamboatman kept intruding nevertheless. I first wanted to be a cabin-boy, so that I could come out with a white apron on and shake a table-cloth over the side, where all my old comrades could see me; later I thought I would rather be the deck-hand who stood on the end of the stage-plank with the coil of rope in his hand, because he was particularly conspicuous. But these were only day-dreams—they were too heavenly to be contemplated as real possibilities. By and by one of our boys went away. He was not heard of for a long time. At last he turned up as apprentice engineer or "striker" on a steamboat. This thing shook the bottom out of all my Sunday-school teachings. That boy had been notoriously worldly and I just the reverse; yet he was exalted to this eminence and I left in obscurity and misery. There was nothing generous about this fellow in his greatness. He would always manage to have a rusty bolt to scrub while his boat tarried at our town, and he would sit on the inside guard and scrub it, where we all could see him and envy him and loathe him. And whenever his boat was laid up he would come home and swell around the town in his blackest and greasiest clothes, so that nobody could help remembering that he was a steamboatman; and he used all sorts of steamboat technicalities in his talk, as if he were so used to them that he forgot common people could not understand them. He would speak of the "labboard" side of a horse in an easy, natural way that would make one wish he was dead. And he was always talking about "St. Looy" like an old citizen; he would refer casually to occasions when he was "coming down Fourth Street," or when he was "passing by the Planter's House," or when there was a fire and he took a turn on the brakes of "the old Big Missouri"; and then he would go on and lie about how many towns the size of ours were burned down there that day. Two or three of the boys had long been persons of consideration among us because they had been to St. Louis once and had a vague general knowledge of its wonders, but the day of their glory was over now. They lapsed into a humble silence and learned to disappear when the ruthless "cub"-engineer approached. This fellow had money, too, and hair-oil. Also an ignorant silver watch and a showy brass watch-chain. He wore a leather belt and used no suspenders. If ever a youth was cordially admired and hated by his comrades, this one was. No girl could withstand his charms. He "cut out" every boy in the village. When his boat blew up at last, it diffused a tranquil contentment among us such as we had not known for months. But when he came home the next week, alive, renowned, and appeared in church all battered up and bandaged, a shining hero, stared at and wondered over by everybody, it seemed to us that the partiality of Providence for an undeserving reptile had reached a point where it was open to criticism.

This creature's career could produce but one result, and it speedily followed. Boy after boy managed to get on the river. The minister's son became an engineer. The doctor's and the postmaster's sons became "mud clerks"; the wholesale liquor dealer's son became a barkeeper on a boat; four sons of the chief merchant and two sons of the county judge became pilots. Pilot was the grandest position of all. The pilot, even in those days of trivial wages, had a princely salary—from a hundred and fifty to two hundred and fifty dollars a month, and no board to pay. Two months of his wages would pay a preacher's salary for a year. Now some of us were left disconsolate. We could not get on the river—at least our parents would not let us.

So, by and by, I ran away. I said I would never come home again till I was a pilot and could come in glory. But somehow I could not manage it. I went meekly aboard a few of the boats that lay packed together like sardines at the long St. Louis wharf, and humbly inquired for the pilots, but got only a cold shoulder and short words from mates and clerks. I had to make the best of this sort of treatment for the time being, but I had comforting day-dreams of a future when I should be a great and honored pilot, with plenty of money, and could kill some of these mates and clerks and pay for them.

Months afterward the hope within me struggled to a reluctant death, and I found myself without an ambition. But I was ashamed to go home. I was in Cincinnati, and I set to work to map out a new career. I had been reading about the recent exploration of the river Amazon by an expedition sent out by our government. It was said that the expedition, owing to difficulties, had not thoroughly explored a part of the country lying about the headwaters, some four thousand miles from the mouth of the river. It was only about fifteen hundred miles from Cincinnati to New Orleans, where I could doubtless get a ship. I had thirty dollars left; I would go and complete the exploration of the Amazon. This was all the thought I gave to the subject. I never was great in matters of detail. I packed my valise, and took passage on an ancient tub called the *Paul Jones,* for New Orleans. For the sum of sixteen dollars I had the scarred and tarnished splendors of "her" main saloon principally to myself, for she was not a creature to attract the eye of wiser travelers.

When we presently got under way and went poking down the broad Ohio, I became a new being and the subject of my own admiration. I was a traveler! A word never had tasted so good in my mouth before. I had an exultant sense of being bound for mysterious lands and distant climes which I never have felt in so uplifting a degree since. I was in such a glorified condition that all ignoble feelings departed out of me, and I was able to look down and pity the untraveled with a compassion that had hardly a trace of contempt in it. Still, when we stopped at villages and wood-yards, I could not help lolling carelessly upon the railings of the boiler-deck to enjoy the envy of the country boys on the bank. If they did not seem to discover me, I presently sneezed to attract their attention, or moved to a position where they could not help seeing me. And as soon as I knew they saw me I gaped and stretched, and gave other signs of being mightily bored with traveling.

I kept my hat off all the time, and stayed where the wind and the sun could strike me, because I wanted to get the bronzed and weather-beaten look of an old traveler. Before the second day was half gone I experienced a joy which filled me with the purest gratitude, for I saw that the skin had begun to blister and peel off my face and neck. I wished that the boys and girls at home could see me now.

We reached Louisville in time—at least the neighborhood of it. We stuck hard and fast on the rocks in the middle of the river and lay there four days. I was now beginning to feel a strong sense of being a part of the boat's family, a sort of infant son to the captain and younger brother to the officers. There is no estimating the pride I took in this grandeur or the affection that began to swell and grow in me for those people. I could not know how the lordly steamboatman scorns that sort of presumption in a mere landsman. I particularly longed to acquire the least trifle of notice from the big stormy mate, and I was on the alert for an opportunity to do him a service to that end. It came at last. The riotous pow-wow of setting a spar was going on down on the forecastle, and I went down there and stood around in the way—or mostly skipping out of it—till the mate suddenly roared a general order for somebody to bring him a capstan bar. I sprang to his side and said: "Tell me where it is—I'll fetch it!"

If a rag-picker had offered to do a diplomatic service for the Emperor of Russia, the monarch could not have been more astounded than the mate was. He even stopped swearing. He stood and stared down at me. It took him ten seconds to scrape his disjointed remains together again. Then he said impressively, "Well, if this don't beat h——l!," and turned to his work with the air of a man who had been confronted with a problem too abstruse for solution.

I crept away and courted solitude for the rest of the day. I did not go to dinner, I stayed away from supper until everybody else had finished. I did not feel so much like a member of the boat's family now as before. However, my spirits returned, in instalments, as we pursued our way down the river. I was sorry I hated the mate so, because it was not in (young) human nature not to admire him. He was huge and muscular, his face was bearded and whiskered all over, he had a red woman and a blue woman tattooed on his right arm—one on each side of a blue anchor with a red rope to it—and in the matter of profanity he was sublime. When he was getting out cargo at a landing, I was always where I could see and hear. He felt all the majesty of his great position and made the world feel it too. When he gave even the simplest order, he discharged it like a blast of lightning and sent a long, reverberating peal of profanity thundering after it. I could not help contrasting the way in which the average landsman would give an order with the mate's way of doing it. If the landsman should wish the gang-plank moved a foot farther forward, he would probably say, "James, or William, one of you push that plank forward, please," but put the mate in his place, and he would roar out, "Here, now, start that gang-plank for'ard! Lively, now! *What*'re you about! Snatch it! *snatch* it! There! there! aft again! aft again! Don't you hear me? Dash it to dash! are you going to *sleep* over it! '*Vast* heaving. 'Vast heaving, I tell you! Going to heave it clear astern? WHERE're you going with that barrel! *for'ard* with it 'fore I make you swallow it, you dash-dash-dash-*dashed* split between a tired mud-turtle and a crippled hearse-horse!"

I wished I could talk like that.

When the soreness of my adventure with the mate had somewhat worn off, I began timidly to make up to the humblest official connected with the boat—the night watchman. He snubbed my advances at first, but I presently ventured to offer him a new chalk pipe, and that softened him. So he allowed me to sit with him by the big bell on the hurricane-deck, and in time he melted into conversation. He could not well have helped it, I hung with such homage on his words and so plainly showed that I felt honored by his notice. He told me the names of dim capes and shadowy islands as we glided by them in the solemnity of the night under the winking stars, and by and by got to talking about himself. He seemed over-sentimental for a man whose salary was six dollars a week—or rather he might have seemed so to an older person than I. But I drank in his words hungrily and with a faith that might have moved mountains if it had been applied judiciously. What was it to me that he was soiled and seedy and fragrant with gin? What was it to me that his grammar was bad, his construction worse, and his profanity so void of art that it was an element of weakness rather than strength in his conversation? He was a wronged man, a man who had seen trouble, and that was enough for me. As he mellowed into his plaintive history his tears dripped upon the lantern in his lap, and I cried too from sympathy. He said he was the son of an English nobleman, either an earl or an alderman, he could not remember which, but believed was both; his father, the nobleman, loved him but his mother hated him from the cradle; and so while he was still a little boy he was sent to "one of them old, ancient colleges," he couldn't remember which; and by and by his father died and his mother seized the property and "shook" him, as he phrased it. After his mother shook him, members of the nobility with whom he was acquainted used their influence to get him the position of "loblolly-boy in a ship," and from that point my watchman threw off all trammels of date and locality and branched out into a narrative that bristled all along with incredible adventures, a narrative that was so reeking with bloodshed and so crammed with hair-breadth escapes and the most engaging and unconscious personal villainies that I sat speechless, enjoying, shuddering, wondering, worshiping.

It was a sore blight to find out afterward that he was a low, vulgar, ignorant, sentimental, half-witted humbug, an untraveled native of the wilds of Illinois, who had absorbed wildcat literature and appropriated its marvels, until in time he had woven odds and ends of the mess into this yarn and then gone on telling it to fledglings like me until he had come to believe it himself.

(1883)

E. M. FORSTER
[1879–1970]

Our Graves in Gallipoli°

FIRST GRAVE   We are important again upon earth. Each morning men mention us.

SECOND GRAVE   Yes, after seven years' silence.

FIRST GRAVE   Every day some eminent public man now refers to the "sanctity of our graves in Gallipoli."

SECOND GRAVE   Why do the eminent men speak of "our" graves, as if they were themselves dead? It is we, not they, who lie on Achi Baba.

FIRST GRAVE   They say "our" out of geniality and in order to touch the great heart of the nation more quickly. *Punch,* the great-hearted jester, showed a picture lately in which the Prime Minister of England, Lloyd George, fertile in counsels, is urged to go to war to protect "the sanctity of our graves in Gallipoli." The elderly artist who designed that picture is not dead and does not mean to die. He hopes to illustrate this war as he did the last, for a sufficient salary. Nevertheless he writes "our" graves, as if he was inside one, and all persons of position now say the same.

SECOND GRAVE   If they go to war, there will be more graves.

FIRST GRAVE   That is what they desire. That is what Lloyd George, prudent in counsels, and lion-hearted Churchill, intend.

SECOND GRAVE   But where will they dig them?

FIRST GRAVE   There is still room over in Chanak. Also, it is well for a nation that would be great to scatter its graves all over the world. Graves in Ireland, graves in Irak, Russia, Persia, India, each with its inscription from the Bible or Rupert Brooke. When England thinks fit, she can launch an expedition to protect the sanctity of her graves, and can follow that by another expedition to protect the sanctity of the additional graves. That is what Lloyd George, prudent in counsels, and lion-hearted Churchill, have planned. Churchill planned this expedition to Gallipoli, where I was killed. He planned the expedition to Antwerp, where my brother was killed. Then he said that Labour is

---

Gallipoli   *During World War I the British army, and especially its Australian contingent, suffered a terrible defeat at Gallipoli in Turkey.*

not fit to govern. Rolling his eyes for fresh worlds, he saw Egypt, and fearing that peace might be established there, he intervened and prevented it. Whatever he undertakes is a success. He is Churchill the Fortunate, ever in office, and clouds of dead heroes attend him. Nothing for schools, nothing for houses, nothing for the life of the body, nothing for the spirit. England cannot spare a penny for anything except for her heroes' graves.

SECOND GRAVE   Is she really putting herself to so much expense on our account?

FIRST GRAVE   For us, and for the Freedom of the Straits. That water flowing below us now—it must be thoroughly free. What freedom is, great men are uncertain, but all agree that the water must be free for all nations; if in peace, then for all nations in peace; if in war, then for all nations in war.

SECOND GRAVE   So all nations now support England.

FIRST GRAVE   It is almost inexplicable. England stands alone. Of the dozens of nations into which the globe is divided, not a single one follows her banner, and even her own colonies hang back.

SECOND GRAVE   Yes . . . inexplicable. Perhaps she fights for some other reason.

FIRST GRAVE   Ah, the true reason of a war is never known until all who have fought in it are dead. In a hundred years' time we shall be told. Meanwhile seek not to inquire. There are rumours that rich men desire to be richer, but we cannot know.

SECOND GRAVE   If rich men desire more riches, let them fight. It is reasonable to fight for our desires.

FIRST GRAVE   But they cannot fight. They must not fight. There are too few of them. They would be killed. If a rich man went into the interior of Asia and tried to take more gold or more oil, he might be seriously injured at once. He must persuade poor men, who are numerous, to go there for him. And perhaps this is what Lloyd George, fertile in counsels, has decreed. He has tried to enter Asia by means of the Greeks. It was the Greeks who, seven years ago, failed to join England after they had promised to do so, and our graves in Gallipoli are the result of this. But Churchill the Fortunate, ever in office, ever magnanimous, bore the Greeks no grudge, and he and Lloyd George persuaded their young men to enter Asia. They have mostly been killed there, so English young men must be persuaded instead. A phrase must be thought of, and "the Gallipoli graves" is the handiest. The clergy must wave their Bibles, the old men their newspapers, the old women their knitting, the unmarried girls must wave white feathers, and all must shout, "Gallipoli graves, Gallipoli graves, Gallipoli, Gally Polly, Gally Polly," until the young men are ashamed and think, What sound can that be but my country's call? and Chanak receives them.

SECOND GRAVE   Chanak is to sanctify Gallipoli.

FIRST GRAVE   It will make our heap of stones for ever England, apparently.

SECOND GRAVE   It can scarcely do that to my portion of it. I was a Turk.

FIRST GRAVE   What! a Turk! You a Turk? And I have lain beside you for seven years and never known!

SECOND GRAVE   How should you have known? What is there to know except that I am your brother?

FIRST GRAVE   I am yours . . .

SECOND GRAVE   All is dead except that. All graves are one. It is their unity that sanctifies them, and some day even the living will learn this.

FIRST GRAVE   Ah, but why can they not learn it while they are still alive?

(1936)

VIRGINIA WOOLF

[1882–1941]

Old Mrs. Grey

There are moments even in England, now, when even the busiest, most contented suddenly let fall what they hold—it may be the week's washing. Sheets and pyjamas crumble and dissolve in their hands, because, though they do not state this in so many words, it seems silly to take the washing round to Mrs. Peel when out there over the fields over the hills, there is no washing; no pinning of clotheslines; mangling and ironing; no work at all, but boundless rest. Stainless and boundless rest; space unlimited; untrodden grass; wild birds flying; hills whose smooth uprise continues that wild flight.

Of all this however only seven foot by four could be seen from Mrs. Grey's corner. That was the size of her front door which stood wide open, though there was a fire burning in the grate. The fire looked like a small spot of dusty light feebly trying to escape from the embarrassing pressure of the pouring sunshine.

Mrs. Grey sat on a hard chair in the corner looking—but at what? Apparently at nothing. She did not change the focus of her eyes when visitors came in. Her eyes had ceased to focus themselves; it may be that they had lost the power. They were aged eyes, blue, unspectacled. They could see, but without looking. She had never used her eyes on anything minute and difficult; merely upon faces, and dishes and fields. And now at the age of ninety-two they saw nothing but a zigzag of pain wriggling across the door, pain that twisted her legs as it wriggled; jerked her body to and fro like a marionette. Her body was wrapped round the pain as a damp sheet is folded over a wire. The wire was spasmodically jerked by a cruel invisible hand. She flung out a foot, a hand. Then it stopped. She sat still for a moment.

In that pause she saw herself in the past at ten, at twenty, at twenty-five. She was running in and out of a cottage with eleven brothers and sisters. The line jerked. She was thrown forward in her chair.

"All dead. All dead," she mumbled. "My brothers and sisters. And my husband gone. My daughter too. But I go on. Every morning I pray God to let me pass."

The morning spread seven foot by four green and sunny. Like a fling of grain the birds settled on the land. She was jerked again by another tweak of the tormenting hand.

"I'm an ignorant old woman. I can't read or write, and every morning when I crawls downstairs, I say I wish it were night; and every night, when I crawls up to bed, I say I wish it were day. I'm only an ignorant old woman. But I prays to God: O let me pass. I'm an ignorant old woman—I can't read or write."

So when the colour went out of the doorway, she could not see the other page which is then lit up; or hear the voices that have argued, sung, talked for hundreds of years.

The jerked limbs were still again.

"The doctor comes every week. The parish doctor now. Since my daughter went, we can't afford Dr. Nicholls. But he's a good man. He says he wonders I don't go. He says my heart's nothing but wind and water. Yet I don't seem able to die."

So we—humanity—insist that the body shall still cling to the wirer. We put out the eyes and the ears; but we pinion it there, with a bottle of medicine, a cup of tea, a dying fire, like a rook on a barn door; but a rook that still lives, even with a nail through it.

(1942)

GEORGE ORWELL

[*1903–1950*]

Shooting an Elephant

In Moulmein, in lower Burma, I was hated by large numbers of people—the only time in my life that I have been important enough for this to happen to me. I was sub-divisional police officer of the town, and in an aimless, petty kind of way anti-European feeling was very bitter. No one had the guts to raise a riot, but if a European woman went through the bazaars alone somebody would probably spit betel juice over her dress. As a police officer I was an obvious target and was baited whenever it seemed safe to do so. When a nimble Burman tripped me up on the football field and the referee (another Burman) looked the other way, the crowd yelled with hideous laughter. This happened more than once. In the end the sneering yellow faces of young men that met me everywhere, the insults hooted after me when I was at a safe distance, got badly on my nerves. The young Buddhist priests were the worst of all. There were several thousands of them in the town and none of them seemed to have anything to do except stand on street corners and jeer at Europeans.

All this was perplexing and upsetting. For at that time I had already made up my mind that imperialism was an evil thing and the sooner I chucked up my job and got out of it the better. Theoretically—and secretly, of course—I was all for the Burmese and all against their oppressors, the British. As for the job I was doing, I hated it more bitterly than I can perhaps make clear. In a job like that you see the dirty work of Empire at close quarters. The wretched prisoners huddling in the stinking cages of the lock-ups, the gray, cowed faces of the long-term convicts, the scarred buttocks of the men who had been flogged with bamboos—all these oppressed me with an intolerable sense of guilt. But I could get nothing into perspective. I was young and ill educated and I had had to think out my problems in the utter silence that is imposed on every Englishman in the East. I did not even know that the British Empire is dying, still less did I know that it is a great deal better than the younger empires that are going to supplant it. All I knew was that I was stuck between my hatred of the empire I served and my rage against the evil-spirited little beasts who tried to make my job impossible. With one part of my mind I thought of the British Raj as an unbreakable tyranny, as something clamped down, in *saecula saeculorum,* upon the will of prostrate peoples; with another part I thought that the greatest joy in the world would be to drive a bayonet into a Buddhist priest's guts. Feelings like these are the normal by-products of imperialism; ask any Anglo-Indian official, if you can catch him off duty.

One day something happened which in a roundabout way was enlightening. It was a tiny incident in itself, but it gave me a better glimpse than I had had before of the real nature of imperialism—the real motives for which despotic governments act. Early one morning the sub-inspector at a police station the other end of the town rang me up on the 'phone and said that an elephant was ravaging the bazaar. Would I please come and do something about it? I did not know what I could do, but I wanted to see what was happening and I got on to a pony and started out. I took my rifle, an old .44 Winchester and much too small to kill an elephant, but I thought the noise might be useful *in terrorem*. Various Burmans stopped me on the way and told me about the elephant's doings. It was not, of course, a wild elephant, but a tame one which had gone "must." It had been chained up, as tame elephants always are when their attack of "must" is due, but on the previous night it had broken its chain and escaped. Its mahout, the only person who could manage it when it was in that state, had set out in pursuit, but had taken the wrong direction and was now twelve hours' journey away, and in the morning the elephant had suddenly reappeared in the town. The Burmese population had no weapons and were quite helpless against it. It had already destroyed somebody's bamboo hut, killed a cow and raided some fruit-stalls and devoured the stock; also it had met the municipal rubbish van and, when the driver jumped out and took to his heels, had turned the van over and inflicted violences upon it.

The Burmese sub-inspector and some Indian constables were waiting for me in the quarter where the elephant had been seen. It was a very poor quarter, a labyrinth of squalid bamboo huts, thatched with palm-leaf, winding all over a steep hillside. I remember that it was a cloudy, stuffy morning at the beginning of the rains. We began questioning the people as to where the elephant had gone and, as usual, failed to get any definite information. That is invariably the case in the East; a story always sounds clear enough at a distance, but the nearer you get to the scene of events the vaguer it becomes. Some of the people said that the elephant had gone in one direction, some said that he had gone in another, some professed not even to have heard of any elephant. I had almost made up my mind that the whole story was a pack of lies, when we heard yells a little distance away. There was a loud, scandalized cry of "Go away, child! Go away this instant!" and an old woman with a switch in her hand came round the corner of a hut, violently shooing away a crowd of naked children. Some more women followed, clicking their tongues and exclaiming; evidently there was something that the children ought not to have seen. I rounded the hut and saw a man's dead body sprawling in the mud. He was an Indian, a black Dravidian coolie, almost naked, and he could not have been dead many minutes. The people said that the elephant had come suddenly upon him round the corner of the hut, caught him with its trunk, put its foot on his back and ground him into the earth. This was the rainy season and the ground was soft, and his face had scored a trench a foot deep and a couple of yards long. He was lying on his belly with arms crucified and head sharply twisted to one side. His face was coated with mud, the eyes wide open, the teeth bared and grinning with an expression of unendurable agony. (Never tell me, by the way, that the dead look peaceful. Most of the corpses I have seen looked devilish.) The friction of the great beast's foot had stripped the skin from his back as neatly as one skins a rabbit. As soon as I saw the dead man I sent an orderly to a friend's house nearby to borrow an elephant rifle. I had already sent back the pony, not wanting it to go mad with fright and throw me if it smelt the elephant.

The orderly came back in a few minutes with a rifle and five cartridges, and meanwhile some Burmans had arrived and told us that the elephant was in the paddy fields below, only a few hundred yards away. As I started forward practically the whole population of the quarter flocked out of the houses and followed me. They had seen the rifle and were all shouting excitedly that I was going to shoot the elephant. They had not shown much interest in the elephant when he was merely ravaging their homes, but it was different now that he was going to be shot. It was a bit of fun to them, as it would be to an English crowd; besides they wanted the meat. It made me vaguely uneasy. I had no intention of shooting the elephant—I had merely sent for the rifle to defend myself if necessary—and it is always unnerving to have a crowd following you. I marched down the hill, looking and feeling a fool, with the rifle over my shoulder and an ever-growing army of people jostling at my heels. At the bottom, when you got away from the huts, there was a metalled road and beyond that a miry waste of paddy fields a thousand yards across, not yet ploughed but soggy from the first rains and dotted with coarse grass. The elephant was standing eight yards from the road, his left side toward us. He took not the slightest notice of the crowd's approach. He was tearing up bunches of grass, beating them against his knees to clean them, and stuffing them into his mouth.

I had halted on the road. As soon as I saw the elephant I knew with perfect certainty that I ought not to shoot him. It is a serious matter to shoot a working elephant—it is comparable to destroying a huge and costly piece of machinery—and obviously one ought not to do it if it can possibly be avoided. And at that distance, peacefully eating, the elephant looked no more dangerous than a cow. I thought then and I think now that his attack of "must" was already passing off; in which case he would merely wander harmlessly about until the mahout came back and caught him. Moreover, I did not in the least want to shoot him. I decided that I would watch him for a little while to make sure that he did not turn savage again, and then go home.

But at that moment I glanced round at the crowd that had followed me. It was an immense crowd, two thousand at the least and growing every minute. It blocked the road for a long distance on either side. I looked at the sea of yellow faces above the garish clothes—faces all happy and excited over this bit of fun, all certain that the elephant was going to be shot. They were watching me as they would watch a conjurer about to perform a trick. They did not like me, but with the magical rifle in my hands I was momentarily worth watching. And suddenly I realized that I should have to shoot the elephant after all. The people expected it of me and I had got to do it; I could feel their two thousand wills pressing me forward, irresistibly. And it was at this moment, as I stood there with the rifle in my hands, that I first grasped the hollowness, the futility of the white man's dominion in the East. Here was I, the white man with his gun, standing in front of the unarmed native crowd—seemingly the leading actor of the piece; but in reality I was only an absurd puppet pushed to and fro by the will of those yellow faces behind. I perceived in this moment that when the white man turns tyrant it is his own freedom that he destroys. He becomes a sort of hollow, posing dummy, the conventionalized figure of a sahib. For it is the condition of his rule that he shall spend his life in trying to impress the "natives," and so in every crisis he has got to do what the "natives" expect of him. He wears a mask, and his face grows to fit it. I had got to shoot the elephant. I had committed myself to doing it when I sent for the rifle. A sahib has got to act like a sahib; he has got to appear resolute, to know his own mind and do definite things. To come all that way, rifle in hand, with two thousand people marching at my heels, and then to trail feebly away, having done nothing—no, that was impossible. The crowd would laugh at me. And my whole life, every white man's life in the East, was one long struggle not to be laughed at.

But I did not want to shoot the elephant. I watched him beating his bunch of grass against his knees with that preoccupied grandmotherly air that elephants have. It seemed to me that it would be murder to shoot him. At that age I was not squeamish about killing animals, but I had never shot an elephant and never wanted to. (Somehow it always seems worse to kill a *large* animal.) Besides, there was the beast's owner to be considered. Alive, the elephant was worth at least a hundred pounds; dead, he would only be worth the value of his tusks, five pounds, possibly. But I had got to act quickly. I turned to some experienced-looking Burmans who had been there when we arrived, and asked them how the elephant had been behaving. They all said the same thing: he took no notice of you if you left him alone, but he might charge if you went too close to him.

It was perfectly clear to me what I ought to do. I ought to walk up to within, say, twenty-five yards of the elephant and test his behavior. If he charged, I could shoot; if he took no notice of me, it would be safe to leave him until the mahout came back. But also I knew that I was going to do no such thing. I was a poor shot with a rifle and the ground was soft mud into which one would sink at every step. If the elephant charged and I missed him, I should have about as much chance as a toad under a steam-roller. But even then I was not thinking particularly of my own skin, only of the watchful yellow faces behind. For at that moment, with the crowd watching me, I was not afraid in the ordinary sense, as I would have been if I had been alone. A white man mustn't be frightened in front of "natives"; and so, in general, he isn't frightened. The sole thought in my mind was that if anything went wrong those two thousand Burmans would see me pursued, caught, trampled on, and reduced to a grinning corpse like that Indian up the hill. And if that happened it was quite probable that some of them would laugh. That would never do. There was only one alternative. I shoved the cartridges into the magazine and lay down on the road to get a better aim.

The crowd grew very still, and a deep, low, happy sigh, as of people who see the theater curtain go up at last, breathed from innumerable throats. They were going to have their bit of fun after all. The rifle was a beautiful German thing with cross-hair sights. I did not then know that in shooting an elephant one would shoot to cut an imaginary bar running from ear-hole to ear-hole. I ought, therefore, as the elephant was sideways on, to have aimed straight at his ear-hole; actually I aimed several inches in front of this, thinking the brain would be further forward.

When I pulled the trigger I did not hear the bang or feel the kick—one never does when a shot goes home—but I heard the devilish roar of glee that went up from the crowd. In that instant, in too short a time, one would have thought, even for the bullet to get there, a mysterious, terrible change had come over the elephant. He neither stirred nor fell, but every line of his body had altered. He looked suddenly stricken, shrunken, immensely old, as though the frightful impact of the bullet had paralyzed him without knocking him down. At last, after what seemed a long time—it might have been five seconds, I dare say—he sagged flabbily to his knees. His mouth slobbered. An enormous senility seemed to have settled upon him. One could have imagined him thousands of years old. I fired again into the same spot. At the second shot he did not collapse but climbed with desperate slowness to his feet and stood weakly upright, with legs sagging and head drooping. I fired a third time. That was the shot that did for him. You could see the agony of it jolt his whole body and knock the last remnant of strength from his legs. But in falling he seemed for a moment to rise, for as his hind legs collapsed beneath him he seemed to tower upward like a huge rock toppling, his trunk reaching skyward like a tree. He trumpeted, for the first and only time. And then down he came, his belly toward me, with a crash that seemed to shake the ground even where I lay.

I got up. The Burmans were already racing past me across the mud. It was obvious that the elephant would never rise again, but he was not dead. He was breathing very rhythmically with long rattling gasps, his great mound of a side painfully rising and falling. His mouth was wide open—I could see far down into caverns of pale pink throat. I waited a long time for him to die, but his breathing did not weaken. Finally I fired my two remaining shots into the spot where I thought his heart must be. The thick blood welled out of him like red velvet, but still he did not die. His body did not even jerk when the shots hit him, the tortured breathing continued without a pause. He was dying, very slowly and in great agony, but in some world remote from me where not even a bullet could damage him further. I felt that I had got to put an end to that dreadful noise. It seemed dreadful to see the great beast lying there, powerless to move and yet powerless to die, and not even to be able to finish him. I sent back for my small rifle and poured shot after shot into his heart and down his throat. They seemed to make no impression. The tortured gasps continued as steadily as the ticking of a clock.

In the end I could not stand it any longer and went away. I heard later that it took him half an hour to die. Burmans were bringing dahs and baskets even before I left, and I was told they had stripped his body almost to the bones by the afternoon.

Afterward, of course, there were endless discussions about the shooting of the elephant. The owner was furious, but he was only an Indian and could do nothing. Besides, legally I had done the right thing, for a mad elephant has to be killed, like a mad dog, if its owner fails to control it. Among the Europeans opinion was divided. The older men said I was right, the younger men said it was a damn shame to shoot an elephant for killing a coolie, because an elephant was worth more than any damn Coringhee coolie. And afterward I was very glad that the coolie had been killed; it put me legally in the right and it gave me a sufficient pretext for shooting the elephant. I often wondered whether any of the others grasped that I had done it solely to avoid looking a fool.

(1936)

LOREN EISELEY

[1907–1977]

The Judgment of the Birds

It is a commonplace of all religious thought, even the most primitive, that the man seeking visions and insight must go apart from his fellows and live for a time in the wilderness. If he is of the proper sort, he will return with a message. It may not be a message from the god he set out to seek, but even if he has failed in that particular, he will have had a vision or seen a marvel, and these are always worth listening to and thinking about.

The world, I have come to believe, is a very queer place, but we have been part of this queerness for so long that we tend to take it for granted. We rush to and fro like Mad Hatters upon our peculiar errands, all the time imagining our surroundings to be dull and ourselves quite ordinary creatures. Actually, there is nothing in the world to encourage this idea, but such is the mind of man, and this is why he finds it necessary from time to time to send emissaries into the wilderness in the hope of learning of great events, or plans in store for him, that will resuscitate his waning taste for life. His great news services, his worldwide radio network, he knows with a last remnant of healthy distrust will be of no use to him in this matter. No miracle can withstand a radio broadcast, and it is certain that it would be no miracle if it could. One must seek, then, what only the solitary approach can give—a natural revelation.

Let it be understood that I am not the sort of man to whom is entrusted direct knowledge of great events or prophecies. A naturalist, however, spends much of his life alone, and my life is no exception. Even in New York City there are patches of wilderness, and a man by himself is bound to undergo certain experiences falling into the class of which I speak. I set mine down, therefore: a matter of pigeons, a flight of chemicals, and a judgment of birds, in the hope that they will come to the eye of those who have retained a true taste for the marvelous, and who are capable of discerning in the flow of ordinary events the point at which the mundane world gives way to quite another dimension.

New York is not, on the whole, the best place to enjoy the downright miraculous nature of the planet. There are, I do not doubt, many remarkable stories to be heard there and many strange sights to be seen, but to grasp a marvel fully it must be savored from all aspects. This cannot be done while one is being jostled and hustled along a crowded street. Nevertheless, in any city there are true wildernesses where a man can be alone. It can happen in a hotel room, or on the high roofs at dawn.

One night on the twentieth floor of a midtown hotel I awoke in the dark and grew restless. On an impulse I climbed upon the broad old-fashioned window sill, opened the curtains, and peered out. It was the hour just before dawn, the hour when men sigh in their sleep or, if awake, strive to focus their wavering eyesight upon a world emerging from the shadows. I leaned out sleepily through the open window. I had expected depths, but not the sight I saw.

I found I was looking down from that great height into a series of curious cupolas or lofts that I could just barely make out in the darkness. As I looked, the outlines of these lofts became more distinct because the light was being reflected from the wings of pigeons who, in utter silence, were beginning to float outward upon the city. In and out through the open slits in the cupolas passed the white-winged birds on their mysterious errands. At this hour the city was theirs, and quietly, without the brush of a single wing tip against stone in that high, eerie place, they were taking over the spires of Manhattan. They were pouring upward in a light that was not yet perceptible to human eyes, while far down in the black darkness of the alleys it was still midnight.

As I crouched half-asleep across the sill, I had a moment's illusion that the world had changed in the night, as in some immense snowfall, and that, if I were to leave, it would have to be as these other inhabitants were doing, by the window. I should have to launch out into that great bottomless void with the simple confidence of young birds reared high up there among the familiar chimney pots and interposed horrors of the abyss.

I leaned farther out. To and fro went the white wings, to and fro. There were no sounds from any of them. They knew man was asleep and this light for a little while was theirs. Or perhaps I had only dreamed about man in this city of wings—which he could surely never have built. Perhaps I, myself, was one of these birds dreaming unpleasantly a moment of old dangers far below as I teetered on a window ledge.

Around and around went the wings. It needed only a little courage, only a little shove from the window ledge, to enter that city of light. The muscles of my hands were already making little premonitory lunges. I wanted to enter that city and go away over the roofs in the first dawn. I wanted to enter it so badly that I drew back carefully into the room and opened the hall door. I found my coat on the chair, and it slowly became clear to me that there was a way down through the floors, that I was, after all, only a man.

I dressed then and went back to my own kind, and I have been rather more than usually careful ever since not to look into the city of light. I had seen, just once, man's greatest creation from a strange inverted angle, and it was not really his at all. I will never forget how those wings went round and round, and how, by the merest pressure of the fingers and a feeling for air, one might go away over the roofs. It is a knowledge, however, that is better kept to oneself. I think of it sometimes in such a way that the wings, beginning far down in the black depths of the mind, begin to rise and whirl till all the mind is lit by their spinning, and there is a sense of things passing away, but lightly, as a wing might veer over an obstacle.

To see from an inverted angle, however, is not a gift allotted merely to the human imagination. I have come to suspect that within their degree it is sensed by animals, though perhaps as rarely as among men. The time has to be right; one has to be, by chance or intention, upon the border of two worlds. And sometimes these two borders may shift or interpenetrate and one sees the miraculous.

I once saw this happen to a crow.

This crow lives near my house, and though I have never injured him, he takes good care to stay up in the very highest trees and, in general, to avoid humanity. His world begins at about the limit of my eyesight.

On the particular morning when this episode occurred, the whole countryside was buried in one of the thickest fogs in years. The ceiling was absolutely zero. All planes were grounded, and even a pedestrian could hardly see his outstretched hand before him.

I was groping across a field in the general direction of the railroad station, following a dimly outlined path. Suddenly out of the fog, at about the level of my eyes, and so closely that I flinched, there flashed a pair of immense black wings and a huge beak. The whole bird rushed over my head with a frantic cawing outcry of such hideous terror as I have never heard in a crow's voice before and never expect to hear again.

He was lost and startled, I thought, as I recovered my poise. He ought not to have flown out in this fog. He'd knock his silly brains out.

All afternoon that great awkward cry rang in my head. Merely being lost in a fog seemed scarcely to account for it—especially in a tough, intelligent old bandit such as I knew that particular crow to be. I even looked once in the mirror to see what it might be about me that had so revolted him that he had cried out in protest to the very stones.

Finally, as I worked my way homeward along the path, the solution came to me. It should have been clear before. The borders of our worlds had shifted. It was the fog that had done it. That crow, and I knew him well, never under normal circumstances flew low near men. He had been lost all right, but it was more than that. He had thought he was high up, and when he encountered me looming gigantically through the fog, he had perceived a ghastly and, to the crow mind, unnatural sight. He had seen a man walking on air, desecrating the very heart of the crow kingdom, a harbinger of the most profound evil a crow mind could conceive of—air-walking men. The encounter, he must have thought, had taken place a hundred feet over the roofs.

He caws now when he sees me leaving for the station in the morning, and I fancy that in that note I catch the uncertainty of a mind that has come to know things are not always what they seem. He has seen a marvel in his heights of air and is no longer as other crows. He has experienced the human world from an unlikely perspective. He and I share a viewpoint in common: our worlds have interpenetrated, and we both have faith in the miraculous.

It is a faith that in my own case has been augmented by two remarkable sights. I once saw some very odd chemicals fly across a waste so dead it might have been upon the moon, and once, by an even more fantastic piece of luck, I was present when a group of birds passed a judgment upon life.

On the maps of the old voyageurs it is called *Mauvaises Terres,* the evil lands, and, slurred a little with the passage through many minds, it has come down to us anglicized as the badlands. The soft shuffle of moccasins has passed through its canyons on the grim business of war and flight, but the last of those slight disturbances of immemorial silences died out almost a century ago. The land, if one can call it a land, is a waste as lifeless as that valley in which lie the kings of Egypt. Like the Valley of the Kings, it is a mausoleum, a place of dry bones in what once was a place of life. Now it has silences as deep as those in the moon's airless chasms.

Nothing grows among its pinnacles; there is no shade except under great toadstools of sandstone whose bases have been eaten to the shape of wine glasses by the wind. Everything is flaking, cracking, disintegrating, wearing away in the long, imperceptible weather of time. The ash of ancient volcanic outbursts still sterilizes its soil, and its colors in that waste are the colors that flame in the lonely sunsets on dead planets. Men come there but rarely, and for one purpose only, the collection of bones.

It was a late hour on a cold, wind-bitten autumn day when I climbed a great hill spined like a dinosaur's back and tried to take my bearings. The tumbled waste fell away in waves in all directions. Blue air was darkening into purple along the bases of the hills. I shifted my knapsack, heavy with the petrified bones of long-vanished creatures, and studied my compass. I wanted to be out of there by nightfall, and already the sun was going sullenly down in the west.

It was then that I saw the flight coming on. It was moving like a little close-knit body of black specks that danced and darted and closed again. It was pouring from the north and heading toward me with the undeviating relentlessness of a compass needle. It streamed through the shadows rising out of monstrous gorges. It rushed over towering pinnacles in the red light of the sun or momentarily sank from sight within their shade. Across that desert of eroding clay and wind-worn stone they came with a faint wild twittering that filled all the air about me as those tiny living bullets hurtled past into the night.

It may not strike you as a marvel. It would not, perhaps, unless you stood in the middle of a dead world at sunset, but that was where I stood. Fifty million years lay under my feet, fifty million years of bellowing monsters moving in a green world now gone so utterly that its very light was traveling on the farther edge of space. The chemicals of all that vanished age lay about me in the ground. Around me still lay the shearing molars of dead titanotheres, the delicate sabers of soft-stepping cats, the hollow sockets that had held the eyes of many a strange, outmoded beast. Those eyes had looked out upon a world as real as ours; dark, savage brains had roamed and roared their challenges into the steaming night.

Now they were still here, or, put it as you will, the chemicals that made them were here about me in the ground. The carbon that had driven them ran blackly in the eroding stone. The stain of iron was in the clays. The iron did not remember the blood it had once moved within, the phosphorus had forgot the savage brain. The little individual moment had ebbed from all those strange combinations of chemicals as it would ebb from our living bodies into the sinks and runnels of oncoming time.

I had lifted up a fistful of that ground. I held it while that wild flight of south-bound warblers hurtled over me into the oncoming dark. There went phosphorus, there went iron, there went carbon, there beat the calcium in those hurrying wings. Alone on a dead planet I watched that incredible miracle speeding past. It ran by some true compass over field and waste land. It cried its individual ecstasies into the air until the gullies rang. It swerved like a single body, it knew itself, and, lonely, it bunched close in the racing darkness, its individual entities feeling about them the rising night. And so, crying to each other their identity, they passed away out of my view.

I dropped my fistful of earth. I heard it roll inanimate back into the gully at the base of the hill: iron, carbon, the chemicals of life. Like men from those wild tribes who had haunted these hills before me seeking visions, I made my sign to the great darkness. It was not a mocking sign, and I was not mocked. As I walked into my camp late that night, one man, rousing from his blankets beside the fire, asked sleepily, "What did you see?"

"I think, a miracle," I said softly, but I said it to myself. Behind me that vast waste began to glow under the rising moon.

I have said that I saw a judgment upon life, and that it was not passed by men. Those who stare at birds in cages or who test minds by their closeness to our own may not care for it. It comes from far away out of my past, in a place of pouring waters and green leaves. I shall never see an episode like it again if I live to be a hundred, nor do I think that one man in a million has ever seen it, because man is an intruder into such silences. The light must be right, and the observer must remain unseen. No man sets up such an experiment. What he sees, he sees by chance.

You may put it that I had come over a mountain, that I had slogged through fern and pine needles for half a long day, and that on the edge of a little glade with one long, crooked branch extending across it, I had sat down to rest with my back against a stump. Through accident I was concealed from the glade, although I could see into it perfectly.

The sun was warm there, and the murmurs of forest life blurred softly away into my sleep. When I awoke, dimly aware of some commotion and outcry in the clearing, the light was slanting down through the pines in such a way that the glade was lit like some vast cathedral. I could see the dust motes of wood pollen in the long shaft of light, and there on the extended branch sat an enormous raven with a red and squirming nestling in his beak.

The sound that awoke me was the outraged cries of the nestling's parents, who flew helplessly in circles about the clearing. The sleek black monster was indifferent to them. He gulped, whetted his beak on the dead branch a moment, and sat still. Up to that point the little tragedy had followed the usual pattern. But suddenly, out of all that area of woodland, a soft sound of complaint began to rise. Into the glade fluttered small birds of half a dozen varieties drawn by the anguished outcries of the tiny parents.

No one dared to attack the raven. But they cried there in some instinctive common misery, the bereaved and the unbereaved. The glade filled with their soft rustling and their cries. They fluttered as though to point their wings at the murderer. There was a dim intangible ethic he had violated, that they knew. He was a bird of death.

And he, the murderer, the black bird at the heart of life, sat on there glistening in the common light, formidable, unmoving, unperturbed, untouchable.

The sighing died. It was then I saw the judgment. It was the judgment of life against death. I will never see it again so forcefully presented. I will never hear it again in notes so tragically prolonged. For in the midst of protest, they forgot the violence. There, in that clearing, the crystal note of a song sparrow lifted hesitantly in the hush. And finally, after painful fluttering, another took the song, and then another, the song passing from one bird to another, doubtfully at first, as though some evil thing were being slowly forgotten. Till suddenly they took heart and sang from many throats joyously together as birds are known to sing. They sang because life is sweet and sunlight beautiful. They sang under the brooding shadow of the raven. In simple truth they had forgotten the raven, for they were the singers of life, and not of death.

I was not of that airy company. My limbs were the heavy limbs of an earthbound creature who could climb mountains, even the mountains of the mind, only by a great effort of will. I knew I had seen a marvel and observed a judgment, but the mind which was my human endowment was sure to question it and to be at me day by day with its heresies until I grew to doubt the meaning of what I had seen. Eventually darkness and subtleties would ring me round once more.

And so it proved until, on the top of a stepladder, I made one more observation upon life. It was cold that autumn evening, and, standing under a suburban street light in a spate of leaves and beginning snow, I was suddenly conscious of some huge and hairy shadows dancing over the pavement. They seemed attached to an odd, globular shape that was magnified above me. There was no mistaking it. I was standing under the shadow of an orb-weaving spider. Gigantically projected against the street, she was about her spinning when everything was going underground. Even her cables were magnified upon the sidewalk and already I was half-entangled in their shadows.

"Good Lord," I thought, "she has found herself a kind of minor sun and is going to upset the course of nature."

I procured a ladder from my yard and climbed up to inspect the situation. There she was, the universe running down around her, warmly arranged among her guy ropes attached to the lamp supports—a great black and yellow embodiment of the life force, not giving up to either frost or stepladders. She ignored me and went on tightening and improving her web.

I stood over her on the ladder, a faint snow touching my cheeks, and surveyed her universe. There were a couple of iridescent green beetle cases turning slowly on a loose strand of web, a fragment of luminescent eye from a moth's wing and a large indeterminable object, perhaps a cicada, that had struggled and been wrapped in silk. There were also little bits and slivers, little red and blue flashes from the scales of anonymous wings that had crashed there.

Some days, I thought, they will be dull and gray and the shine will be out of them; then the dew will polish them again and drops hang on the silk until everything is gleaming and turning in the light. It is like a mind, really, where everything changes but remains, and in the end you have these eaten-out bits of experience like beetle wings.

I stood over her a moment longer, comprehending somewhat reluctantly that her adventure against the great blind forces of winter, her seizure of this warming globe of light, would come to nothing and was hopeless. Nevertheless it brought the birds back into my mind, and that faraway song which had traveled with growing strength around a forest clearing years ago—a kind of heroism, a world where even a spider refuses to lie down and die if a rope can still be spun on to a star. Maybe man himself will fight like this in the end, I thought, slowly realizing that the web and its threatening yellow occupant had been added to some luminous store of experience, shining for a moment in the fogbound reaches of my brain.

The mind, it came to me as I slowly descended the ladder, is a very remarkable thing; it has gotten itself a kind of courage by looking at a spider in a street lamp. Here was something that ought to be passed on to those who will fight our final freezing battle with the void. I thought of setting it down carefully as a message to the future: *In the days of the frost seek a minor sun.*

But as I hesitated, it became plain that something was wrong. The marvel was escaping—a sense of bigness beyond man's power to grasp, the essence of life in its great dealings with the universe. It was better, I decided, for the emissaries returning from the wilderness, even if they were merely descending from a stepladder, to record their marvel, not to define its meaning. In that way it would go echoing on through the minds of men, each grasping at that beyond out of which the miracles emerge, and which, once defined, ceases to satisfy the human need for symbols.

In the end I merely made a mental note: One specimen of Epeira observed building a web in a street light. Late autumn and cold for spiders. Cold for men, too. I shivered and left the lamp glowing there in my mind. The last I saw of Epeira she was hauling steadily on a cable. I stepped carefully over her shadow as I walked away.

(1956)

JAMES BALDWIN

[1924–1989]

Notes of a Native Son

I

On the 29th of July, in 1943, my father died. On the same day, a few hours later, his last child was born. Over a month before this, while all our energies were concentrated in waiting for these events, there had been, in Detroit, one of the bloodiest race riots of the century. A few hours after my father's funeral, while he lay in state in the undertaker's chapel, a race riot broke out in Harlem. On the morning of the 3rd of August, we drove my father to the graveyard through a wilderness of smashed plate glass.

The day of my father's funeral had also been my nineteenth birthday. As we drove him to the graveyard, the spoils of injustice, anarchy, discontent, and hatred were all around us. It seemed to me that God himself had devised, to mark my father's end, the most sustained and brutally dissonant of codas. And it seemed to me, too, that the violence which rose all about us as my father left the world had been devised as a corrective for the pride of his eldest son. I had declined to believe in that apocalypse which had been central to my father's vision; very well, life seemed to be saying, here is something that will certainly pass for an apocalypse until the real thing comes along. I had inclined to be contemptuous of my father for the conditions of his life, for the conditions of our lives. When his life had ended I began to wonder about that life and also, in a new way, to be apprehensive about my own.

I had not known my father very well. We had got on badly, partly because we shared, in our different fashions, the vice of stubborn pride. When he was dead I realized that I had hardly ever spoken to him. When he had been dead a long time I began to wish I had. It seems to be typical of life in America, where opportunities, real and fancied, are thicker than anywhere else on the globe, that the second generation has no time to talk to the first. No one, including my father, seems to have known exactly how old he was, but his mother had been born during slavery. He was of the first generation of free men. He, along with thousands of other Negroes, came North after 1919 and I was part of that generation which had never seen the landscape of what Negroes sometimes call the Old Country.

He had been born in New Orleans and had been a quite young man there during the time that Louis Armstrong, a boy, was running errands for the dives and honky-tonks of what was always presented to me as one of the most wicked of cities—to this day, whenever I think of New Orleans, I also helplessly think of Sodom and Gomorrah. My father never mentioned Louis Armstrong, except to forbid us to play his records; but there was a picture of him on our wall for a long time. One of my father's strong-willed female relatives had placed it there and forbade my father to take it down. He never did, but he eventually maneuvered her out of the house and when, some years later, she was in trouble and near death, he refused to do anything to help her.

He was, I think, very handsome. I gather this from photographs and from my own memories of him, dressed in his Sunday best and on his way to preach a sermon somewhere, when I was little. Handsome, proud, and ingrown, "like a toe-nail," somebody said. But he looked to me, as I grew older, like pictures I had seen of African tribal chieftains: he really should have been naked, with war-paint on and barbaric mementos, standing among spears. He could be chilling in the pulpit and indescribably cruel in his personal life and he was certainly the most bitter man I have ever met; yet it must be said that there was something else in him, buried in him, which lent him his tremendous power and, even, a rather crushing charm. It had something to do with his blackness, I think—he was very black—with his blackness and his beauty, and with the fact that he knew that he was black but did not know that he was beautiful. He claimed to be proud of his blackness but it had also been the cause of much humiliation and it had fixed bleak boundaries to his life. He was not a young man when we were growing up and he had already suffered many kinds of ruin; in his outrageously demanding and protective way he loved his children, who were black like him and menaced, like him; and all these things sometimes showed in his face when he tried, never to my knowledge with any success, to establish contact with any of us. When he took one of his children on his knee to play, the child always became fretful and began to cry; when he tried to help one of us with our homework the absolutely unabating tension which emanated from him caused our minds and our tongues to become paralyzed, so that he, scarcely knowing why, flew into a rage and the child, not knowing why, was punished. If it ever entered his head to bring a surprise home for his children, it was, almost unfailingly, the wrong surprise and even the big watermelons he often brought home on his back in the summertime led to the most appalling scenes. I do not remember, in all those years, that one of his children was ever glad to see him come home. From what I was able to gather of his early life, it seemed that this inability to establish contact with other people had always marked him and had been one of the things which had driven him out of New Orleans. There was something in him, therefore, groping and tentative, which was never expressed and which was buried with him. One saw it most clearly when he was facing new people and hoping to impress them. But he never did, not for long. We went from church to smaller and more improbable church, he found himself in less and less demand as a minister, and by the time he died none of his friends had come to see him for a long time. He had lived and died in an intolerable bitterness of spirit and it frightened me, as we drove him to the graveyard through those unquiet, ruined streets, to see how powerful and overflowing this bitterness could be and to realize that this bitterness now was mine.

When he died I had been away from home for a little over a year. In that year I had had time to become aware of the meaning of all my father's bitter warnings, had discovered the secret of his proudly pursed lips and rigid carriage: I had discovered the weight of white people in the world. I saw that this had been for my ancestors and now would be for me an awful thing to live with and that the bitterness which had helped to kill my father could also kill me.

He had been ill a long time—in the mind, as we now realized, reliving instances of his fantastic intransigence in the new light of his affliction and endeavoring to feel a sorrow for him which never, quite, came true. We had not known that he was being eaten up by paranoia, and the discovery that his cruelty, to our bodies and our minds, had been one of the symptoms of his illness was not, then, enough to enable us to forgive him. The younger children felt, quite simply, relief that he would not be coming home anymore. My mother's observation that it was he, after all, who had kept them alive all these years meant nothing because the problems of keeping children alive are not real for children. The older children felt, with my father gone, that they could invite their friends to the house without fear that their friends would be insulted or, as had sometimes happened with me, being told that their friends were in league with the devil and intended to rob our family of everything we owned. (I didn't fail to wonder, and it made me hate him, what on earth we owned that anybody else would want.)

His illness was beyond all hope of healing before anyone realized that he was ill. He had always been so strange and had lived, like a prophet, in such unimaginably close communion with the Lord that his long silences which were punctuated by moans and hallelujahs and snatches of old songs while he sat at the living-room window never seemed odd to us. It was not until he refused to eat because, he said, his family was trying to poison him that my mother was forced to accept as a fact what had, until then, been only an unwilling suspicion. When he was committed, it was discovered that he had tuberculosis and, as it turned out, the disease of his mind allowed the disease of his body to destroy him. For the doctors could not force him to eat, either, and, though he was fed intravenously, it was clear from the beginning that there was no hope for him.

In my mind's eye I could see him, sitting at the window, locked up in his terrors; hating and fearing every living soul including his children who had betrayed him, too, by reaching towards the world which had despised him. There were nine of us. I began to wonder what it could have felt like for such a man to have had nine children whom he could barely feed. He used to make little jokes about our poverty, which never, of course, seemed very funny to us; they could not have seemed very funny to him, either, or else our all too feeble response to them would never have caused such rages. He spent great energy and achieved, to our chagrin, no small amount of success in keeping us away from the people who surrounded us, people who had all-night rent parties to which we listened when we should have been sleeping, people who cursed and drank and flashed razor blades on Lenox Avenue. He could not understand why, if they had so much energy to spare, they could not use it to make their lives better. He treated almost everybody on our block with a most uncharitable asperity and neither they, nor, of course, their children were slow to reciprocate.

The only white people who came to our house were welfare workers and bill collectors. It was almost always my mother who dealt with them, for my father's temper, which was at the mercy of his pride, was never to be trusted. It was clear that he felt their very presence in his home to be a violation: this was conveyed by his carriage, almost ludicrously stiff, and by his voice, harsh and vindictively polite. When I was around nine or ten I wrote a play which was directed by a young, white schoolteacher, a woman, who then took an interest in me, and gave me books to read and, in order to corroborate my theatrical bent, decided to take me to see what she somewhat tactlessly referred to as "real" plays. Theatergoing was forbidden in our house, but, with the really cruel intuitiveness of a child, I suspected that the color of this woman's skin would carry the day for me. When, at school, she suggested taking me to the theater, I did not, as I might have done if she had been a Negro, find a way of discouraging her, but agreed that she should pick me up at my house one evening. I then, very cleverly, left all the rest to my mother, who suggested to my father, as I knew she would, that it would not be very nice to let such a kind woman make the trip for nothing. Also, since it was a schoolteacher, I imagine that my mother countered the idea of sin with the idea of "education," which word, even with my father, carried a kind of bitter weight.

Before the teacher came my father took me aside to ask *why* she was coming, what *interest* she could possibly have in our house, in a boy like me. I said I didn't know but I, too, suggested that it had something to do with education. And I understood that my father was waiting for me to say something—I didn't quite know what; perhaps that I wanted his protection against this teacher and her "education." I said none of these things and the teacher came and we went out. It was clear, during the brief interview in our living room, that my father was agreeing very much against his will and that he would have refused permission if he had dared. The fact that he did not dare caused me to despise him: I had no way of knowing that he was facing in that living room a wholly unprecedented and frightening situation.

Later, when my father had been laid off from his job, this woman became very important to us. She was really a very sweet and generous woman and went to a great deal of trouble to be of help to us, particularly during one awful winter. My mother called her by the highest name she knew. She said she was a "christian." My father could scarcely disagree but during the four or five years of our relatively close association he never trusted her and was always trying to surprise in her open, Midwestern face the genuine, cunningly hidden, and hideous motivation. In later years, particularly when it began to be clear that this "education" of mine was going to lead me to perdition, he became more explicit and warned me that my white friends in high school were not really my friends and that I would see, when I was older, how white people would do anything to keep a Negro down. Some of them could be nice, he admitted, but none of them were to be trusted and most of them were not even nice. The best thing was to have as little to do with them as possible. I did not feel this way and I was certain, in my innocence, that I never would.

But the year which preceded my father's death had made a great change in my life. I had been living in New Jersey, working in defense plants, working and living among southerners, white and black. I knew about the south, of course, and about how southerners treated Negroes and how they expected them to behave, but it had never entered my mind that anyone would look at me and expect *me* to behave that way. I learned in New Jersey that to be a Negro meant, precisely, that one was never looked at but was simply at the mercy of the reflexes the color of one's skin caused in other people. I acted in New Jersey as I had always acted, that is as though I thought a great deal of myself—I had to *act* that way—with results that were, simply, unbelievable. I had scarcely arrived before I had earned the enmity, which was extraordinarily ingenious, of all my superiors and nearly all my co-workers. In the beginning, to make matters worse, I simply did not know what was happening. I did not know what I had done, and I shortly began to wonder what *anyone* could possibly do, to bring about such unanimous, active, and unbearably vocal hostility. I knew about jim-crow but I had never experienced it. I went to the same self-service restaurant three times and stood with all the Princeton boys before the counter, waiting for a hamburger and coffee; it was always an extraordinarily long time before anything was set before me; but it was not until the fourth visit that I learned that, in fact, nothing had ever been set before me: I had simply picked something up. Negroes were not served there, I was told, and they had been waiting for me to realize that I was always the only Negro present. Once I was told this, I determined to go there all the time. But now they were ready for me and, though some dreadful scenes were subsequently enacted in that restaurant, I never ate there again.

It was the same story all over New Jersey, in bars, bowling alleys, diners, places to live. I was always being forced to leave, silently, or with mutual imprecations. I very shortly became notorious and children giggled behind me when I passed and their elders whispered or shouted—they really believed that I was mad. And it did begin to work on my mind, of course; I began to be afraid to go anywhere and to compensate for this I went places to which I really should not have gone and where, God knows, I had no desire to be. My reputation in town naturally enhanced my reputation at work and my working day became one long series of acrobatics designed to keep me out of trouble. I cannot say that these acrobatics succeeded. It began to seem that the machinery of the organization I worked for was turning over, day and night, with but one aim: to eject me. I was fired once, and contrived, with the aid of a friend from New York, to get back on the payroll; was fired again, and bounced back again. It took a while to fire me for the third time, but the third time took. There were no loopholes anywhere. There was not even any way of getting back inside the gates.

That year in New Jersey lives in my mind as though it were the year during which, having an unsuspected predilection for it, I first contracted some dread, chronic disease, the unfailing symptom of which is a kind of blind fever, a pounding in the skull and fire in the bowels. Once this disease is contracted, one can never be really carefree again, for the fever, without an instant's warning, can recur at any moment. It can wreck more important things than race relations. There is not a Negro alive who does not have this rage in his blood—one has the choice, merely, of living with it consciously or surrendering to it. As for me, this fever has recurred in me, and does, and will until the day I die.

My last night in New Jersey, a white friend from New York took me to the nearest big town, Trenton, to go to the movies and have a few drinks. As it turned out, he also saved me from, at the very least, a violent whipping. Almost every detail of that night stands out very clearly in my memory. I even remember the name of the movie we saw because its title impressed me as being so patly ironical. It was a movie about the German occupation of France, starring Maureen O'Hara and Charles Laughton and called *This Land Is Mine*. I remember the name of the diner we walked into when the movie ended: it was the "American Diner." When we walked in the counterman asked what we wanted and I remember answering with the casual sharpness which had become my habit: "We want a hamburger and a cup of coffee, what do you think we want?" I do not know why, after a year of such rebuffs, I so completely failed to anticipate his answer, which was, of course, "We don't serve Negroes here." This reply failed to discompose me, at least for the moment. I made some sardonic comment about the name of the diner and we walked out into the streets.

This was the time of what was called the "brown-out," when the lights in all American cities were very dim. When we re-entered the streets something happened to me which had the force of an optical illusion, or a nightmare. The streets were very crowded and I was facing north. People were moving in every direction but it seemed to me, in that instant, that all of the people I could see, and many more than that, were moving toward me, against me, and that everyone was white. I remember how their faces gleamed. And I felt, like a physical sensation, a *click* at the nape of my neck as though some interior string connecting my head to my body had been cut. I began to walk. I heard my friend call after me, but I ignored him. Heaven only knows what was going on in his mind, but he had the good sense not to touch me—I don't know what would have happened if he had—and to keep me in sight. I don't know what was going on in my mind, either; I certainly had no conscious plan. I wanted to do something to crush these white faces, which were crushing me. I walked for perhaps a block or two until I came to an enormous, glittering, and fashionable restaurant in which I knew not even the intercession of the Virgin would cause me to be served. I pushed through the doors and took the first vacant seat I saw, at a table for two, and waited.

I do not know how long I waited and I rather wonder, until today, what I could possibly have looked like. Whatever I looked like, I frightened the waitress who shortly appeared, and the moment she appeared all of my fury flowed towards her. I hated her for her white face, and for her great, astounded, frightened eyes. I felt that if she found a black man so frightening I would make her fright worth-while.

She did not ask me what I wanted, but repeated, as though she had learned it somewhere, "We don't serve Negroes here." She did not say it with the blunt, decisive hostility to which I had grown so accustomed, but, rather, with a note of apology in her voice, and fear. This made me colder and more murderous than ever. I felt I had to do something with my hands. I wanted her to come close enough for me to get her neck between my hands.

So I pretended not to have understood her, hoping to draw her closer. And she did step a very short step closer, with her pencil poised incongruously over her pad, and repeated the formula: ". . . don't serve Negroes here."

Somehow, with the repetition of that phrase, which was already ringing in my head like a thousand bells of a nightmare, I realized that she would never come any closer and that I would have to strike from a distance. There was nothing on the table but an ordinary water-mug half full of water, and I picked this up and hurled it with all my strength at her. She ducked and it missed her and shattered against the mirror behind the bar. And, with that sound, my frozen blood abruptly thawed, I returned from wherever I had been, I *saw,* for the first time, the restaurant, the people with their mouths open, already, as it seemed to me, rising as one man, and I realized what I had done, and where I was, and I was frightened. I rose and began running for the door. A round, potbellied man grabbed me by the nape of the neck just as I reached the doors and began to beat me about the face. I kicked him and got loose and ran into the streets. My friend whispered, *"Run!"* and I ran.

My friend stayed outside the restaurant long enough to misdirect my pursuers and the police, who arrived, he told me, at once. I do not know what I said to him when he came to my room that night. I could not have said much. I felt, in the oddest, most awful way, that I had somehow betrayed him. I lived it over and over and over again, the way one relives an automobile accident after it has happened and one finds oneself alone and safe. I could not get over two facts, both equally difficult for the imagination to grasp, and one was that I could have been murdered. But the other was that I had been ready to commit murder. I saw nothing very clearly but I did see this: that my life, my *real* life, was in danger, and not from anything other people might do but from the hatred I carried in my own heart.

2

I had returned home around the second week in June—in great haste because it seemed that my father's death and my mother's confinement were both but a matter of hours. In the case of my mother, it soon became clear that she had simply made a miscalculation. This had always been her tendency and I don't believe that a single one of us arrived in the world, or has since arrived anywhere else, on time. But none of us dawdled so intolerably about the business of being born as did my baby sister. We sometimes amused ourselves, during those endless, stifling weeks, by picturing the baby sitting within in the safe, warm dark, bitterly regretting the necessity of becoming a part of our chaos and stubbornly putting it off as long as possible. I understood her perfectly and congratulated her on showing such good sense so soon. Death, however, sat as purposefully at my father's bedside as life stirred within my mother's womb and it was harder to understand why he so lingered in that long shadow. It seemed that he had bent, and for a long time, too, all of his energies towards dying. Now death was ready for him but my father held back.

All of Harlem, indeed, seemed to be infected by waiting. I had never before known it to be so violently still. Racial tensions throughout this country were exacerbated during the early years of the war, partly because the labor market brought together hundreds of thousands of ill-prepared people and partly because Negro soldiers, regardless of where they were born, received their military training in the south. What happened in defense plants and army camps had repercussions, naturally, in every Negro ghetto. The situation in Harlem had grown bad enough for clergymen, policemen, educators, politicians, and social workers to assert in one breath that there was no "crime wave" and to offer, in the very next breath, suggestions as to how to combat it. These suggestions always seemed to involve playgrounds, too. Playground or not, crime wave or not, the Harlem police force had been augmented in March, and the unrest grew—perhaps, in fact, partly as a result of the ghetto's instinctive hatred of policemen. Perhaps the most revealing news item, out of the steady parade of reports of muggings, stabbings, shootings, assaults, gang wars, and accusations of police brutality is the item concerning six Negro girls who set upon a white girl in the subway because, as they all too accurately put it, she was stepping on their toes. Indeed she was, all over the nation.

I had never before been so aware of policemen, on foot, on horseback, on corners, everywhere, always two by two. Nor had I ever been so aware of small knots of people. They were on stoops and on corners and in doorways, and what was striking about them, I think, was that they did not seem to be talking. Never, when I passed these groups, did the usual sound of a curse or a laugh ring out and neither did there seem to be any hum of gossip. There was certainly, on the other hand, occurring between them communication extraordinarily intense. Another thing that was striking was the unexpected diversity of the people who made up these groups. Usually, for example, one would see a group of sharpies standing on the street corner, jiving the passing chicks; or a group of older men, usually, for some reason, in the vicinity of a barber shop, discussing baseball scores, or the numbers, or making rather chilling observations about women they had known. Women, in a general way, tended to be seen less often together—unless they were church women, or very young girls, or prostitutes met together for an unprofessional instant. But that summer I saw the strangest combinations:

large, respectable, churchly matrons standing on the stoops or the corners with their hair tied up, together with a girl in sleazy satin whose face bore the marks of gin and the razor, or heavyset, abrupt, no-nonsense older men, in company with the most disreputable and fanatical "race" men, or these same "race" men with the sharpies, or these sharpies with the churchly women. Seventh Day Adventists and Methodists and Spiritualists seemed to be hobnobbing with Holyrollers and they were all, alike, entangled with the most flagrant disbelievers; something heavy in their stance seemed to indicate that they had all, incredibly, seen a common vision, and on each face there seemed to be the same strange, bitter shadow.

The churchly women and the matter-of-fact, no-nonsense men had children in the Army. The sleazy girls they talked to had lovers there, the sharpies and the "race" men had friends and brothers there. It would have demanded an unquestioning patriotism, happily as uncommon in this country as it is undesirable, for these people not to have been disturbed by the bitter letters they received, by the newspaper stories they read, not to have been enraged by the posters, then to be found all over New York, which described the Japanese as "yellowbellied Japs." It was only the "race" men, to be sure, who spoke ceaselessly of being revenged—how this vengeance was to be exacted was not clear—for the indignities and dangers suffered by Negro boys in uniform; but everybody felt a directionless, hopeless bitterness, as well as that panic which can scarcely be suppressed when one knows that a human being one loves is beyond one's reach, and in danger. This helplessness and this gnawing uneasiness does something, at length, to even the toughest mind. Perhaps the best way to sum all this up is to say that the people I knew felt, mainly, a peculiar kind of relief when they knew that their boys were being shipped out of the south, to do battle overseas. It was, perhaps, like feeling that the most dangerous part of a dangerous journey had been passed and that now, even if death should come, it would come with honor and without the complicity of their countrymen. Such a death would be, in short, a fact with which one could hope to live.

It was on the 28th of July, which I believe was a Wednesday, that I visited my father for the first time during his illness and for the last time in his life. The moment I saw him I knew why I had put off this visit so long. I had told my mother that I did not want to see him because I hated him. But this was not true. It was only that I *had* hated him and I wanted to hold on to this hatred. I did not want to look on him as a ruin: it was not a ruin I had hated. I imagine that one of the reasons people cling to their hates so stubbornly is because they sense, once hate is gone, that they will be forced to deal with pain.

We traveled out to him, his older sister and myself, to what seemed to be the very end of a very Long Island. It was hot and dusty and we wrangled, my aunt and I, all the way out, over the fact that I had recently begun to smoke and, as she said, to give myself airs. But I knew that she wrangled with me because she could not bear to face the fact of her brother's dying. Neither could I endure the reality of her despair, her unstated bafflement as to what had happened to her brother's life, and her own. So we wrangled and I smoked and from time to time she fell into a heavy reverie. Covertly, I watched her face, which was the face of an old woman; it had fallen in, the eyes were sunken and lightless; soon she would be dying, too.

In my childhood—it had not been so long ago—I had thought her beautiful. She had been quick-witted and quick-moving and very generous with all the children and each of her visits had been an event. At one time one of my brothers and myself had thought of running away to live with her. Now she could no longer produce out of her handbag some unexpected and yet familiar delight. She made me feel pity and re-vulsion and fear. It was awful to realize that she no longer caused me to feel affection. The closer we came to the hospital the more querulous she became and at the same time, naturally, grew more dependent on me. Between pity and guilt and fear I began to feel that there was another me trapped in my skull like a jack-in-the-box who might escape my control at any moment and fill the air with screaming.

She began to cry the moment we entered the room and she saw him lying there, all shriveled and still, like a little black monkey. The great, gleaming apparatus which fed him and would have compelled him to be still even if he had been able to move brought to mind, not beneficence, but torture; the tubes entering his arm made me think of pictures I had seen when a child, of Gulliver, tied down by the pygmies on that island. My aunt wept and wept, there was a whistling sound in my father's throat; nothing was said; he could not speak. I wanted to take his hand, to say something. But I do not know what I could have said, even if he could have heard me. He was not really in that room with us, he had at last really embarked on his journey; and though my aunt told me that he said he was going to meet Jesus, I did not hear anything except that whistling in his throat. The doctor came back and we left, into that unbearable train again, and home. In the morning came the telegram saying that he was dead. Then the house was suddenly full of relatives, friends, hysteria, and confusion and I quickly left my mother and the children to the care of those impressive women, who, in Negro communities at least, automatically appear at times of bereavement armed with lotions, proverbs, and patience, and an ability to cook. I went downtown. By the time I re-turned, later the same day, my mother had been carried to the hospital and the baby had been born.

3

For my father's funeral I had nothing black to wear and this posed a nagging problem all day long. It was one of those problems, simple, or impossible of solution, to which the mind insanely clings in order to avoid the mind's real trouble. I spent most of that day at the downtown apartment of a girl I knew, celebrating my birthday with whiskey and wondering what to wear that night. When planning a birthday celebration one naturally does not expect that it will be up against competition from a funeral and this girl had anticipated taking me out that night, for a big dinner and a night club after-wards. Sometime during the course of that long day we decided that we would go out anyway, when my father's funeral service was over. I imagine I decided it, since, as the funeral hour approached, it became clearer and clearer to me that I would not know what to do with myself when it was over. The girl, stifling her very lively concern as to the possible effects of the whiskey on one of my father's chief mourners, concen-trated on being conciliatory and practically helpful. She found a black shirt for me some-where and ironed it and, dressed in the darkest pants and jacket I owned, and slightly drunk, I made my way to my father's funeral.

The chapel was full, but not packed, and very quiet. There were, mainly, my fa-ther's relatives, and his children, and here and there I saw faces I had not seen since childhood, the faces of my father's one-time friends. They were very dark and solemn now, seeming somehow to suggest that they had known all along that something like this would happen. Chief among the mourners was my aunt, who had quarreled with my father all his life; by which I do not mean to suggest that her mourning was insincere or that she had not loved him. I suppose that she was one of the few people in the world who had, and their incessant quarreling proved precisely the strength of the tie that bound them. The only other person in the world, as far as I knew, whose relationship to my father rivaled my aunt's in depth was my mother, who was not there.

It seemed to me, of course, that it was a very long funeral. But it was, if anything, a rather shorter funeral than most, nor, since there were no overwhelming, uncontrollable expressions of grief, could it be called—if I dare to use the word—successful. The minister who preached my father's funeral sermon was one of the few my father had still been seeing as he neared his end. He presented to us in his sermon a man whom none of us had ever seen—a man thoughtful, patient, and forbearing, a Christian inspiration to all who knew him, and a model for his children. And no doubt the children, in their disturbed and guilty state, were almost ready to believe this; he had been remote enough to be anything and, anyway, the shock of the incontrovertible, that it was really our father lying up there in that casket, prepared the mind for anything. His sister moaned and this grief-stricken moaning was taken as corroboration. The other faces held a dark, non-committal thoughtfulness. This was not the man they had known, but they had scarcely expected to be confronted with *him;* this was, in a sense deeper than questions of fact, the man they had not known, and the man they had not known may have been the real one. The real man, whoever he had been, had suffered and now he was dead: this was all that was sure and all that mattered now. Every man in the chapel hoped that when his hour came he, too, would be eulogized, which is to say forgiven, and that all of his lapses, greeds, errors, and strayings from the truth would be invested with coherence and looked upon with charity. This was perhaps the last thing human beings could give each other and it was what they demanded, after all, of the Lord. Only the Lord saw the midnight tears, only He was present when one of His children, moaning and wringing hands, paced up and down the room. When one slapped one's child in anger the recoil in the heart reverberated through heaven and became part of the pain of the universe. And when the children were hungry and sullen and distrustful and one watched them, daily, growing wilder, and further away, and running headlong into danger, it was the Lord who knew what the charged heart endured as the strap was laid to the backside; the Lord alone who knew what one *would* have said if one had had, like the Lord, the gift of the living word. It was the Lord who knew of the impossibility every parent in that room faced: how to prepare the child for the day when the child would be despised and how to *create* in the child—by what means?—a stronger antidote to this poison than one had found for oneself. The avenues, side streets, bars, billiard halls, hospitals, police stations, and even the playgrounds of Harlem—not to mention the houses of correction, the jails, and the morgue—testified to the potency of the poison while remaining silent as to the efficacy of whatever antidote, irresistibly raising the question of whether or not such an antidote existed; raising, which was worse, the question of whether or not an antidote was desirable; perhaps poison should be fought with poison. With these several schisms in the mind and with more terrors in the heart than could be named, it was better not to judge the man who had gone down under an impossible burden. It was better to remember: *Thou knowest this man's fall; but thou knowest not his wrassling.*

While the preacher talked and I watched the children—years of changing their diapers, scrubbing them, slapping them, taking them to school, and scolding them had had the perhaps inevitable result of making me love them, though I am not sure I knew this then—my mind was busily breaking out with a rash of disconnected impressions. Snatches of popular songs, indecent jokes, bits of books I had read, movie sequences, faces, voices, political issues—I thought I was going mad; all these impressions suspended, as it were, in the solution of the faint nausea produced in me by the heat and liquor. For a moment I had the impression that my alcoholic breath, inefficiently disguised with chewing gum, filled the entire chapel. Then someone began singing one of my father's favorite songs and, abruptly, I was with him, sitting on his knee, in the hot, enormous, crowded church which was the first church we attended. It was the Abyssinia Baptist Church on 138th Street. We had not gone there long. With this image, a host of others came. I had forgotten, in the rage of my growing up, how proud my father had been of me when I was little. Apparently, I had had a voice and my father had liked to show me off before the members of the church. I had forgotten what he had looked like when he was pleased but now I remembered that he had always been grinning with pleasure when my solos ended. I even remembered certain expressions on his face when he teased my mother—had he loved her? I would never know. And when had it all begun to change? For now it seemed that he had not always been cruel. I remembered being taken for a haircut and scraping my knee on the footrest of the barber's chair and I remembered my father's face as he soothed my crying and applied the stinging iodine. Then I remembered our fights, fights which had been of the worst possible kind because my technique had been silence.

I remembered the one time in all our life together when we had really spoken to each other.

It was on a Sunday and it must have been shortly before I left home. We were walking, just the two of us, in our usual silence, to or from church. I was in high school and had been doing a lot of writing and I was, at about this time, the editor of the high school magazine. But I had also been a Young Minister and had been preaching from the pulpit. Lately, I had been taking fewer engagements and preached as rarely as possible. It was said in the church, quite truthfully, that I was "cooling off."

My father asked me abruptly, "You'd rather write than preach, wouldn't you?"

I was astonished at his question—because it was a real question. I answered, "Yes."

That was all we said. It was awful to remember that that was all we had *ever* said.

The casket now was opened and the mourners were being led up the aisle to look for the last time on the deceased. The assumption was that the family was too overcome with grief to be allowed to make this journey alone and I watched while my aunt was led to the casket and, muffled in black, and shaking, led back to her seat. I disapproved of forcing the children to look on their dead father, considering that the shock of his death, or, more truthfully, the shock of death as a reality, was already a little more than a child could bear, but my judgment in this matter had been overruled and there they were, bewildered and frightened and very small, being led, one by one, to the casket. But there is also something very gallant about children at such moments. It has something to do with their silence and gravity and with the fact that one cannot help them. Their legs, somehow, seem *exposed,* so that it is at once incredible and terribly clear that their legs are all they have to hold them up.

I had not wanted to go to the casket myself and I certainly had not wished to be led there, but there was no way of avoiding either of these forms. One of the deacons led me up and I looked on my father's face. I cannot say that it looked like him at all. His blackness had been equivocated by powder and there was no suggestion in that casket of what his power had or could have been. He was simply an old man dead, and it was hard to believe that he had ever given anyone either joy or pain. Yet, his life filled that room. Further up the avenue his wife was holding his newborn child. Life and death so close together, and love and hatred, and right and wrong, said something to me which I did not want to hear concerning man, concerning the life of man.

After the funeral, while I was downtown desperately celebrating my birthday, a Negro soldier, in the lobby of the Hotel Braddock, got into a fight with a white policeman over a Negro girl. Negro girls, white policemen, in or out of uniform, and Negro males—in or out of uniform—were part of the furniture of the lobby of the Hotel Braddock and this was certainly not the first time such an incident had occurred. It was destined, however, to receive an unprecedented publicity, for the fight between the policeman and the soldier ended with the shooting of the soldier. Rumor, flowing immediately to the streets outside, stated that the soldier had been shot in the back, an instantaneous and revealing invention, and that the soldier had died protecting a Negro woman. The facts were somewhat different—for example, the soldier had not been shot in the back, and was not dead, and the girl seems to have been as dubious a symbol of womanhood as her white counterpart in Georgia usually is, but no one was interested in the facts. They preferred the invention because this invention expressed and corroborated their hates and fears so perfectly. It is just as well to remember that people are always doing this. Perhaps many of those legends, including Christianity, to which the world clings began their conquest of the world with just some such concerted surrender to distortion. The effect, in Harlem, of this particular legend was like the effect of a lit match in a tin of gasoline. The mob gathered before the doors of the Hotel Braddock simply began to swell and to spread in every direction, and Harlem exploded.

The mob did not cross the ghetto lines. It would have been easy, for example, to have gone over to Morningside Park on the west side or to have crossed the Grand Central railroad tracks at 125th Street on the east side, to wreak havoc in white neighborhoods. The mob seems to have been mainly interested in something more potent and real than the white face, that is, in white power, and the principal damage done during the riot of the summer of 1943 was to white business establishments in Harlem. It might have been a far bloodier story, of course, if, at the hour the riot began, these establishments had still been open. From the Hotel Braddock the mob fanned out, east and west along 125th Street, and for the entire length of Lenox, Seventh, and Eighth avenues. Along each of these avenues, and along each major side street—116th, 125th, 135th, and so on—bars, stores, pawnshops, restaurants, even little luncheonettes had been smashed open and entered and looted—looted, it might be added, with more haste than efficiency. The shelves really looked as though a bomb had struck them. Cans of beans and soup and dog food, along with toilet paper, corn flakes, sardines and milk tumbled every which way, and abandoned cash registers and cases of beer leaned crazily out of the splintered windows and were strewn along the avenues. Sheets, blankets, and clothing of every description formed a kind of path, as though people had dropped them while running. I truly had not realized that Harlem *had* so many stores until I saw them all smashed open; the first time the word *wealth* ever entered my mind in relation to Harlem was when I saw it scattered in the streets. But one's first, incongruous impression of plenty was countered immediately by an impression of waste. None of this was doing anybody any good. It would have been better to have left the plate glass as it had been and the goods lying in the stores.

It would have been better, but it would also have been intolerable, for Harlem had needed something to smash. To smash something is the ghetto's chronic need. Most of the time it is the members of the ghetto who smash each other, and themselves. But as long as the ghetto walls are standing there will always come a moment when these outlets do not work. That summer, for example, it was not enough to get into a fight on Lenox Avenue, or curse out one's cronies in the barber shops. If ever, indeed, the violence which fills Harlem's churches, pool halls, and bars erupts outward in a more direct fashion, Harlem and its citizens are likely to vanish in an apocalyptic flood. That this is not likely to happen is due to a great many reasons, most hidden and powerful among them the Negro's real relation to the white American. This relation prohibits, simply, anything as uncomplicated and satisfactory as pure hatred. In order really to hate white people, one has to blot so much out of the mind—and the heart—that this hatred itself becomes an exhausting and self-destructive pose. But this does not mean, on the other hand, that love comes easily: the white world is too powerful, too complacent, too ready with gratuitous humiliation, and, above all, too ignorant and too innocent for that. One is absolutely forced to make perpetual qualifications and one's own reactions are always canceling each other out. It is this, really, which has driven so many people mad, both white and black. One is always in the position of having to decide between amputation and gangrene. Amputation is swift but time may prove that the amputation was not necessary—or one may delay the amputation too long. Gangrene is slow, but it is impossible to be sure that one is reading one's symptoms right. The idea of going through life as a cripple is more than one can bear, and equally unbearable is the risk of swelling up slowly, in agony, with poison. And the trouble, finally, is that the risks are real even if the choices do not exist.

"But as for me and my house," my father had said, "we will serve the Lord." I wondered, as we drove him to a resting place, what this line had meant for him. I had heard him preach it many times. I had preached it once myself, proudly giving it an interpretation different from my father's. Now the whole thing came back to me, as though my father and I were on our way to Sunday school and I were memorizing the golden text: *And if it seem evil unto you to serve the Lord, choose you this day whom you will serve; whether the gods which your fathers served that were on the other side of the flood, or the gods of the Amorites, in whose land ye dwell: but as for me and my house, we will serve the Lord.* I suspected in these familiar lines a meaning which had never been there for me before. All of my father's texts and songs, which I had decided were meaningless, were arranged before me at his death like empty bottles, waiting to hold the meaning which life would give them for me. This was his legacy: nothing is ever escaped. That bleakly memorable morning I hated the unbelievable streets and the Negroes and whites who had, equally, made them that way. But I knew that it was folly, as my father would have said, this bitterness was folly. It was necessary to hold on to the things that mattered. The dead man mattered, the new life mattered; blackness and whiteness did not matter; to believe that they did was to acquiesce in one's own destruction. Hatred, which could destroy so much, never failed to destroy the man who hated and this was an immutable law.

It began to seem that one would have to hold in the mind forever two ideas which seemed to be in opposition. The first idea was acceptance, the acceptance, totally without rancor, of life as it is, and men as they are: in the light of this idea, it goes without saying that injustice is a commonplace. But this did not mean that one could be complacent, for the second idea was of equal power: that one must never, in one's own life, accept these injustices as commonplace but must fight them with all one's strength. This fight begins, however, in the heart and it now had been laid to my charge to keep my own heart free of hatred and despair. This intimation made my heart heavy and, now that my father was irrecoverable, I wished that he had been beside me so that I could have searched his face for the answers which only the future would give me now.

(1955)

A SAMPLING OF CONTEMPORARY ESSAYS

T O M   W O L F E

[b. 1931]

The Right Stuff

What an extraordinary grim stretch that had been . . . and yet thereafter Pete and Jane would keep running into pilots from other Navy bases, from the Air Force, from the Marines, who had been through their own extraordinary grim stretches. There was an Air Force pilot named Mike Collins, a nephew of former Army Chief of Staff J. Lawton Collins. Mike Collins had undergone eleven weeks of combat training at Nellis Air Force Base, near Las Vegas, and in that eleven weeks twenty-two of his fellow trainees had died in accidents, which was an extraordinary rate of two per week. Then there was a test pilot, Bill Bridgeman. In 1952, when Bridgeman was flying at Edwards Air Force Base, sixty-two Air Force pilots died in the course of thirty-six weeks of training, an extraordinary rate of 1.7 per week. Those figures were for fighter-pilot trainees only; they did not include the test pilots, Bridgeman's own confreres, who were dying quite regularly enough.

Extraordinary, to be sure; except that every veteran of flying small high-performance jets seemed to have experienced these bad strings.

In time, the Navy would compile statistics showing that for a career Navy pilot, i.e., one who intended to keep flying for twenty years as Conrad did, there was a 23 percent probability that he would die in an aircraft accident. This did not even include combat deaths, since the military did not classify death in combat as accidental. Furthermore, there was a better than even chance, a 56 percent probability, to be exact, that at some point a career Navy pilot would have to eject from his aircraft and attempt to come down by parachute. In the era of jet fighters, ejection meant being exploded out of the cockpit by a nitroglycerine charge, like a human cannonball. The ejection itself was so hazardous—men lost knees, arms, and their lives on the rim of the cockpit or had the skin torn off their faces when they hit the "wall" of air outside—that many pilots chose to wrestle their aircraft to the ground rather than try it . . . and died that way instead.

The statistics were not secret, but neither were they widely known, having been eased into print rather obliquely in a medical journal. No pilot, and certainly no pilot's wife, had any need of the statistics in order to know the truth, however. The funerals took care of that in the most dramatic way possible. Sometimes, when the young wife of a fighter pilot would have a little reunion with the girls she went to school with, an odd fact would dawn on her: *they* have not been going to funerals. And then Jane Conrad would look at Pete . . . Princeton, Class of 1953 . . . Pete had already worn his great dark sepulchral bridge coat more than most boys of the Class of '53 had worn their tuxedos. How many of those happy young men had buried more than a dozen friends, comrades, and co-workers? (Lost through violent death in the execution of everyday duties.) At the time, the 1950's, students from Princeton took great pride in going into what they considered highly competitive, aggressive pursuits, jobs on Wall Street, on Madison Avenue, and at magazines such as *Time* and *Newsweek*. There was much fashionably brutish talk of what "dog-eat-dog" and "cutthroat" competition they found there; but in the rare instances when one of these young men died on the job, it was likely to be from choking on a chunk of Chateaubriand, while otherwise blissfully boiled, in an expense-account restaurant in Manhattan. How many would have gone to work, or stayed at work, on cutthroat Madison Avenue if there had been a 23 percent chance, nearly one chance in four, of dying from it? Gentlemen, we're having this little problem with chronic violent death . . .

And yet was there any basic way in which Pete (or Wally Schirra or Jim Lovell or any of the rest of them) was different from other college boys his age? There didn't seem to be, other than his love of flying. Pete's father was a Philadelphia stockbroker who in Pete's earliest years had a house in the Main Line suburbs, a limousine, and a chauffeur. The Depression eliminated the terrific brokerage business, the house, the car, and the servants; and by and by his parents were divorced and his father moved to Florida. Perhaps because his father had been an observation balloonist in the First World War—an adventurous business, since the balloons were prized targets of enemy aircraft—Pete was fascinated by flying. He went to Princeton on the Holloway Plan, a scholarship program left over from the Second World War in which a student trained with midshipmen from the Naval Academy during the summers and graduated with a commission in the Regular Navy. So Pete graduated, received his commission, married Jane, and headed off to Pensacola, Florida, for flight training.

Then came the difference, looking back on it.

A young man might go into military flight training believing that he was entering some sort of technical school in which he was simply going to acquire a certain set of skills. Instead, he found himself all at once enclosed in a fraternity. And in this fraternity, even though it was military, men were not rated by their outward rank as ensigns, lieutenants, commanders, or whatever. No, herein the world was divided into those who had it and those who did not. This quality, that *it,* was never named, however, nor was it talked about in any way.

As to just what this ineffable quality was . . . well, it obviously involved bravery. But it was not bravery in the simple sense of being willing to risk your life. The idea seemed to be that any fool could do that, if that was all that was required, just as any fool could throw away his life in the process. No, the idea here (in the all-enclosing fraternity) seemed to be that a man should have the ability to go up in a hurtling piece of machinery and put his hide on the line and then have the moxie, the reflexes, the experience, the coolness, to pull it back in the last yawning moment—and then to go up again *the next day,* and the next day, and every next day, even if the series should prove infinite—and, ultimately, in its best expression, do so in a cause that means something to thousands, to a people, a nation, to humanity, to God. Nor was there *a test* to show whether or not a pilot had this righteous quality. There was, instead, a seemingly infinite series of tests. A career in flying was like climbing one of those ancient Babylonian pyramids made up of a dizzy progression of steps and ledges, a ziggurat, a pyramid extraordinarily high and steep; and the idea was to prove at every foot of the way up that pyramid that you were one of the elected and anointed ones who had *the right stuff* and could move higher and higher and even—ultimately, God willing, one day— that you might be able to join that special few at the very top, that elite who had the capacity to bring tears to men's eyes, the very Brotherhood of the Right Stuff itself.

None of this was to be mentioned, and yet it was acted out in a way that a young man could not fail to understand. When a new flight (i.e., a class) of trainees arrived at Pensacola, they were brought into an auditorium for a little lecture. An officer would tell them: "Take a look at the man on either side of you." Quite a few actually swiveled their heads this way and that, in the interest of appearing diligent. Then the officer would say: "One of the three of you is not going to make it!"—meaning, not get his wings. That was the opening theme, the *motif* of primary training. We already know that one-third of you do not have the right stuff—it only remains to find out who.

Furthermore, that was the way it turned out. At every level in one's progress up that staggeringly high pyramid, the world was once more divided into those men who had the right stuff to continue the climb and those who had to be *left behind* in the most obvious way. Some were eliminated in the course of the opening classroom work, as either not smart enough or not hardworking enough, and were left behind. Then came the basic flight instruction, in single-engine, propeller-driven trainers, and a few more— even though the military tried to make this stage easy—were washed out and left behind. Then came more demanding levels, one after the other, formation flying, instrument flying, jet training, all-weather flying, gunnery, and at each level more were washed out and left behind. By this point easily a third of the original candidates had been, indeed, eliminated . . . from the ranks of those who might prove to have the right stuff.

In the Navy, in addition to the stages that Air Force trainees went through, the neophyte always had waiting for him, out in the ocean, a certain grim gray slab; namely, the deck of an aircraft carrier; and with it perhaps the most difficult routine in military flying, carrier landings. He was shown films about it, he heard lectures about it, and he knew that carrier landings were hazardous. He first practiced touching down on the shape of a flight deck painted on an airfield. He was instructed to touch down and gun right off. This was safe enough—the shape didn't move, at least—but it could do terrible things to, let us say, the gyroscope of the soul. *That shape!—it's so damned small!* And more candidates were washed out and left behind. Then came the day, without warning, when those who remained were sent out over the ocean for the first of many days of reckoning with the slab. The first day was always a clear day with little wind and a calm sea. The carrier was so steady that it seemed, from up there in the air, to

be resting on pilings, and the candidate usually made his first carrier landing success-
fully, with relief and even *élan*. Many young candidates looked like terrific aviators up
to that very point—and it was not until they were actually standing on the carrier deck
that they first began to wonder if they had the proper stuff, after all. In the training film
the flight deck was a grand piece of gray geometry, perilous, to be sure, but an amaz-
ing abstract shape as one looks down upon it on the screen. And yet once the newcomer's two feet were on it . . . *Geometry*—my God, man, this is a . . . skillet! It *heaved*,
it moved up and down underneath his feet, it pitched up, it pitched down, it rolled to
port (this great beast *rolled!*) and it rolled to starboard, as the ship moved into the wind
and, therefore, into the waves, and the wind kept sweeping across, sixty feet up in the
air out in the open sea, and there were no railings whatsoever. This was a *skillet!*—a
frying pan!—a short-order grill!—not gray but black, smeared with skid marks from
one end to the other and glistening with pools of hydraulic fluid and the occasional
jet-fuel slick, all of it still hot, sticky, greasy, runny, virulent from God knows what
traumas—still ablaze!—consumed in detonations, explosions, flames, combustion,
roars, shrieks, whines, blasts, horrible shudders, fracturing impacts, as little men in
screaming red and yellow and purple and green shirts with black Mickey Mouse helmets over their ears skittered about on the surface as if for their very lives (you've said
it now!), hooking fighter planes onto the catapult shuttles so that they can explode their
afterburners and be slung off the deck in a red-mad fury with a *kaboom!* that pounds
through the entire deck—a procedure that seems absolutely controlled, orderly, sublime, however, compared to what he is about to watch as aircraft return to the ship for
what is known in the engineering stoicisms of the military as "recovery and arrest."
To say that an F-4 was coming back onto this heaving barbecue from out of the sky
at a speed of 135 knots . . . that might have been the truth in the training lecture, but
it did not begin to get across the idea of what the newcomer saw from the deck itself,
because it created the notion that perhaps the plane was gliding in. On the deck one
knew differently! As the aircraft came closer and the carrier heaved on into the waves
and the plane's speed did not diminish and the deck did not grow steady—indeed, it
pitched up and down five or ten feet per greasy heave—one experienced a neural alarm
that no lecture could have prepared him for: This is not an *airplane* coming toward me,
it is a brick with some poor sonofabitch riding it *(someone much like myself!),* and it is
not *gliding,* it is *falling,* a fifty-thousand-pound brick, headed not for a stripe on the deck
but for *me*—and with a horrible *smash!* it hits the skillet, and with a blur of momen-
tum as big as a freight train's it hurtles toward the far end of the deck—another blind-
ing storm!—another roar as the pilot pushes the throttle up to full military power and
another smear of rubber screams out over the skillet—and this is nominal!—quite
okay!—for a wire stretched across the deck has grabbed the hook on the end of the
plane as it hit the deck tail down, and the smash was the rest of the fifteen-ton brute
slamming onto the deck, as it tripped up, so that it is now straining against the wire at
full throttle, in case it hadn't held and the plane had "boltered" off the end of the deck
and had to struggle up into the air again. And already the Mickey Mouse helmets are
running toward the fiery monster . . .

And the candidate, looking on, begins to *feel* that great heaving sun-blazing death-
board of a deck wallowing in his own vestibular system—and suddenly he finds himself backed up against his own limits. He ends up going to the flight surgeon with so-
called conversion symptoms. Overnight he develops blurred vision or numbness in his
hands and feet or sinusitis so severe that he cannot tolerate changes in altitude. On one

level the symptom is real. He really cannot see too well or use his fingers or stand the pain. But somewhere in his subconscious he knows it is a plea and a beg-off; he shows not the slightest concern (the flight surgeon notes) that the condition might be permanent and affect him in whatever life awaits him outside the arena of the right stuff.

Those who remained, those who qualified for carrier duty—and even more so those who later on qualified for *night* carrier duty—began to feel a bit like Gideon's warriors. *So many have been left behind!* The young warriors were now treated to a deathly sweet and quite unmentionable sight. They could gaze at length upon the crushed and wilted pariahs who had washed out. They could inspect those who did not have that righteous stuff.

The military did not have very merciful instincts. Rather than packing up these poor souls and sending them home, the Navy, like the Air Force and the Marines, would try to make use of them in some other role, such as flight controller. So the washout has to keep taking classes with the rest of his group, even though he can no longer touch an airplane. He sits there in the classes staring at sheets of paper with cataracts of sheer human mortification over his eyes while the rest steal looks at him . . . this man reduced to an ant, this untouchable, this poor sonofabitch. And in what test had he been found wanting? Why, it seemed to be nothing less than *manhood* itself. Naturally, this was never mentioned, either. Yet there it was. *Manliness, manhood, manly courage* . . . there was something ancient, primordial, irresistible about the challenge of this stuff, no matter what a sophisticated and rational age one might think he lived in.

Perhaps because it could not be talked about, the subject began to take on superstitious and even mystical outlines. A man either had it or he didn't! There was no such thing as having *most* of it. Moreover, it could blow at any seam. One day a man would be ascending the pyramid at a terrific clip, and the next—bingo!—he would reach his own limits in the most unexpected way. Conrad and Schirra met an Air Force pilot who had had a great pal at Tyndall Air Force Base in Florida. This man had been the budding ace of the training class; he had flown the hottest fighter-style trainer, the T-38, like a dream; and then he began the routine step of being checked out in the T-33. The T-33 was not nearly as hot an aircraft as the T-38; it was essentially the old P-80 jet fighter. It had an exceedingly small cockpit. The pilot could barely move his shoulders. It was the sort of airplane of which everybody said, "You don't get into it, you *wear* it." Once inside a T-33 cockpit this man, this budding ace, developed claustrophobia of the most paralyzing sort. He tried everything to overcome it. He even went to a psychiatrist, which was a serious mistake for a military officer if his superiors learned of it. But nothing worked. He was shifted over to flying jet transports, such as the C-135. Very demanding and necessary aircraft they were, too, and he was still spoken of as an excellent pilot. But as everyone knew—and, again, it was never explained in so many words—only those who were assigned to fighter squadrons, the "fighter jocks," as they called each other with a self-satisfied irony, remained in the true fraternity. Those assigned to transports were not humiliated like washouts—*somebody* had to fly those planes—nevertheless, they, too, had been *left behind* for lack of the right stuff.

Or a man could go for a routine physical one fine day, feeling like a million dollars, and be grounded for *fallen arches*. It happened!—just like that! (And try raising them.) Or for breaking his wrist and losing only *part* of its mobility. Or for a minor deterioration of eyesight, or for any of hundreds of reasons that would make no difference to a man in an ordinary occupation. As a result all fighter jocks began looking upon doctors as their natural enemies. Going to see a flight surgeon was a no-gain proposition; a pilot could only hold his own or lose in the doctor's office. To be grounded for a medical reason was no humiliation, looked at objectively. But it was a humiliation, nonetheless!—for it meant you no longer had that indefinable, unutterable, integral stuff. (It could blow at *any* seam.)

All the hot young fighter jocks began trying to test the limits themselves in a superstitious way. They were like believing Presbyterians of a century before who used to probe their own experience to see if they were truly among *the elect*. When a fighter pilot was in training, whether in the Navy or the Air Force, his superiors were continually spelling out strict rules for him, about the use of the aircraft and conduct in the sky. They repeatedly forbade so-called hot-dog stunts, such as outside loops, buzzing, flat-hatting, hedgehopping and flying under bridges. But somehow one got the message that the man who truly *had* it could ignore those rules—not that he should make a point of it, but that he *could*—and that after all there was only one way to find out—and that in some strange unofficial way, peeking through his fingers, his instructor halfway expected him to challenge all the limits. They would give a lecture about how a pilot should never fly without a good solid breakfast—eggs, bacon, toast, and so forth—because if he tried to fly with his blood-sugar level too low, it could impair his alertness. Naturally, the next day every hot dog in the unit would get up and have a breakfast consisting of one cup of black coffee and take off and go up into a vertical climb until the weight of the ship exactly canceled out the upward pull of the engine and his air speed was zero, and he would hang there for one thick adrenal instant— and then fall like a rock, until one of three things happened: he keeled over nose first and regained his aerodynamics and all was well, he went into a spin and fought his way out of it, or he went into a spin and had to eject or crunch it, which was always supremely possible.

Likewise, "hassling"—mock dogfighting—was strictly forbidden, and so naturally young fighter jocks could hardly wait to go up in, say, a pair of F-100s and start the duel by making a pass at each other at 800 miles an hour, the winner being the pilot who could slip in behind the other one and get locked in on his tail ("wax his tail"), and it was not uncommon for some eager jock to try too tight an outside turn and have his engine flame out, whereupon, unable to restart it, he has to eject . . . and he shakes his fist at the victor as he floats down by parachute and his half-a-million-dollar aircraft goes *kaboom!* on the palmetto grass or the desert floor, and he starts thinking about how he can get together with the other guy back at the base in time for the two of them to get their stories straight before the investigation: "I don't know what happened, sir. I was pulling up after a target run, and it just flamed out on me." Hassling was forbidden, and hassling that led to the destruction of an aircraft was a serious court-martial offense, and the man's superiors knew that the engine hadn't *just flamed out,* but every unofficial impulse on the base seemed to be saying: "Hell, we wouldn't give you a nickel for a pilot who hasn't done some crazy rat-racing like that. It's all part of the right stuff."

The other side of this impulse showed up in the reluctance of the young jocks to admit it when they had maneuvered themselves into a bad corner they couldn't get out of. There were two reasons why a fighter pilot hated to declare an emergency. First, it triggered a complex and very public chain of events at the field: all other incoming flights were held up, including many of one's comrades who were probably low on fuel; the fire trucks came trundling out to the runway like yellow toys (as seen from way up there), the better to illustrate one's hapless state; and the bureaucracy began to crank up the paper monster for the investigation that always followed. And second, to declare an emergency, one first had to reach that conclusion in his own mind, which to the young pilot was the same as saying: "A minute ago I still *had it*—now I need your help!" To have a bunch of young fighter pilots up in the air thinking this way used to drive flight controllers crazy. They would see a ship beginning to drift off the radar, and they couldn't rouse the pilot on the microphone for anything other than a few meaningless mumbles, and they would know he was probably out there with engine failure at a low altitude, trying to reignite by lowering his auxiliary generator rig, which had a little propeller that was supposed to spin in the slipstream like a child's pinwheel.

"Whiskey Kilo Two Eight, do you want to declare an emergency?"

This would rouse him!—to say: "Negative, negative, Whiskey Kilo Two Eight is not declaring an emergency."

Kaboom. Believers in the right stuff would rather crash and burn.

One fine day, after he had joined a fighter squadron, it would dawn on the young pilot exactly how the losers in the great fraternal competition were now being left behind. Which is to say, not by instructors or other superiors or by failures at prescribed levels of competence, but by death. At this point the essence of the enterprise would begin to dawn on him. Slowly, step by step, the ante had been raised until he was now involved in what was surely the grimmest and grandest gamble of manhood. Being a fighter pilot—for that matter, simply taking off in a single-engine jet fighter of the Century series, such as an F-102, or any of the military's other marvelous bricks with fins on them—presented a man, on a perfectly sunny day, with more ways to get himself killed than his wife and children could imagine in their wildest fears. If he was barreling down the runway at two hundred miles an hour, completing the takeoff run, and the board started lighting up red, should he (a) abort the takeoff (and try to wrestle with the monster, which was gorged with jet fuel, out in the sand beyond the end of the runway) or (b) eject (and hope that the goddamned human cannonball trick works at zero altitude and he doesn't shatter an elbow or a kneecap on the way out) or (c) continue the takeoff and deal with the problem aloft (knowing full well that the ship may be on fire and therefore seconds away from exploding)? He would have one second to sort out the options and act, and this kind of little workaday decision came up all the time. Occasionally a man would look coldly at the binary problem he was now confronting every day—Right Stuff/Death—and decide it wasn't worth it and voluntarily shift over to transports or reconnaissance or whatever. And his comrades would wonder, for a day or so, what evil virus had invaded his soul . . . as they left him behind. More often, however, the reverse would happen. Some college graduate would enter Navy aviation through the Reserves, simply as an alternative to the Army draft, fully intending to return to civilian life, to some waiting profession or family business; would become involved in the obsessive business of ascending the ziggurat pyramid of flying; and, at the end of his enlistment, would astound everyone back home and very likely himself as well by signing up for another one. What on earth got into him? He couldn't explain it. After all, the very words for it had been amputated. A Navy study showed that two-thirds of the fighter pilots who were rated in the top rungs of their groups—i.e., the hottest young pilots—reenlisted when the time came, and practically all were college graduates. By this point, a young fighter jock was like the preacher in *Moby Dick* who climbs up into the pulpit on a rope ladder and then pulls the ladder up behind him; except the pilot could not use the words necessary to express the vital lessons. Civilian life, and even home and hearth, now seemed not only far away but far *below,* back down many levels of the pyramid of the right stuff.

A fighter pilot soon found he wanted to associate only with other fighter pilots. Who else could understand the nature of the little proposition (right stuff/death) they were all dealing with? And what other subject could compare with it? It was riveting! To talk about it in so many words was forbidden, of course. The very words *death, danger, bravery, fear* were not to be uttered except in the occasional specific instance or for ironic effect. Nevertheless, the subject could be adumbrated in *code* or *by example.* Hence the endless evenings of pilots huddled together talking about flying. On these long and drunken evenings (the band of their family life) certain theorems would be propounded and demonstrated—and all by *code* and *example.* One theorem was: There are no *accidents* and no fatal flaws in the machines; there are only pilots with the wrong stuff. (I.e., blind Fate can't kill me.) When Bud Jennings crashed and burned in the swamps at Jacksonville, the other pilots in Pete Conrad's squadron said: *How could he have been so stupid?* It turned out that Jennings had gone up in the SNJ with his cockpit canopy opened in a way that was expressly forbidden in the manual, and carbon monoxide had been sucked in from the exhaust, and he passed out and crashed. All agreed that Bud Jennings was a good guy and a good pilot, but his epitaph on the ziggurat was: *How could he have been so stupid?* This seemed shocking at first, but by the time Conrad had reached the end of that bad string at Pax River, he was capable of his own corollary to the theorem: viz., no single factor ever killed a pilot; there was always a chain of mistakes. But what about Ted Whelan, who fell like a rock from 8,100 feet when his parachute failed? Well, the parachute was merely part of the chain: first, someone should have caught the structural defect that resulted in the hydraulic leak that triggered the emergency; second, Whelan did not check out his seat-parachute rig, and the drogue failed to separate the main parachute from the seat; but even after those two mistakes, Whelan had fifteen or twenty seconds, as he fell, to disengage himself from the seat and open the parachute manually. Why just stare at the scenery coming up to smack you in the face! And everyone nodded. (He failed—but I wouldn't have!) Once the theorem and the corollary were understood, the Navy's statistics about one in every four Navy aviators dying meant nothing. The figures were averages, and averages applied to those with average stuff.

A riveting subject, especially if it were one's own hide that was on the line. Every evening at bases all over America, there were military pilots huddled in officers clubs eagerly cutting the right stuff up in coded slices so they could talk about it. What more compelling topic of conversation was there in the world? In the Air Force there were even pilots who would ask the tower for priority landing clearance so that they could make the beer call on time, at 4 p.m. sharp, at the Officers Club. They would come right out and state the reason. The drunken rambles began at four and sometimes went on for ten or twelve hours. Such conversations! They diced that righteous stuff up into little bits, bowed ironically to it, stumbled blindfolded around it, groped, lurched, belched, staggered, bawled, sang, roared, and feinted at it with self-deprecating humor. Nevertheless!—they never mentioned it by name. No, they used the approved codes, such as: "Like a jerk I got myself into a hell of a corner today." They told of how they "lucked out of it." To get across the extreme peril of his exploit, one would use certain oblique cues. He would say, "I looked over at Robinson"—who would be known to the listeners as a non-com who sometimes rode backseat to read radar—"and he wasn't talking any more, he was just staring at the radar, like this, giving it that *zombie* look. Then I *knew* I was in trouble!" Beautiful! Just right! For it would also be known to the listeners that the non-coms advised one another: "*Never* fly with a lieutenant. *Avoid* captains and majors. Hell, man, do yourself a favor: don't fly with anybody below colonel." Which in turn said: "Those young bucks shoot dice with death!" And yet once in the air the non-com had his own standards. He was determined to remain as outwardly cool as the pilot, so that when the pilot did something that truly petrified him, he would say nothing; instead, he would turn silent, catatonic, like a zombie. Perfect! *Zombie.* There you had it, compressed into a single word all of the foregoing. I'm a hell of a pilot! I shoot dice with death! And now all you fellows know it! And I haven't spoken of that unspoken stuff even once!

The talking and drinking began at the beer call, and then the boys would break for dinner and come back afterward and get more wasted and more garrulous or else more quietly fried, drinking good cheap PX booze until 2 A.M. The night was young! Why not get the cars and go out for a little proficiency run? It seemed that every fighter jock thought himself an ace driver, and he would do anything to obtain a hot car, especially a sports car, and the drunker he was, the more convinced he would be about his driving skills, as if the right stuff, being indivisible, carried over into any enterprise whatsoever, under any conditions. A little proficiency run, boys! (There's only one way to find out!) And they would roar off in close formation from, say, Nellis Air Force Base, down Route 15, into Las Vegas, barreling down the highway, rat-racing, sometimes four abreast, jockeying for position, piling into the most listless curve in the desert flats as if they were trying to root each other out of the groove at the Rebel 500—and then bursting into downtown Las Vegas with a rude fraternal roar like the Hell's Angels—and the natives chalked it up to youth and drink and the bad element that the Air Force attracted. They knew nothing about the right stuff, of course.

More fighter pilots died in automobiles than in airplanes. Fortunately, there was always some kindly soul up the chain to certify the papers "line of duty," so that the widow could get a better break on the insurance. That was okay and only proper because somehow the system itself had long ago said *Skol!* and *Quite right!* to the military cycle of Flying & Drinking and Drinking & Driving, as if there were no other way. Every young fighter jock knew the feeling of getting two or three hours' sleep and then waking up at 5:30 A.M. and having a few cups of coffee, a few cigarettes, and then carting his poor quivering liver out to the field for another day of flying. There were those who arrived not merely hungover but still drunk, slapping oxygen tank cones over their faces and trying to burn the alcohol out of their systems, and then going up, remarking later: "I don't *advise* it, you understand, but it *can* be done." (Provided you have the right stuff, you miserable pudknocker.)

Air Force and Navy airfields were usually on barren or marginal stretches of land and would have looked especially bleak and Low Rent to an ordinary individual in the chilly light of dawn. But to a young pilot there was an inexplicable bliss to coming out to the flight line while the sun was just beginning to cook up behind the rim of the horizon, so that the whole field was still in shadow and the ridges in the distance were in silhouette and the flight line was a monochrome of Exhaust Fume Blue, and every little red light on top of the water towers or power stanchions looked dull, shriveled, congealed, and the runway lights, which were still on, looked faded, and even the land-ing lights on a fighter that had just landed and was taxiing in were no longer dazzling, as they would be at night, and looked instead like shriveled gobs of candlepower out there—and yet it was beautiful, exhilarating!—for he was revved up with adrenalin, anxious to take off before the day broke, to burst up into the sunlight over the ridges before all those thousands of comatose souls down there, still dead to the world, snug in home and hearth, even came to their senses. To take off in an F-100F at dawn and cut on the afterburner and hurtle twenty-five thousand feet up into the sky in thirty seconds, so suddenly that you felt not like a bird but like a trajectory, yet with full con-trol, full control of *four tons* of thrust, all of which flowed from your will and through your fingertips, with the huge engine right beneath you, so close that it was as if you were riding it bareback, until all at once you were supersonic, an event registered on earth by a tremendous cracking boom that shook windows, but up here only by the fact that you now felt utterly free of the earth—to describe it, even to wife, child, near ones and dear ones, seemed impossible. So the pilot kept it to himself, along with an even more indescribable . . . an even more sinfully inconfessable . . . feeling of supe-riority, appropriate to him and to his kind, lone bearers of the right stuff.

From *up here* at dawn the pilot looked down upon poor hopeless Las Vegas (or Yuma, Corpus Christi, Meridian, San Bernardino, or Dayton) and began to wonder: How can all of them down there, those poor souls who will soon be waking up and trudg-ing out of their minute rectangles and inching along their little noodle highways to-ward whatever slots and grooves make up their everyday lives—how could they live like that, with such earnestness, if they had the faintest idea of what it was like up here in this righteous zone?

But of course! Not only the washed-out, grounded, and dead pilots had been left behind—but also all of those millions of sleepwalking souls who never even attempted the great gamble. The entire world below . . . *left behind.* Only at this point can one begin to understand just how big, how titanic, the ego of the military pilot could be. The world was used to enormous egos in artists, actors, entertainers of all sorts, in politi-cians, sports figures, and even journalists, because they had such familiar and conve-nient ways to show them off. But that slim young man over there in uniform, with the enormous watch on his wrist and the withdrawn look on his face, that young of-ficer who is so shy that he can't even open his mouth unless the subject is flying—that young pilot—well, my friends, his ego is even *bigger!*—so big, it's *breathtaking!* Even in the 1950's it was difficult for civilians to comprehend such a thing, but *all* military officers and many enlisted men tended to feel superior to civilians. It was really quite ironic, given the fact that for a good thirty years the rising business classes in the cities had been steering their sons away from the military, as if from a bad smell, and the of-ficer corps had never been held in lower esteem. Well, career officers returned the con-tempt in trumps. They looked upon themselves as men who lived by higher standards of behavior than civilians, as men who were the bearers and protectors of the most im-portant values of American life, who maintained a sense of discipline while civilians abandoned themselves to hedonism, who maintained a sense of honor while civilians lived by opportunism and greed. Opportunism and greed: there you had your much-vaunted corporate business world. Khrushchev was right about one thing: when it came time to hang the capitalist West, an American businessman would sell him the rope. When the showdown came—and the showdowns always came—not all the wealth in the world or all the sophisticated nuclear weapons and radar and missile systems it could buy would take the place of those who had the uncritical willingness to face danger, those who, in short, had the right stuff.

In fact, the feeling was so righteous, so exalted, it could become religious. Civilians seldom understood this, either. There was no one to teach them. It was no longer the fashion for serious writers to describe the glories of war. Instead, they dwelt upon its horrors, often with cynicism or disgust. It was left to the occasional pilot with a literary flair to provide a glimpse of the pilot's self-conception in its heavenly or spiritual aspect. When a pilot named Robert Scott flew his P-43 over Mount Everest, quite a feat at the time, he brought his hand up and snapped a salute to his fallen adversary. He thought he had *defeated* the mountain, surmounting all the forces of nature that had made it formidable. And why not? "God is my co-pilot," he said—that became the title of his book—and he meant it. So did the most gifted of all the pilot authors, the Frenchman Antoine de Saint-Exupéry. As he gazed down upon the world . . . from up there . . . during transcontinental flights, the good Saint-Ex saw civilization as a series of tiny fragile patches clinging to the otherwise barren rock of Earth. He felt like a lonely sentinel, a protector of those vulnerable little oases, ready to lay down his life in their behalf, if necessary; a saint, in short, true to his name, flying up here at the right hand of God. The good Saint-Ex! And he was not the only one. He was merely the one who put it into words most beautifully and anointed himself before the altar of the right stuff.

(1979)

ALICE WALKER

[b. 1944]

In Search of Our Mothers' Gardens

I described her own nature and temperament. Told how they needed a larger life for their expression. . . . I pointed out that in lieu of proper channels, her emotions had overflowed into paths that dissipated them. I talked, beautifully I thought, about an art that would be born, an art that would open the way for women the likes of her. I asked her to hope, and build up an inner life against the coming of that day. . . . I sang, with a strange quiver in my voice, a promise song.

—"AVEY," JEAN TOMER, *CANE*
The poet speaking to a prostitute who falls asleep while he's talking

When the poet Jean Toomer walked through the South in the early twenties, he discovered a curious thing: black women whose spirituality was so intense, so deep, so *unconscious,* they were themselves unaware of the richness they held. They stumbled blindly through their lives: creatures so abused and mutilated in body, so dimmed and confused by pain, that they considered themselves unworthy even of hope. In the self-less abstractions their bodies became to the men who used them, they became more than "sexual objects," more even than mere women: they became "Saints." Instead of being perceived as whole persons, their bodies became shrines: what was thought to be their minds became temples suitable for worship. These crazy Saints stared out at the world, wildly, like lunatics—or quietly, like suicides; and the "God" that was in their gaze was as mute as a great stone.

Who were these Saints? These crazy, loony, pitiful women?

Some of them, without a doubt, were our mothers and grandmothers.

In the still heat of the post-Reconstruction South, this is how they seemed to Jean Toomer: exquisite butterflies trapped in an evil honey, toiling away their lives in an era, a century, that did not acknowledge them, except as "the *mule* of the world." They dreamed dreams that no one knew—not even themselves, in any coherent fashion—and saw visions no one could understand. They wandered or sat about the country-side crooning lullabies to ghosts, and drawing the mother of Christ in charcoal on court-house walls.

They forced their minds to desert their bodies and their striving spirits sought to rise, like frail whirlwinds from the hard red clay. And when those frail whirlwinds fell, in scattered particles, upon the ground, no one mourned. Instead, men lit candles to cel-ebrate the emptiness that remained, as people do who enter a beautiful but vacant space to resurrect a God.

Our mothers and grandmothers, some of them: moving to music not yet written. And they waited.

They waited for a day when the unknown thing that was in them would be made known; but guessed, somehow in their darkness, that on the day of their revelation they would be long dead. Therefore to Toomer they walked, and even ran, in slow motion. For they were going nowhere immediate, and the future was not yet within their grasp. And men took our mothers and grandmothers, "but got no pleasure from it." So complex was their passion and their calm.

To Toomer, they lay vacant and fallow as autumn fields, with harvest time never in sight: and he saw them enter loveless marriages, without joy; and become prostitutes, without resistance; and become mothers of children, without fulfillment.

For these grandmothers and mothers of ours were not Saints, but Artists; driven to a numb and bleeding madness by the springs of creativity in them for which there was no release. They were Creators, who lived lives of spiritual waste, because they were so rich in spirituality—which is the basis of Art—that the strain of enduring their un-used and unwanted talent drove them insane. Throwing away this spirituality was their pathetic attempt to lighten the soul to a weight their work-worn, sexually abused bod-ies could bear.

What did it mean for a black woman to be an artist in our grandmothers' time? In our great-grandmothers' day? It is a question with an answer cruel enough to stop the blood.

Did you have a genius of a great-great-grandmother who died under some ignorant and depraved white overseer's lash? Or was she required to bake biscuits for a lazy back-water tramp, when she cried out in her soul to paint watercolors of sunsets, or the rain falling on the green and peaceful pasturelands? Or was her body broken and forced to bear children (who were more often than not sold away from her)—eight, ten, fifteen, twenty children—when her one joy was the thought of modeling heroic figures of re-bellion, in stone or clay?

How was the creativity of the black woman kept alive, year after year and century after century, when for most of the years black people have been in America, it was a punishable crime for a black person to read or write? And the freedom to paint, to sculpt, to expand the mind with action did not exist. Consider, if you can bear to imagine it, what might have been the result if singing, too, had been forbidden by law. Listen to the voices of Bessie Smith, Billie Holiday, Nina Simone, Roberta Flack, and Aretha Franklin, among others, and imagine those voices muzzled for life. Then you may begin to comprehend the lives of our "crazy," "Sainted" mothers and grand-mothers. The agony of the lives of women who might have been Poets, Novelists, Essayists, and Short-Story Writers (over a period of centuries), who died with their real gifts stifled within them.

And, if this were the end of the story, we would have cause to cry out in my para-phrase of Okot p'Bitek's great poem:

> O, my clanswomen
> Let us all cry together!
> Come,
> Let us mourn the death of our mother,
> The death of a Queen
> The ash that was produced
> By a great fire!
> O, this homestead is utterly dead
> Close the gates
> With *lacari* thorns,
> For our mother
> The creator of the Stool is lost!
> And all the young men
> Have perished in the wilderness!

But this is not the end of the story, for all the young women—our mothers and grandmothers, *ourselves*—have not perished in the wilderness. And if we ask ourselves why, and search for and find the answer, we will know beyond all efforts to erase it from our minds, just exactly who, and of what, we black American women are.

One example, perhaps the most pathetic, most misunderstood one, can provide a backdrop for our mothers' work: Phillis Wheatley, a slave in the 1700s.

Virginia Woolf, in her book *A Room of One's Own,* wrote that in order for a woman to write fiction she must have two things, certainly: a room of her own (with key and lock) and enough money to support herself.

What then are we to make of Phillis Wheatley, a slave, who owned not even her-self? This sickly, frail black girl who required a servant of her own at times—her health was so precarious—and who, had she been white, would have been easily considered the intellectual superior of all the women and most of the men in the society of her day.

Virginia Woolf wrote further, speaking of course not of our Phillis, that "any woman born with a great gift in the sixteenth century [insert "eighteenth century," insert "black woman," insert "born or made a slave"] would certainly have gone crazed, shot her-self, or ended her days in some lonely cottage outside the village, half witch, half wizard [insert "Saint"], feared and mocked at. For it needs little skill and psychology to be sure that a highly gifted girl who had tried to use her gift of poetry would have been so thwarted and hindered by contrary instincts [add "chains, guns, the lash, the owner-ship of one's body by someone else, submission to an alien religion"], that she must have lost her health and sanity to a certainty."

The key words, as they relate to Phillis, are "contrary instincts." For when we read the poetry of Phillis Wheatley—as when we read the novels of Nella Larsen or the oddly false-sounding autobiography of that freest of all black women writers, Zora Hurston—evidence of "contrary instincts" is everywhere. Her loyalties were com-pletely divided, as was, without question, her mind.

But how could this be otherwise? Captured at seven, a slave of wealthy, doting whites who instilled in her the "savagery" of the Africa they "rescued" her from . . . one wonders if she was even able to remember her homeland as she had known it, or as it really was.

Yet, because she did try to use her gift for poetry in a world that made her a slave, she was "so thwarted and hindered by . . . contrary instincts, that she . . . lost her health. . . ." In the last years of her brief life, burdened not only with the need to ex-press her gift but also with a penniless, friendless "freedom" and several small children for whom she was forced to do strenuous work to feed, she lost her health, certainly. Suffering from malnutrition and neglect and who knows what mental agonies, Phillis Wheatley died.

So torn by "contrary instincts" was black, kidnapped, enslaved Phillis that her de-scription of "the Goddess"—as she poetically called the Liberty she did not have—is ironically, cruelly humorous. And, in fact, has held Phillis up to ridicule for more than a century. It is usually read prior to hanging Phillis's memory as that of a fool. She wrote:

> The Goddess comes, she moves divinely fair,
> Olive and laurel binds her *golden* hair.
> Wherever shines this native of the skies,
> Unnumber'd charms and recent graces rise. [My italics]

It is obvious that Phillis, the slave, combed the "Goddess's" hair every morning; prior, perhaps, to bringing in the milk, or fixing her mistress's lunch. She took her imagery from the one thing she saw elevated above all others.

With the benefit of hindsight we ask, "How could she?"

But at last, Phillis, we understand. No more snickering when your stiff, struggling, ambivalent lines are forced on us. We know now that you were not an idiot or a trai-tor; only a sickly little black girl, snatched from your home and country and made a slave; a woman who still struggled to sing the song that was your gift, although in a land of barbarians who praised you for your bewildered tongue. It is not so much what you sang, as that you kept alive, in so many of our ancestors, *the notion of song*.

Black women are called, in the folklore that so aptly identifies one's status in society, "the *mule* of the world," because we have been handed the burdens that everyone else— *everyone* else—refused to carry. We have also been called "Matriarchs," "Superwomen," and "Mean and Evil Bitches." Not to mention "Castraters" and "Sapphire's Mama." When we have pleaded for understanding, our character has been distorted; when we have asked for simple caring, we have been handed empty inspirational appellations, then stuck in the farthest corner. When we have asked for love, we have been given children. In short, even our plainer gifts, our labors of fidelity and love, have been knocked down our throats. To be an artist and a black woman, even today, lowers our status in many respects, rather than raises it: and yet, artists we will be.

Therefore we must fearlessly pull out of ourselves and look at and identify with our lives the living creativity some of our great-grandmothers were not allowed to know. I stress *some* of them because it is well known that the majority of our great-grandmothers knew, even without "knowing" it, the reality of their spirituality, even if they didn't recognize it beyond what happened in the singing at church—and they never had any intention of giving it up.

How they did it—those millions of black women who were not Phillis Wheatley, or Lucy Terry or Frances Harper or Zora Hurston or Nella Larsen or Bessie Smith; or Elizabeth Catlett, or Katherine Dunham, either—brings me to the title of this essay, "In Search of Our Mothers' Gardens," which is a personal account that is yet shared, in its theme and its meaning, by all of us. I found, while thinking about the far-reaching world of the creative black woman, that often the truest answer to a question that really matters can be found very close.

In the late 1920s my mother ran away from home to marry my father. Marriage, if not running away, was expected of seventeen-year-old girls. By the time she was twenty, she had two children and was pregnant with a third. Five children later, I was born. And this is how I came to know my mother: she seemed a large, soft, loving-eyed woman who was rarely impatient in our home. Her quick, violent temper was on view only a few times a year, when she battled with the white landlord who had the misfortune to suggest to her that her children did not need to go to school.

She made all the clothes we wore, even my brothers' overalls. She made all the towels and sheets we used. She spent the summers canning vegetables and fruits. She spent the winter evenings making quilts enough to cover all our beds.

During the "working" day, she labored beside—not behind—my father in the fields. Her day began before sunup, and did not end until late at night. There was never a moment for her to sit down, undisturbed, to unravel her own private thoughts; never a time free from interruption—by work or the noisy inquiries of her many children. And yet, it is to my mother—and all our mothers who were not famous—that I went in search of the secret of what has fed that muzzled and often mutilated, but vibrant, creative spirit that the black woman has inherited, and that pops out in wild and unlikely places to this day.

But when, you will ask, did my overworked mother have time to know or care about feeding the creative spirit?

The answer is so simple that many of us have spent years discovering it. We have constantly looked high, when we should have looked high—and low.

For example: in the Smithsonian Institution in Washington, D.C., there hangs a quilt unlike any other in the world. In fanciful, inspired, and yet simple and identifiable figures, it portrays the story of the Crucifixion. It is considered rare, beyond price. Though it follows no known pattern of quiltmaking, and though it is made of bits and pieces of worthless rags, it is obviously the work of a person of powerful imagination and deep spiritual feeling. Below this quilt I saw a note that says it was made by "an anonymous Black woman in Alabama, a hundred years ago."

If we could locate this "anonymous" black woman from Alabama, she would turn out to be one of our grandmothers—an artist who left her mark in the only materials she could afford, and in the only medium her position in society allowed her to use.

As Virginia Woolf wrote further, in *A Room of One's Own:*

> Yet genius of a sort must have existed among women as it must have existed among the working class. [Change this to "slaves" and "the wives and daughters of sharecroppers."] Now and again an Emily Brontë or a Robert Burns [change this to "a Zora Hurston or a Richard Wright"] blazes out and proves its presence. But certainly it never got itself on to paper. When, however, one reads of a witch being ducked, of a woman possessed by devils [or "Sainthood"], of a wise woman selling herbs [our root workers], or even a very remarkable man who had a mother, then I think we are on the track of a lost novelist, a suppressed poet, or some mute and inglorious Jane Austen. . . . Indeed, I would venture to guess that Anon, who wrote so many poems without signing them, was often a woman. . . .

And so our mothers and grandmothers have, more often than not anonymously, handed on the creative spark, the seed of the flower they themselves never hoped to see: or like a sealed letter they could not plainly read.

And so it is, certainly, with my own mother. Unlike "Ma" Rainey's songs, which retained their creator's name even while blasting forth from Bessie Smith's mouth, no song or poem will bear my mother's name. Yet so many of the stories that I write, that we all write, are my mother's stories. Only recently did I fully realize this: that through years of listening to my mother's stories of her life, I have absorbed not only the stories themselves, but something of the manner in which she spoke, something of the urgency that involves the knowledge that her stories—like her life—must be recorded. It is probably for this reason that so much of what I have written is about characters whose counterparts in real life are so much older than I am.

But the telling of these stories, which came from my mother's lips as naturally as breathing, was not the only way my mother showed herself as an artist. For stories, too, were subject to being distracted, to dying without conclusion. Dinners must be started, and cotton must be gathered before the big rains. The artist that was and is my mother showed itself to me only after many years. This is what I finally noticed:

Like Mem, a character in *The Third Life of Grange Copeland,* my mother adorned with flowers whatever shabby house we were forced to live in. And not just your typical straggly country stand of zinnias, either. She planted ambitious gardens—and still does—with over fifty different varieties of plants that bloom profusely from early March until late November. Before she left home for the fields, she watered her flowers, chopped up the grass, and laid out new beds. When she returned from the fields she might divide clumps of bulbs, dig a cold pit, uproot and replant roses, or prune branches from her taller bushes or trees—until night came and it was too dark to see.

Whatever she planted grew as if by magic, and her fame as a grower of flowers spread over three counties. Because of her creativity with her flowers, even my memories of poverty are seen through a screen of blooms—sunflowers, petunias, roses, dahlias, forsythia, spirea, delphiniums, verbena . . . and on and on.

And I remember people coming to my mother's yard to be given cuttings from her flowers; I hear again the praise showered on her because whatever rocky soil she landed on, she turned into a garden. A garden so brilliant with colors, so original in its design, so magnificent with life and creativity, that to this day people drive by our house in Georgia—perfect strangers and imperfect strangers—and ask to stand or walk among my mother's art.

I notice that it is only when my mother is working in her flowers that she is radiant, almost to the point of being invisible—except as Creator: hand and eye. She is involved in work her soul must have. Ordering the universe in the image of her personal conception of Beauty.

Her face, as she prepares the Art that is her gift, is a legacy of respect she leaves to me, for all that illuminates and cherishes life. She has handed down respect for the possibilities—and the will to grasp them.

For her, so hindered and intruded upon in so many ways, being an artist has still been a daily part of her life. This ability to hold on, even in very simple ways, is work black women have done for a very long time.

This poem is not enough, but it is something, for the woman who literally covered the holes in our walls with sunflowers:

> They were women then
> My mama's generation
> Husky of voice—Stout of
> Step
> With fists as well as
> Hands
> How they battered down
> Doors
> And ironed
> Starched white
> Shirts
> How they led
> Armies
> Headragged Generals
> Across mined
> Fields
> Booby-trapped
> Kitchens
> To discover books
> Desks
> A place for us
> How they knew what we
> *Must* know
> Without knowing a page
> Of it
> Themselves.

Guided by my heritage of a love of beauty and a respect for strength—in search of my mother's garden, I found my own.

And perhaps in Africa over two hundred years ago, there was just such a mother; perhaps she painted vivid and daring decorations in oranges and yellows and greens on the walls of her hut; perhaps she sang—in a voice like Roberta Flack's—*sweetly* over the compounds of her village; perhaps she wove the most stunning mats or told the most ingenious stories of all the village storytellers. Perhaps she was herself a poet—though only her daughter's name is signed to the poems that we know.

Perhaps Phillis Wheatley's mother was also an artist.

Perhaps in more than Phillis Wheatley's biological life is her mother's signature made clear.

(1983)

BERNARD COOPER
[1951]

Burl's

FROM THE LOS ANGELES TIMES MAGAZINE

I loved the restaurant's name, a compact curve of a word. Its sign, five big letters rimmed in neon, hovered above the roof. I almost never saw the sign with its neon lit; my parents took me there for early summer dinners, and even by the time we left—father cleaning his teeth with a toothpick, mother carrying steak bones in a doggie bag—the sky was still bright. Heat rippled off the cars parked along Hollywood Boulevard, the asphalt gummy from hours of sun.

With its sleek architecture, chrome appliances, and arctic temperature, Burl's offered a refuge from the street. We usually sat at one of the booths in front of the plate-glass windows. During our dinner, people came to a halt before the news-vending machine on the corner and burrowed in their pockets and purses for change.

The waitresses at Burl's wore brown uniforms edged in checked gingham. From their breast pockets frothed white lace handkerchiefs. In between reconnaissance missions to the table, they busied themselves behind the counter and shouted "Tuna to travel" or "Scorch that patty" to a harried short-order cook who manned the grill. Miniature pitchers of cream and individual pats of butter were extracted from an industrial refrigerator. Coca-Cola shot from a glinting spigot. Waitresses dodged and bumped one another, frantic as atoms.

My parents usually lingered after the meal, nursing cups of coffee while I played with the beads of condensation on my glass of ice water, tasted Tabasco sauce, or twisted pieces of my paper napkin into mangled animals. One evening, annoyed with my restlessness, my father gave me a dime and asked me to buy him a *Herald Examiner* from the vending machine in front of the restaurant.

Shouldering open the heavy glass door, I was seared by a sudden gust of heat. Traffic roared past me and stirred the air. Walking toward the newspaper machine, I held the dime so tightly it seemed to melt in my palm. Duty made me feel large and important. I inserted the dime and opened the box, yanking a *Herald* from the spring contraption that held it as tight as a mousetrap. When I turned around, paper in hand, I saw two women walking toward me.

Their high heels clicked on the sun-baked pavement. They were tall, broad-shouldered women who moved with a mixture of haste and defiance. They'd teased their hair into nearly identical black beehives. Dangling earrings flashed in the sun, brilliant as prisms. Each of them wore the kind of clinging, strapless outfit my mother referred to as a cocktail dress. The silky fabric—one dress was purple, the other pink—accentuated their breasts and hips and rippled with insolent highlights. The dresses exposed their bare arms, the slope of their shoulders, and the smooth, powdered plane of flesh where their cleavage began.

I owned at the time a book called *Things for Boys and Girls to Do.* There were pages to color, intricate mazes, and connect-the-dots. But another type of puzzle came to mind as I watched those women walking toward me: What's Wrong With This Picture? Say the drawing of a dining room looked normal at first glance; on closer inspection, a chair was missing its leg and the man who sat atop it wore half a pair of glasses.

The women had Adam's apples.

The closer they came, the shallower my breathing was. I blocked the sidewalk, an incredulous child stalled in their path. When they saw me staring, they shifted their purses and linked their arms. There was something sisterly and conspiratorial about their sudden closeness. Though their mouths didn't move, I thought they might have been communicating without moving their lips, so telepathic did they seem as they joined arms and pressed together, synchronizing their heavy steps. The pages of the *Herald* fluttered in the wind. I felt them against my arm, light as batted lashes.

The woman in pink shot me a haughty glance and yet she seemed pleased that I'd taken notice, hungry to be admired by a man, or even an awestruck eight-year-old boy. She tried to stifle a grin, her red lipstick more voluptuous than the lips it painted. Rouge deepened her cheekbones. Eye shadow dusted her lips, a clumsy abundance of blue. Her face was like a page in *Things for Boys and Girls to Do,* colored by a kid who went outside the lines.

At close range, I saw that her wig was slightly askew. I was certain it was a wig because my mother owned several; three Styrofoam heads lined a shelf in my mother's closet; upon them were perched a Page-Boy, an Empress, and a Baby-Doll, all in shades of auburn. The woman in the pink dress wore her wig like a crown of glory.

But it was the woman in the purple dress who passed nearest me, and I saw that her jaw was heavily powdered, a half-successful attempt to disguise the telltale shadow of a beard. Just as I noticed this, her heel caught on a crack in the pavement and she reeled on her stilettos. It was then that I witnessed a rift in her composure, a window through which I could glimpse the shades of maleness that her dress and wig and makeup obscured. She shifted her shoulders and threw out her hands like a surfer riding a curl. The instant she regained her balance, she smoothed her dress, patted her hair, and sauntered onward.

Any woman might be a man. The fact of it clanged through the chambers of my brain. In broad day, in the midst of traffic, with my parents drinking coffee a few feet away, I felt as if everything I understood, everything I had taken for granted up to that moment—the curve of the earth, the heat of the sun, the reliability of my own eyes—had been squeezed out of me. Who were those men? Did they help each other get inside those dresses? How many other people and things were not what they seemed? From the back, the impostors looked like women once again, slinky and curvaceous, purple and pink. I watched them disappear into the distance, their disguises so convincing that other people on the street seemed to take no notice, and for a moment I wondered if I had imagined the whole encounter, a visitation by two unlikely muses.

Frozen in the middle of the sidewalk, I caught my reflection in the window of Burl's, a silhouette floating between his parents. They faced one another across a table. Once the solid embodiments of woman and man, pedestrians and traffic appeared to pass through them.

★

There were some mornings, seconds before my eyes opened and my senses gathered into consciousness, that the child I was seemed to hover above the bed, and I couldn't tell what form my waking would take—the body of a boy or the body of a girl. Finally stirring, I'd blink against the early light and greet each incarnation as a male with mild surprise. My sex, in other words, didn't seem to be an absolute fact so much as a pleasant, recurring accident.

By the age of eight, I'd experienced this groggy phenomenon several times. Those ethereal moments above my bed made waking up in the tangled blankets, a boy steeped in body heat, all the more astonishing. That this might be an unusual experience never occurred to me; it was one among a flood of sensations I could neither name nor ignore.

And so, shocked as I was when those transvestites passed me in front of Burl's, they confirmed something about which I already had an inkling: the hazy border between the sexes. My father, after all, raised his pinky when he drank from a teacup, and my mother looked as faded and plain as my father until she fixed her hair and painted her face.

Like most children, I once thought it possible to divide the world into male and female columns. Blue/Pink. Rooster/Hens. Trousers/Skirts. Such divisions were easy, not to mention comforting, for they simplified matter into compatible pairs. But there also existed a vast range of things that didn't fit neatly into either camp: clocks, milk, telephones, grass. There were nights I fell into a fitful sleep while trying to sex the world correctly.

Nothing typified the realms of male and female as clearly as my parents' walk-in closets. Home alone for any length of time, I always found my way inside them. I could stare at my parents' clothes for hours, grateful for the stillness and silence, haunting the very heart of their privacy.

The overhead light in my father's closet was a bare bulb. Whenever I groped for the chain in the dark, it wagged back and forth and resisted my grasp. Once the light clicked on, I saw dozens of ties hanging like stalactites. A monogrammed silk bathrobe sagged from a hook, a gift my father had received on a long-ago birthday and, thinking it fussy, rarely wore. Shirts were cramped together along the length of an aluminum pole, their starched sleeves sticking out as if in a halfhearted gesture of greeting. The medicinal odor of mothballs permeated the boxer shorts that were folded and stacked in a built-in drawer. Immaculate underwear was proof of a tenderness my mother couldn't otherwise express; she may not have touched my father often, but she laundered his boxers with infinite care. Even back then, I suspected that a sense of duty was the final erotic link between them.

Sitting in a neat row on the closet floor were my father's boots and slippers and dress shoes. I'd try on his wingtips and clomp around, slipping out of them with every step. My wary, unnatural stride made me all the more desperate to effect some authority. I'd whisper orders to imagined lackeys and take my invisible wife in my arms. But no matter how much I wanted them to fit, those shoes were as cold and hard as marble.

My mother's shoes were just as uncomfortable, but a lot more fun. From a brightly colored array of pumps and slingbacks, I'd pick a pair with the glee and deliberation of someone choosing a chocolate. Whatever embarrassment I felt was overwhelmed by the exhilaration of being taller in a pair of high heels. Things will look like this some-day, I said to myself, gazing out from my new and improved vantage point as if from a crow's nest. Calves elongated, arms akimbo, I gauged each step so that I didn't fall over and moved with what might have passed for grace had someone seen me, a possibility I scrupulously avoided by locking the door.

Back and forth I went. The longer I wore a pair of heels, the better my balance. In the periphery of my vision, the shelf of wigs looked like a throng of kindly bystanders. Light streamed down from a high window, causing crystal bottles to glitter, the air ripe with perfume. A makeup mirror above the dressing table invited my self-absorption. Sound was muffled. Time slowed. It seemed as if nothing bad could happen as long as I stayed within those walls.

Though I'd never been discovered in my mother's closet, my parents knew that I was drawn toward girlish things—dolls and jump rope and jewelry—as well as to the games and preoccupations that were expected of a boy. I'm not sure now if it was my effeminacy itself that bothered them as much as my ability to slide back and forth, with-out the slightest warning, between male and female mannerisms. After I'd finished build-ing the model of an F-17 bomber, say, I'd sit back to examine my handiwork, purs-ing my lips in concentration and crossing my legs at the knee.

One day my mother caught me standing in the middle of my bedroom doing an imitation of Mary Injijikian, a dark, overeager Armenian girl with whom I believed myself to be in love, not only because she was pretty but because I wanted to be like her. Collector of effortless A's, Mary seemed to know all the answers in class. Before the teacher had even finished asking a question, Mary would let out a little grunt and practically levitate out of her seat, as if her hand were filled with helium. "Could we please hear from someone else today besides Miss Injijikian," the teacher would say. *Miss Injijikian.* Those were the words I was repeating over and over to myself when my mother caught me. To utter them was rhythmic, delicious, and under their spell I raised my hand and wiggled like Mary. I heard a cough and spun around. My mother froze in the doorway. She clutched the folded sheets to her stomach and turned with-out saying a word. My sudden flush of shame confused me. Weren't boys supposed to swoon over girls? Hadn't I seen babbling, heartsick men in a dozen movies?

Shortly after the Injijikian incident, my parents decided to send me to gymnastics class at the Los Angeles Athletic Club, a brick relic of a building on Olive Street. One of the oldest establishments of its kind in Los Angeles, the club prohibited women from the premises. My parents didn't have to say it aloud: they hoped a fraternal atmosphere would toughen me up and tilt me toward the male side of my nature.

My father drove me downtown so I could sign up for the class, meet the instructor, and get a tour of the place. On the way there, he reminisced about sports. Since he'd grown up in a rough Philadelphia neighborhood, sports consisted of kick-the-can or rolling a hoop down the street with a stick. The more he talked about his physical prowess, the more convinced I became that my daydreams and shyness were a disappointment to him.

The hushed lobby of the athletic club was paneled in dark wood. A few solitary figures were hidden in wing chairs. My father and I introduced ourselves to a man at the front desk who seemed unimpressed by our presence. His aloofness unnerved me, which wasn't hard considering that no matter how my parents put it, I knew their sending me here was a form of disapproval, a way of banishing the part of me they didn't care to know.

A call went out over the intercom for someone to show us around. While we waited, I noticed that the sand in the standing ashtrays had been raked into perfect furrows. The glossy leaves of the potted plants looked as if they'd been polished by hand. The place seemed more like a well-tended hotel than an athletic club. Finally, a stoop-shouldered old man hobbled toward us, his head shrouded in a cloud of white hair. He wore a T-shirt that said "Instructor"; his arms were so wrinkled and anemic, I thought I might have misread it. While we followed him to the elevator, I readjusted my expectations, which had involved fantasies of a hulking drill sergeant barking orders at a flock of scrawny boys.

The instructor, mumbling to himself and never turning around to see if we were behind him, showed us where the gymnastics class took place. I'm certain the building was big, but the size of the room must be exaggerated by a trick of memory, because when I envision it, I picture a vast and windowless warehouse. Mats covered the wooden floor. Here and there, in remote and lonely pools of light, stood a pommel horse, a balance beam, and parallel bars. Tiers of bleachers rose into darkness. Unlike the cloistered air of a closet, the room seemed incomplete without a crowd.

Next we visited the dressing room, empty except for a naked middle-aged man. He sat on a narrow bench and clipped his formidable toenails. Moles dotted his back. He glistened like a fish.

We continued to follow the instructor down an aisle lined with numbered lockers. At the far end, steam billowed from the doorway that led to the showers. Fresh towels stacked on a nearby table made me think of my mother; I knew she liked to have me at home with her—I was often her only companion—and I resented her complicity in the plan to send me here.

The tour ended when the instructor gave me a sign-up sheet. Only a few names preceded mine. They were signatures, or so I imagined, of other soft and wayward sons.

When the day of the first gymnastics class arrived, my mother gave me money and a gym bag and sent me to the corner of Hollywood and Western to wait for a bus. The sun was bright, the traffic heavy. While I sat there, an argument raged inside my head, the familiar, battering debate between the wish to be like other boys and the wish to be like myself. Why shouldn't I simply get up and go back home, where I'd be left alone to read and think? On the other hand, wouldn't life be easier if I liked athletics, or learned to like them?

No sooner did I steel my resolve to get on the bus than I thought of something better: I could spend the morning wandering through Woolworth's, then tell my parents

I'd gone to the class. But would my lie stand up to scrutiny? As I practiced describing phantom gymnastics, I became aware of a car circling the block. It was a large car in whose shaded interior I could barely make out the driver, but I thought it might be the man who owned the local pet store. I'd often gone there on the pretext of looking at the cocker spaniel puppies huddled together in their pen, but I really went to gawk at the owner, whose tan chest, in the V of his shirt, was the place I most wanted to rest my head. Every time the man moved, counting stock or writing a receipt, his shirt parted, my mouth went dry, and I smelled the musk of sawdust and dogs.

I found myself hoping that the driver was the man who ran the pet store. I was thrilled by the unlikely possibility that the sight of me, slumped on a bus bench in my T-shirt and shorts, had caused such a man to circle the block. Up to that point in my life, lovemaking hovered somewhere in the future, an impulse a boy might aspire to but didn't indulge. And there I was, sitting on a bus bench in the middle of the city, dreaming I could seduce an adult. I showered the owner of the pet store with kisses and, as aquariums bubbled, birds sang, and mice raced in a wire wheel, slipped my hand beneath his shirt. The roar of traffic brought me to my senses. I breathed deeply and blinked against the sun. I crossed my legs at the knee in order to hide an erection. My fantasy left me both drained and changed. The continent of sex had drifted closer.

The car made another round. This time the driver leaned across the passenger seat and peered at me through the window. He was a complete stranger, whose gaze filled me with fear. It wasn't the surprise of not recognizing him that frightened me, it was what I did recognize—the unmistakable shame in his expression, and the weary temptation that drove him in circles. Before the car behind him honked, he mouthed "hello" and cocked his head. What now, he seemed to be asking. A bold, unbearable question.

I bolted to my feet, slung the gym bag over my shoulder, and hurried toward home. Now and then I turned around to make sure he wasn't trailing me, both relieved and disappointed when I didn't see his car. Even after I became convinced that he wasn't at my back—my sudden flight had scared him off—I kept turning around to see what was making me so nervous, as if I might spot the source of my discomfort somewhere on the street. I walked faster and faster, trying to outrace myself. Eventually, the bus I was supposed to have taken roared past. Turning the corner, I watched it bob eastward.

Closing the kitchen door behind me, I vowed never to leave home again. I was resolute in this decision without fully understanding why, or what it was I hoped to avoid; I was only aware of the need to hide and a vague notion, fading fast, that my trouble had something to do with sex. Already the mechanism of self-deception was at work. By the time my mother rushed into the kitchen to see why I'd returned so early, the thrill I'd felt while waiting for the bus had given way to indignation.

I poured out the story of the man circling the block and protested, with perhaps too great a passion, my own innocence. "I was just sitting there," I said again and again. I was so determined to deflect suspicion away from myself, and to justify my missing the class, that I portrayed the man as a grizzled pervert who drunkenly veered from lane to lane as he followed me halfway home.

My mother cinched her housecoat. She seemed moved and shocked by what I told her, if a bit incredulous, which prompted me to be more dramatic. "It wouldn't be safe," I insisted, "for me to wait at the bus stop again."

No matter how overwrought my story, I knew my mother wouldn't question it, wouldn't bring the subject up again; sex of any kind, especially sex between a man and a boy, was simply not discussed in our house. The gymnastics class, my parents agreed, was something I could do another time.

And so I spent the remainder of that summer at home with my mother, stirring cake batter, holding the dustpan, helping her fold the sheets. For a while I was proud of myself for engineering a reprieve from the athletic club. But as the days wore on, I began to see that my mother had wanted me with her all along, and forcing that to happen wasn't such a feat. Soon a sense of compromise set in; by expressing disgust for the man in the car, I'd expressed disgust for an aspect of myself. Now I had all the time in the world to sit around and contemplate my desire for men. The days grew long and stifling and hot, an endless sentence of self-examination.

Only trips to the pet store offered any respite. Every time I went there, I was too electrified with longing to think about longing in the abstract. The bell tinkled above the door, animals stirred within their cages, and the handsome owner glanced up from his work.

I handed my father the *Herald*. He opened the paper and disappeared behind it. My mother stirred her coffee and sighed. She gazed at the sweltering passersby and probably thought herself lucky. I slid into the vinyl booth and took my place beside my parents.

For a moment, I considered asking them about what had happened on the street, but they would have reacted with censure and alarm, and I sensed there was more to the story than they'd ever be willing to tell me. Men in dresses were only the tip of the iceberg. Who knew what other wonders existed—a boy, for example, who wanted to kiss a man—exceptions the world did its best to keep hidden.

It would be years before I heard the word "transvestite," so I struggled to find a word for what I'd seen. "He-she" came to mind, as lilting as "Injijikian." "Burl's" would have been perfect, like "boys" and "girls" spliced together, but I can't claim to have thought of this back then.

I must have looked stricken as I tried to figure it all out, because my mother put down her coffee cup and asked if I was O.K. She stopped just short of feeling my forehead. I assured her I was fine, but something within me had shifted, had given way to a heady doubt. When the waitress came and slapped down our check—"Thank You," it read, "Dine out more often"—I wondered if her lofty hairdo or the breasts on which her nametag quaked were real. Wax carnations bloomed at every table. Phony wood paneled the walls. Plastic food sat in a display case: fried eggs, a hamburger sandwich, a sundae topped with a garish cherry.

(1995)

Acknowledgments

JAMES BALDWIN "Notes of a Native Son" from *Notes of a Native Son* by James Baldwin. Copyright © 1955, renewed 1983, by James Baldwin. Reprinted by permission of Beacon Press, Boston.

KING-KOK CHEUNG "Feminism and History in 'On Discovery'" an excerpt from "Provocative Silences" from *Articulate Silences: Hisaye Yamamoto, Maxine Hong Kingston and Joy Kogawa* by King-Kok Cheung. Copyright © 1993 by Cornell University. Used by permission of the publisher, Cornell University Press.

KING-KOK CHEUNG "On 'Woman Warrior,'" an excerpt from "Provocative Silences" from *Articulate Silences: Hisaye Yamamoto, Maxine Hong Kingston and Joy Kogawa* by King-Kok Cheung. Copyright © 1993 by Cornell University. Used by permission of the publisher, Cornell University Press.

BERNARD COOPER "Burl's" from *Truth Serum*. Copyright © 1996 by Bernard Cooper. Reprinted by permission of Houghton Mifflin Company. All rights reserved.

JOAN DIDION Part 1 from "Los Angeles Notebook" from *Slouching Towards Bethlehem* by Joan Didion. Copyright © 1966, 1968, renewed © 1996 by Joan Didion. Reprinted by permission of Farrar, Straus & Giroux, LLC.

ANNIE DILLARD "Living Like Weasels" from *Teaching a Stone to Talk* by Annie Dillard. Copyright © 1982 by Annie Dillard. Reprinted by permission of HarperCollins Publishers, Inc.

ANNIE DILLARD "What Essays Can Do" Excerpt from Introduction by Annie Dillard to *Best American Essays 1988*, edited by Annie Dillard and Series Editor Robert Atwan. Copyright © 1988 by Ticknor & Fields. Reprinted by permission of Annie Dillard.

GRETEL EHRLICH "About Men" from *The Solace of Open Spaces* by Gretel Ehrlich. Copyright © 1985 by Gretel Ehrlich. Used by permission of Viking Penguin, a division of Penguin Putnam Inc.

LOREN EISELEY "The Judgment of the Birds" from *The Immense Journey* by Loren Eiseley. Copyright © 1957 by Loren Eiseley. Used by permission of Random House, Inc.

E.B. WHITE "The Geese" from *Essays of E.B. White* by E.B. White. Copyright © 1971 by E.B. White. Originally appeared in The New Yorker. Reprinted by permission of HarperCollins Publishers, Inc.

E.B. WHITE "The Ring of Time" from *The Points of My Compass* by E.B. White. Copyright © 1956 by E.B. White. Originally appeared in The New Yorker. Reprinted by permission of HarperCollins Publishers, Inc.

THOMAS WOLFE Excerpt from *The Right Stuff* by Tom Wolfe. Copyright © 1979 by Tom Wolfe. Reprinted by permission of Farrar, Straus & Giroux, LLC.

VIRGINIA WOOLF "Old Mrs. Grey" from *The Death of the Moth and Other Essays* by Virginia Woolf, copyright 1942 by Harcourt, Inc. and renewed 1970 by Marjorie T. Parsons. Reprinted by permission of the publisher.

VIRGINIA WOOLF "The Death of the Moth" from *The Death of the Moth and Other Essays* by Virgina Woolf, copyright 1942 by Harcourt, Inc. and renewed 1970 by Marjorie T. Parsons. Reprinted by permission of the publisher.

Index

Selection titles appear in italics, and first lines of poems appear in roman type. Page numbers in roman type indicate the opening page of a selection; italic numbers indicate discussion. Bold page numbers indicate complete sections on specific authors.